The Life and Death
of Thelma Todd

Lawrence's sweetheart; Thelma Todd at fourteen, ca. 1920 (courtesy of Edna Todd Bixby).

The Life and Death
of Thelma Todd

WILLIAM DONATI

McFarland & Company, Inc., Publishers
Jefferson, North Carolina, and London

ALSO BY WILLIAM DONATI

*Lucky Luciano: The Rise and Fall
of a Mob Boss* (McFarland, 2010)

LIBRARY OF CONGRESS CATALOGUING-IN-PUBLICATION DATA

Donati, William.
The life and death of Thelma Todd / William Donati.
p.   cm.
Includes bibliographical references and index.
Includes filmography.

ISBN 978-0-7864-6518-7
softcover : acid free paper ∞

1. Todd, Thelma, 1905–1935.
2. Actors — United States — Biography.
I. Title.
PN2287.T575D77 2012   791.4302'8092—dc23   [B]   2011049233

BRITISH LIBRARY CATALOGUING DATA ARE AVAILABLE

On the cover: Thelma Todd publicity photo;
background © 2011 Shutterstock

Manufactured in the United States of America

*McFarland & Company, Inc., Publishers
Box 611, Jefferson, North Carolina 28640
www.mcfarlandpub.com*

To Bill and Edna Todd

Contents

Acknowledgments

I am indebted to the following individuals and institutions for helping make this book possible: Leith Adams, William Bakewell, Lina Basquette, Greg Blackton, Pat Broeske, Joe Cobb, Don Collins, Ned Comstock, Eartha Dengler, Rosario Drago, Benny Drinnon, Will Fowler, Anita Garvin, Dorothy Granger, Jim Heimann, Almeda King, Rena Lundigan, Ida Lupino, Scott MacQueen, Harry Mines, Ken Skulski, William Studer, Adam Todd, Roy Windham, and Mike Velez.

And: Columbia University, New York; the Federal Bureau of Investigation, Washington; the Lawrence History Center, Lawrence, MA; the Lawrence Public Library; the Los Angeles County Public Library; the Los Angeles County Public Records; the Academy of Motion Picture Arts and Sciences, Beverly Hills; the Lied Library, the University of Nevada, Las Vegas; the University of Southern California, Los Angeles; the Hal Roach Collection, the Warner Archives and the Cinema-Television Library and Archives at USC.

Research by Kathy Flynn provides a wonderful look at the Contarino brothers and their motion picture endeavors in Lawrence. She interviewed Rosario Contarino for the Lawrence History Center, thereby documenting his memories as an ambitious filmmaker. Research by film historian J.B. Kaufman regarding the Paramount Pictures School was of immense assistance. The knowledge of cinema scholars Kevin Brownlow and Anthony Slide remains invaluable for those interested in the silent screen era.

Most of all, I am deeply grateful to Thelma's cousins, William Todd and Edna Todd Bixby. They were most generous with interviews and correspondence. They allowed me to view family scrapbooks and photographs. Not only did they open their family archives to me, but they opened their homes as well.

Extensive use has been made of printed materials, specifically newspapers, magazines, and books. The fine writers of the past have left a window to another era. Sources are acknowledged; citations allow readers to determine where information originated. A special debt is owed to the newspaper reporters of the thirties, especially those who covered Thelma's death in Los Angeles.

Thelma's tragedy is that she died so young without achieving all of her dreams.

My fondest wish is that Thelma Todd is remembered for her screen contribution, for the joy she brought to audiences around the world. Thelma's wish was to appear in motion pictures, and she succeeded. Although her life was a short one, it was quite eventful.

Prologue

The pungent odor of formaldehyde permeated the county morgue, filling the nostrils and stinging the eyes. The reporters and police officers watched as the white sheet was removed. Their faces were transfixed, expectant, gathered to witness an unseemly event. Men around the world had dreamed about getting under the sheets with Thelma Todd, noted Agness Underwood, witnessing her first autopsy. There she lay, exposed to prying eyes, the famous porcelain skin now pink. She was no longer a vibrant woman emanating warmth and laughter. She was no longer a breathtaking beauty; she was only a corpse.

Bright lights illuminated the curly blonde locks. The autopsy surgeon held an electric saw. The scalp was detached and pushed over the forehead, covering the familiar face, now rigid in death. Reporter Agness Underwood grimaced but remained on her feet, stiffening as the jagged teeth of a saw split the skull, revealing the brain. When it was over, Underwood found herself alone.[1] This was Thelma's exit from Hollywood; the entrance was nicer.

Thelma Todd's bright future proclaimed the headline in 1927: "Miss Todd was very proud when the Elks of her home state chose her as Miss Massachusetts of 1924, but she was even prouder yesterday when she was informed by B.P. Schulberg that she was to play opposite Richard Dix, this time in his next starring vehicle, a film version of James Forbes's play *The Traveling Salesman*, which Malcolm St. Clair will direct for Paramount."[2] The first months in Hollywood were exciting — until the telephone rang. She had expected an evening of re-takes at the studio. But instead of a bright soundstage, she found a party with a loud gramophone, willing starlets, and eager executives. A voice from the curling smoke offered Thelma a drink, but she angrily walked away. The leers of the cigar chompers turned to steel. "They'll never get me on the casting couch," she fumed.[3] Thelma Todd never made *The Traveling Salesman*.

The beginning wasn't so nice after all. The ending, either.

"This Horrible Thing Happened"

Anita Garvin walked briskly along a wintry street in New York City. As she passed a newsstand, she suddenly stopped: "I saw a face and I thought, 'Oh, it looks like Thelma.'

1

That's who it was. She was very intelligent. She had a lot of money and beauty. She had everything going for her. Then this horrible thing happened ... I think she was murdered. Everybody who knew her, knew that she didn't commit suicide, and I believe she didn't. At the time there were stories going around. That's all I can figure out; she was murdered."

William Bakewell was also in New York when he learned the tragic news: "I knew Thelma very well. I was in a play when that happened, but it was Ida who told me about the end. She had a party at the Trocadero ... I know that Thelma had quite a bit to drink, champagne, and I think she just fell asleep with the motor running. Now they make a big thing out of it. Everybody's gone and they tend to embellish things."

Ida Lupino, the hostess of the party, recalled Thelma's last words: "She hadn't driven her own car. There was a driver. She leaned out of the window, just before it took off, and she said, 'Goodbye, all of you!' The car drove off. My father said to my mother, 'Oh, my God, Connie, she knows she's booked. I don't think we are going to see her today.' Then I told them on the way home in the car what Thelma had told me, that she wasn't going to live to see another birthday, and that she wasn't going to make it. Dad said, 'No darling, I don't think she is; it's her heart.'"

Lina Basquette had seen Thelma shortly before the tragic end: "I once attempted suicide, maybe Thelma succeeded."

The mysterious death of Thelma Todd has intrigued the curious for decades. What really happened to her?

ONE

Fascinating Youth

William Todd pondered a momentous decision. Should he join the great Irish exodus? William and Eliza Shaw Todd lived in the gatekeeper's cottage on an estate in the district of Ballyloughan in Northern Ireland. As the landowner's caretaker, William was highly trusted for his honesty. He was also renowned as a master carpenter who could transform pieces of wood into a beautiful chair, cabinet, or bookcase. But at age 37, William was dissatisfied with his humble life. There were five sons to feed and another child on the way. Eliza, his wife, had been born in Scotland and spoke English with a burr. Her sister was living prosperously in America. Immigrants wrote home that America was a land of opportunity. In 1882, to improve their children's lives, the Todd family bade farewell to Ireland.

William and Eliza packed their trunks and prepared to join the three million Irish-born immigrants who lived abroad. The terrible famines of the early half of the century had already forced many Irish to abandon their island in droves. Miners, factory workers, and farmers had poured into New York and Boston, eager for a new life.

When the ship docked in Boston Harbor, the Todds gave thanks for a safe crossing. The oldest son, John, age eight, helped his father and mother shepherd his siblings onto a train. William Todd had but $9.00 in his pocket. Twenty-eight miles later, the Todds arrived at their final destination, Lawrence, Massachusetts, a city of immigrants and industry. Founded in 1845, it was named after the Lawrence brothers who had helped build the city and its mills. Lawrence was only a little over seven square miles, surrounded by the bordering towns of Methuen, Andover, and North Andover. The city owed its good fortune to the mighty Merrimack River which crossed its center, creating north and south regions, flowing to the Atlantic Ocean 20 miles to the east.

Along the banks of the Merrimack enormous textile mills had been built to harness the river's power, assisted by "the Great Stone Dam," a structure that stretched nine hundred feet. The population of 85,000 depended heavily on the Merrimack, a river that turned more spindles than any other river in America. The smokestacks of the mills towered above the skyline, belching dark smoke, a common sight for the thousands of laborers who dressed before dawn, then trod through the mill gates as shrill whistles sounded.

The many nationalities that inhabited Lawrence spent their salaries in shops on Essex Street, not far from the picturesque Lawrence Common. Elm and maple trees towered above

3

the 17 acres of parkland, dominated by a granite monument dedicated to the Grand Army of the Republic: "In Memory of Her Brave Men, Whose Sacrifice and Death Preserved the Union." City Hall faced the Common. Atop its spire perched a golden eagle, a symbol of the city's soaring prosperity. As a carpenter, William Todd had chosen his new town wisely, for Lawrence, like many cities in Massachusetts, favored homes built of wood. As Todd hammered and sawed for others, he began a house of his own at 22 Bowdoin Street in South Lawrence. Nearby was the residence of Daniel Saunders, an illustrious city father. The Saunders' residence on South Broadway had been part of "the underground railroad" for fleeing slaves.

The Todd home on Bowdoin Street was overrun with six sons: John, Adam, Henry, William Junior, David, and Charles. William Todd liked to jest that Charles was "the only son who could be president."[1] Two daughters, Elizabeth and Alice, came later. The eight children attended the Weatherby School. Every Sunday morning the entire family walked a mile to the Presbyterian Church on Haverhill Street. The children filled hours with Bible study, choir practice, and evening services. William forbade the Sunday newspaper, card playing, and theatre attendance. His strong religious beliefs were exhibited in his power as a faith healer. Friends and strangers alike came to his door for help. Quoting Scriptures, with a symbolic pocketknife in hand, he made the sign of the cross over the afflicted area. He invoked the name of Saint Anthony in the prayers, hoping to cure the sick, and never charged a fee for his healing.

William was a kind father, adored by his children. His past was recalled by the many animals that filled the backyard, where chickens, rabbits, and a horse roamed. The creatures often escaped into the home, to the children's delight. Though new immigrants, the Todds were members of a long tradition of Irish arrivals. Ingrained in the city's social structure was a network of charitable organizations which operated under the banner of the "Lawrence Provident Association." William and Eliza assisted the needy and taught their children to do the same.

Maturing into manhood, John, the oldest son, was a handsome youth with finely chiseled features, dark hair, and dapper moustache. He accepted a rather lowly job in a bleach factory and dutifully contributed to the family earnings. John later moved to Boston where he studied carpet cleaning and repair. Ambitious and articulate, John Todd displayed skill as an orator, a talent he carefully developed. On a visit to Graniteville, Vermont, John fell in love with Alice Edwards, a native of Quebec. Alice was a hearty woman with a booming laugh. She had been captivated by John's good looks and charm. Though plump and rather plain, Alice brightened a room with her sparkling sense of humor. She had an assertive personality and was proud of her heritage, boasting that her family had descended from Pilgrims who arrived on the *Mayflower*.

The newlyweds made their home at 306 South Broadway, close to the Todd family home. John and his brother Adam became partners as Todd Brothers–Carpet Renovators. Their office was at 325 Methuen Street, but they spent most of the day circulating the city in a horse-drawn wagon, offering to clean rugs. Alice worked in a woolen mill until her son William was born in 1903. On July 29, 1906, a daughter was born at the home on South Broadway. Her parents named her Thelma Alice Todd. The Todd brothers prospered. As businessmen they learned to be civic-minded and sociable. John and Alice were members of the South Congregational Church on South Broadway. John joined the Elks, the Knights of Pythias, and other fraternal organizations. He made no secret of his ambition for a city career. Befriended by fellow businessmen, who were swayed by his charm and eloquence, John Todd was soon a rising prospect for city office.

Lawrencians revised the city charter in 1910 and elected a five member commission to replace the outdated 25 man board. John was a good bookkeeper and felt the moment was opportune to solidify his plan. He believed he could be of service to the community and fiercely spoke out against Mayor Scanlon's administration. But the bright future soon dimmed. Tragedy struck while the family vacationed in North Randolph, Vermont. William, age seven, was playing in a dairy creamery when a flywheel suddenly shattered; the pieces struck and killed him. The boy's body was returned to Lawrence and buried in Bellevue Cemetery. Only his initials W.E.T. — William Edwards Todd — marked his tombstone, the tiny remembrance of a brief life. The terrible accident devastated John and Alice. Thelma became the center of parental affection.

The Irish, once dirt poor shanty dwellers, were firmly in control of the city government by 1912. John Todd made his bid for election. He denounced Mayor Scanlon and his aldermen as "a ring." In the fall, John Todd campaigned for election as Commissioner of Health and Charities, challenging incumbent alderman Robert S. Maloney. But the election was overshadowed by a bitter labor dispute, a confrontation that shook the city to its foundation and brought unwanted notoriety. Local laborers were upset over the mill owners' response to a new law that limited work to 54 hours per week. The legislation was designed to protect women and children. The owners not only reduced hours to comply with the law, but they also reduced wages as well. The move ignited pent-up anger. Half of the city's population, those over 14, worked in the textile factories. The volatile situation soon alarmed the entire community. The Italian branch of the International Workers of the World tried to close the mills by calling for a citywide strike. Rosario Contarino, 16, had been born in Italy to a middle class family. Despite being well-educated, the teenager spoke little English. He found work in the mills and earned a weekly salary of $4.40 for removing spools of yarn from machinery. Like other immigrants, mostly non-union, he joined his countrymen in the strike. The Italians formed the backbone of the upheaval, as the I.W.W. encouraged thousands of foreign-born mill workers to strike. Violence in the mills and streets brought the state militia to Lawrence. Arturo Giovannitti and Big Bill Haywood, I.W.W. leaders, also arrived. Trying to prevent entry to the factories, strikers smashed trolley car windows, and a policeman was stabbed. Shots from the militia killed striker Annie LoPezzi. A cache of dynamite was uncovered by authorities, who later determined it had been planted by a prominent mill owner.

After two months of strife, a significant concession was made to the workers. They returned to the mills with increased wages but were angry that three strike leaders had been indicted in the death of Annie LoPezzi. After the leaders were acquitted in November, citizens breathed a sigh of relief, but bitterness lingered. In the aftermath of the gloomy atmosphere fostered by the strike, John Todd was embroiled in a fierce election. Todd hammered away at the incompetence of his rival: "Your treasury is practically empty and they will attempt perhaps to blind you with false statements and figures. You can protect yourself and progress by smashing the ring at city hall!"[2]

Alderman Robert Maloney fired back. At a city hall rally he defended the use of funds for the paupers' home: "I am proud to say that I have always given them chicken on Sundays, that I will continue to do so as long as I am in office, and will save money for the city at that!" John Todd campaigned from neighborhood to neighborhood, speaking on street corners, pumping hands. He pounded away at Maloney, telling voters the incumbent had squandered taxpayer money. The candidate was usually accompanied by his beaming wife and six-year-old daughter, a beautiful child with golden curls, brightened by egg yolks, carefully added to the shampoo by her mother.

The voter turnout was heavy, especially in the race for Commissioner of Health and Charities. Among the four contenders, the battle was between Todd and Maloney. Of the 17,357 votes cast, John Todd received 4,266 and Maloney 4,016. John Todd won by a mere 250 votes, but it was enough to proclaim a glorious victory. Family and friends gathered at the patriarch's home where William Todd joyfully hailed his son as the victor. The new alderman moved his family from South Broadway to the Town Farm at 121 Marston Street. They settled in a residence adjacent to the home for paupers. Little Thelma was popular with both the residents and staff. Lena Bourdelais, chief nurse, was especially delighted with the pretty child who was admired by all for her cheery personality. Thelma's long blonde tresses attracted immediate attention as she chatted happily with those confined to "the poor house." During his two year term John Todd managed the Town Farm, Tuberculosis Hospital, and Health Department. He devised a clever plan to save town funds. The plan was to use city garbage, picked up in "honey carts," to feed and raise hogs. The animals were then slaughtered and fed to the residents of the Town Farm. Robert Maloney, bitter and seeking to regain office, spread the false story that Alderman Todd was raising hogs for his own profit.

As the 1914 election drew near, an incident took place that made John Todd the center of attention. While Mayor White conducted business out of town, John Todd was temporary mayor; unexpectedly, he banned three motion pictures. Todd notified theatres that *In the Clutches of the Gangsters*, *The Fatal Wedding*, and *Rose of the Alley* could not be shown in Lawrence because the films ridiculed Jews: "While I am the authority I will not permit the exhibition of any picture that will cast reflection on the character, mode of living or habits of any race, creed or color, or which has a tendency toward ridicule."[3]

Though Protestants, the Todds were respectful of other religious views. They never engaged in the religious disputes

John Shaw Todd in March 1904 (courtesy of Edna Todd Bixby).

which plagued their native Ireland. William Todd, though a staunch Protestant, welcomed the priests from nearby St. Patrick's Catholic Church into his home for tea. But the family relished political fervor and the rematch between Todd and Maloney was merciless, as both attacked each other, exchanging charges of mishandling taxpayer funds.

"The city treasury did not get this $5,498.89. Where is it, John?" asked Maloney.[4]

"Maloney surrenders," answered Todd.[5] "He makes rash statements and no attempt to show how he gets his sum totals. Why such a vicious attack in the form of a letter, at the last moment, when the gong is about to ring and Bob Maloney about to take the count?"

Whether it was because of John Todd's defense of Hebrews or the scheme to raise hogs, Maloney triumphed by 68 votes. The defeated candidate bowed his head to democracy: "The people have made their choice. I am willing to abide by it."[6] Though publicly gracious, the accusations of dishonesty had poisoned Todd's political dreams. Disillusioned, he had a warning for other dreamers that he recited to family members: "Keep out of politics. It's a dirty game."[7]

The Todds packed their belongings and left the Town Farm for a new home at 100 Blanchard Street in South Lawrence. John Todd became assistant supervisor of the city street department, a job he held for several years. He never again ventured into the political arena. But his short two years in office would have an unexpected advantage. His daughter inherited his love of the crowd and the common touch of mingling with one and all. As Thelma grew older, she emulated her mother's sense of humor. In the family Thelma's mother was known as "Big Alice," while her sister-in-law was "Little Alice."

The large family always gathered during the Christmas holidays, despite the icy wind that swept in from the Atlantic, covering the city with sleet and snow; sons, daughters, spouses, and children dutifully came to the home on Bowdoin Street. The Christmas festivities were happy events, always filled with gaiety, especially when Alice Todd arrived. Alice made an impression wherever she went. William "Bill" Todd, Thelma's young cousin, once blurted, "Here comes Aunt Alice in a new pink dress, and I hope she doesn't laugh as loud!"

Thelma's beauty made her the center of attention. But at seven she was a tomboy, riding her bicycle on Bowdoin Street, romping in bloomies and middies, when most little girls wore frills and lace. Thelma loved to play baseball and swim; nevertheless, each Sunday Alice dressed her daughter immaculately for church service. She entered Saunders School, next door to her grandparents' home. At age 13, Thelma graduated from Packard Grammar School. She was photographed with her classmates and proudly displayed her diploma, beautifully gowned in a white dress with black silk stockings. She was the prettiest girl in the class. Thelma had yet to discover boys, but she had a great passion beside sports — motion pictures. Lawrence was filled with ornate movie palaces, like the Bijou on Appleton Street, a theatre that boasted:

> Best Moving Pictures, Illustrated Songs and Special Comedy Performances. Come to the Bijou and see Marvelous scenic effects produced by the Bijouscope, on the Carr Patent Radium screen. FLICKERLESS, CLEAR AS A BELL, DAYLIGHT PICTURES. Accompanied by realistic effects. Grand-Startling-Sublime-Free! Valuable presents will be given to patrons of this theatre, watch for announcements. Admission 5 cents Any Seat–Anywhere–Anytime Afternoon Evenings Sundays[8]

Alice and Thelma loved motion pictures. They usually boarded a trolley that clanged down South Broadway and shuttled past South Congregational Church, where Thelma sang in the choir each Sunday. The trolley passed Saint Patrick's Church and continued onto the O'Leary Bridge, a long span that stretched over the Merrimack River near the dam. The trolley soon arrived at Theatre Row where four marquees were brightly lit: the Broadway, the Empire, the Modern, and the Strand. The managers of all four theatres knew Thelma. Like millions of other girls, Thelma dreamed of being a screen actress.

On the other side of town, the Cosmopolitan Theatre on Newbury Street delighted 350 patrons, mostly Italians, who were greeted by the Contarino family, immigrants from Catania, Sicily. Rosario Contarino, the former mill worker, sold tickets. Peter, his brother, was the projectionist. As the lights dimmed, Emmanuele, their father, counted the box office receipts. The Contarinos had come to America as tourists but never returned to Italy, where the family owned property; instead, Emmanuele bought the Cosmopolitan Theatre in 1919. The Contarino boys watched the films over and over. They studied the productions and told their father that they would one day make movies just as good as the ones from Hollywood.

Thelma's cousins, Bill and Edna Todd, grew up at 26 Bowdoin. Alice and Thelma would stop by almost every day to visit. The Todd clan was close. Thelma and her cousins spent summers at Foster Pond. John Todd also liked to take the children to Johnson's Pond, a fresh water swimming hole, where fishing was prohibited, but Uncle John would drop a line in the pond and pull up a fish. When only a teenager, Thelma had a full figure with shapely hips. Bill Todd always enjoyed her visits to his home, since she burst with fun and laughter. She would jut out her hip playfully, "Come on, I'll give you a camel ride,"[9] Thelma shouted. Her eyes sparkled as she bounced her little cousin around the room. Bill Todd

At Foster Pond. Back row: Elizabeth Todd Henderson, Bill Todd. Front row: Alice Edward Todd, Thelma, Edna Dutton Todd, Edna Todd (courtesy of Edna Todd Bixby).

noticed the effect his gorgeous cousin had on men: "Wherever she went, heads would turn." Bill and Thelma often visited their grandfather, now a widower. Thelma was especially fond of Bill's mother, known in the family as "Big Edna," a cheerful woman who was married to Uncle Charles, a carpenter and the youngest brother. Thelma and Aunt Edna would grow close over the years.

Within view of City Hall, across the tree-lined Common, was Lawrence High School. Students chose one of five programs on enrollment: the college preparatory course, the normal school course, the commercial course, the mechanic arts, or household arts. At fourteen, Thelma chose the normal school program, the path to a teaching career.

In 1920, Thelma's first year in high school, her grandfather died. William had been active to the end, but he had fallen and suffered serious injuries. He died peacefully on his birthday in the home he had built, surrounded by his large family. Thereafter, a shadow fell on the family. Bill Todd was carefully watched by the family after two young cousins, both named William, met with tragic childhood accidents. Thelma's brother had died in the creamery and Kenneth William Todd, while playing in an excavated dirt pit, suffocated when mounds of dirt collapsed on him.

As the loveliest girl in Lawrence High School, Thelma had many admirers. She stayed busy with the school newspaper and contributed to Gossip Notes for *The Bulletin*. Most afternoons Thelma would walk home with Almeda King, a neighborhood friend. If the girls felt daring, Thelma would put out her thumb. "She always got us a ride," recalls King.[10] "Thelma was so attractive and lots of fun, too." Almeda worked at a bakery across from Saint Patrick's Church. Almeda came to know the entire Todd clan. She found John Todd

As a staff writer for *The Bulletin* of Lawrence High School (collection of the Lawrence History Center, Lawrence, Massachusetts).

handsome. "Alice was a smart dresser, what we called then 'a nifty-looking woman.' She always looked nice and was a fine conversationalist. She had good timing and always knew when to say the right thing."

Older men were crazy about Thelma, King noted. But those who couldn't catch her eye grew resentful: "Some of the fellows thought she was uppity. They used to hang out at the pool room, just staring as she passed by." Thelma was also close to the McMahon sisters, Ann and Katherine, school chums from a Catholic family. Single dates were forbidden, so the teenagers went out in a group, usually to enjoy a film. Thelma's first boyfriend was Jean Campopiano. One day, Jean excitedly told Thelma that his friends, Rosario and Peter Contarino, were going to make a movie. Jean knew that Thelma wanted to be an actress, so he urged her to audition. She rushed home, to 6 Brookfield Street, the new family residence, and excitedly asked her parents for permission. Thelma had already appeared in church plays; one role had been the bride in *Tom Thumb's Wedding*. On a Thursday evening, she lined up outside the Cosmopolitan Theatre on Newbury Street. She hoped to win the lead in *The Life of Saint Genevieve*. Young women from as far away as Boston and Manchester anxiously awaited their turn to audition on the Cosmopolitan stage. The Contarino brothers watched as the eager sang, recited, danced, or merely stood. When Thelma stepped into the spotlight Rosario Contarino sat up in his seat. This beautiful girl should be given a chance, he told his brother. Eva McKenna, a Lawrence native, won the lead, but Thelma was hired as an extra. The brothers started Aurora Films.

The Contarinos, who were in their twenties, bought a camera in Boston for $1,200; afterward, they purchased three acres of land in Methuen for $3,000. Shares in the company were sold at $100 each, until $100,000 was raised; an attorney incorporated the company as the Aurora Film Corporation in 1922. They sold $49,000 in shares and kept the remainder, valued at $51,000. Local theatre owners had assured the brothers that Italians would crowd the theatres to see a film about Saint Genevieve, and they would be wealthy men. What was formerly Weisner's Field became the headquarters of Aurora Films, a huge barn-shaped structure 200 feet long by 75 feet wide. Children peered through glass walls as the cast assembled in colorful costumes, wigs, and plumed hats. Behind the building was an outdoor set with a cobblestone street and a saloon. Thelma arrived on the set filled with awe and excitement.

Unexpectedly, a city inspector came to the barn, curious about the use of young girls in the production but, after looking around, he left satisfied that nothing illegal was underway. The company went on location to Searles Castle, a lavish estate, where 100 extras, dressed as soldiers, were dutifully paid $10 each per day. Thelma earned $50. Peter Contarino wore a black beret and gave directions in heavily-accented English. Rosario, his camera mounted on a tripod, cranked furiously. Though her appearance was minor, Thelma excitedly told her friends about her performance. She was now a screen actress. The dream to be a famous star in Hollywood seemed a possibility. The Contarinos spent $22,000 on *The Life of St. Genevieve* and planned a second film. They even opened studios in Boston and Memphis.

The Contarinos liked Thelma. The brothers gave her a key scene in *Tangled Hearts*, their next production, a comedy about a wealthy man whose wife is so obsessed with household duties that she ignores him. Based on the novel by William Galt, the brothers felt they had a winner. Cast members were paid high salaries, and the company even went on location

Already an actress in *Tom Thumb's Wedding*, date unknown (courtesy of Edna Todd Bixby).

to Rye Beach in New Hampshire, where Thelma and Angelo Carallo were photographed emerging from a beach house, holding hands, and sitting on a bench.

Rosario Drago, an actor in the film, came to appreciate Thelma's vivacious charm and friendliness. Drago had an idea. He suggested to Thelma that they should send their photographs to Hollywood studios. After Rudolph Valentino's international success, Drago felt he had a chance at stardom. The young Italian was astounded when a letter arrived from Fox Pictures. The letter was from William Fox, the studio president. Drago was offered a role in *Asleep in the Deep*. There was no mention of Thelma. Despite his previous enthusiasm, Drago lost his nerve. He was afraid to accept the Hollywood offer. The young man was frightened that his poor English would make him a laughingstock in sophisticated Los Angeles.

While Thelma waited anxiously for the release of the two films, she began a part-time job at Woolworths on Essex Street, along with her friend Kathleen Barnes. Thelma attracted male admirers who came in the store just to talk to her. Carl Eidam, a high school assistant headmaster, fell in love with her. Eidam proposed and offered to marry her once she finished school, but Thelma rejected Eidam's offer; she was more intent on a career than a wedding. Thelma joined the graduating class of 1923 assembled at Lawrence High for a final farewell. After a dinner of roast spring chicken, the graduates danced to the music of Bardsley's Orchestra. Principal Lawrence J. O'Leary addressed the crowd. He praised the *Bulletin* staff, saying that he was "justly proud" of the year's publications.[11] Thelma, despite her column in the school paper, told friends she would train to be a teacher, rather than a reporter. Thelma enrolled in the Lowell Normal College, but she hoped that the Contarinos would succeed with the unreleased films, so more films could be made, and her screen career would take off. But the fledgling entrepreneurs faced deadly obstacles.

In New York City, a major market, the Contarinos discovered that the distribution company that serviced theatres in Italian neighborhoods was controlled by extortionists. The company demanded that the Contarinos share a major portion of the profits. They refused. Instead, Rosario located a theatre in New York, a former church, whose owner agreed to screen *The Life of Saint Genevieve*. When the brothers arrived, crowds were waiting to enter the theatre, but a man stepped forward and warned: "If you put it on, we'll put you away."[12] Crowds milled outside, anxiously waiting to buy tickets, but the theatre owner was so frightened he refused to open the doors. The brothers received the same treatment in Chicago, where Al Capone controlled the projectionist union. The brothers were told that 50 percent of the profits had to be surrendered or there would be no screening of their motion pictures. They discovered that even the Boston market was controlled from New York. The shareholders fumed over the delay. The film only earned $8,500. The brothers next made a film called *Mussolino*, about a bandit Robin Hood.

Tremount Campbell, a Metro agent in Boston expressed interest in distributing *Tangled Hearts* and offered $125,000, but the shareholders wanted an immediate return. The Contarinos arranged a week's run at the Empire Theatre in Lawrence. In May 1924, local newspapers advertisements hailed the unseen picture: "An all-star cast of great merit ... made locally ... made under the master-hand of the great director Peter Contarino. Love! Passion! Romance! Intrigue! Tragedy! Smiles! Tears! Laughs! Thrills!" The screening was a success, but Rosario was surprised when the Metro agent abandoned the distribution deal. The agent was angry the film had already been premiered. The discouraged brothers faced financial ruin. They had no choice but to sell both pictures to a mob-controlled distribution company which made huge profits. After shareholders were paid, the Contarino brothers were destitute. "The Mafia took everything," Rosario lamented.[13]

Thelma concentrated on her teaching career. She was assigned a class at Hood Elementary School, as a substitute teacher, where she taught eighth graders. But she also had another job. Thelma modeled clothes and furs for local shops. Doykos Furriers arranged to have her photographed at the La Fond Gallery. She won a beauty contest at Hampton Beach and was chosen to be the first Snow Queen, reigning over the winter festival on Lightning Hill. Thelma's good looks brought modeling assignments in Boston. In a shoe store she was photographed wearing the latest in beaded garters. Thelma was chosen as the best model in the Fall Fashion Revue at the Empire Theatre. She was awarded an expensive dress from Cherry and Webb and received gold coins from Florence Fredericks, the woman who staged the event. Thelma combined style and substance, beauty and brains, as she pursued her diverse careers. Alice Todd guided her. Though both parents were extremely proud of Thelma, it was Alice who encouraged Thelma to capitalize on her beauty. John Todd had never achieved financial success, a situation that became a major disappointment to his wife. Alice pushed Thelma toward a modeling career.

Thelma became the center of a controversy when Lowell College unexpectedly changed the rules for obtaining a teaching position. Previously, all students were guaranteed employment after six months of practice teaching. However, after Thelma enrolled, a new system went into effect. Thelma and her classmates protested that they were being treated unfairly. Thelma was the student leader. She appeared before a distinguished school committee and voiced her opinions "ably and logically," recorded the *Evening Tribune*.[14] The committee debated with her, but Thelma, 18, refused to retreat. Although the panel upheld the new regulations, they admired Thelma's presentation and courage. Soon after, the school controversy was rendered inconsequential. Her life changed dramatically in the spring of 1925.

John Todd's Elk Lodge 65 announced it would sponsor a beauty pageant to select Miss Lawrence. The winner would enter the Miss Massachusetts competition. Thelma's mother and friends urged Thelma to compete, but in the midst of the excitement, Thelma's parents were worried. John Todd was in failing health due to heart disease. He had suffered a light stroke and walked with a limp. Drawn and gaunt, he had retired from the street department in 1920. He wore owlish glasses that gave him a professorial air as he shuffled along. Always yearning for the country life, John became superintendent of Donovan's Dairy Farm in North Andover. Thelma and her cousins enjoyed visits to the farm. Her father delighted in showing them the grazing herds, vats of milk, and the ferocious, snorting bull, all reminders of his youth in Ireland.

Alice had grown plump in middle age. The couple's life now revolved around their lovely daughter. Since there were never sufficient funds to purchase a home, Alice liked to move frequently, renting houses they could never own. In 1924, the Todds moved to 592 Andover Street, an address that was destined to be their last residence in Lawrence.

On June 1, 1925, the streets leading to Rosewood Amusement Park were jammed with automobiles. Reporters from Boston came to Lawrence to cover the beauty contest. A reporter from the *Evening Tribune* captured the excitement as the swelling crowd poured through the park gates on the scenic Merrimack River and into the ballroom where Fletcher Henderson's Orchestra performed. An air of excitement permeated the huge hall, decorated with bowers of wisteria blossoms and colored bunting. Bright lights illuminated a stage where Wyatt Kimball was greeted with applause. Kimball, the sole judge, was a renowned artist, world traveler, and member of the diplomatic service. While secretary of the American consulate in Plymouth, England, Kimball had won acclaim with a portrait of Queen Victoria. A resident of Concord, New Hampshire, Kimball was regarded as a connoisseur of beauty. The crowd stirred as the 15 entrants moved into the spotlight. As each passed before Kimball, cheers broke forth from throngs of supporters. Thelma came forward, dressed in a simple frock of robin's egg blue crepe. Her long blonde tresses shone brightly. Applause exploded. Kimball deliberated, then turned to the audience; a hushed silence swept the packed ballroom: "Miss Todd is a young lady ideally fitted to represent your city at the coming state contest. She is stunning and striking in appearance, two qualities which are necessary to success."[15] Thelma was crowned Miss Lawrence.

The Todd clan was elated. Thelma prepared for the forthcoming state contest. She posed for photographs and gave interviews. A special dress was designed for her to wear. In the flurry of excitement a telegram arrived at the Todd home on Andover Street. Thelma caught her breath as she read the news. Movie magnate Jessie L. Lasky asked her to visit Paramount Pictures in Astoria, Long Island. In April, Lasky had announced a nationwide search for students to attend the Paramount School. Those eligible were men between 18 and 30, and women from 16 to 25. Tuition would be $500 along with living expenses. Lasky explained the purpose of the school: "Our aim in founding the Paramount School embraces more than teaching how to act. It is hoped that our students in the course of their studies will become imbued with a lofty conception of the screen artists' opportunities and

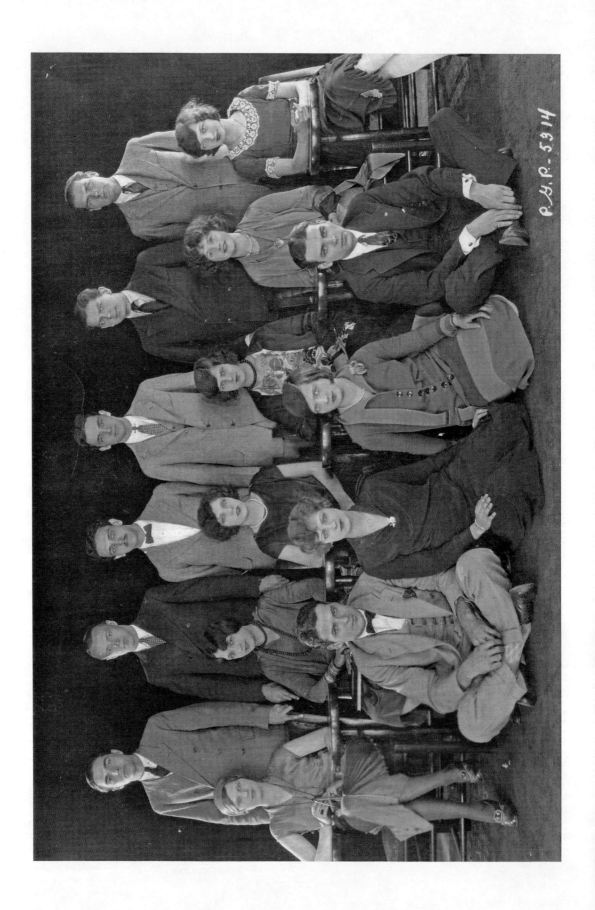

responsibilities. The student will learn what it means to appear simultaneously on the screen of thousands of theatres; he will be taught the great responsibility which is placed upon him as a public figure; he will be shown the pitfalls that lurk in the path of the young and popular player; and he will be taught those principals of right living and right thinking that will make him worthy to be a part of the greatest force for enlightenment and recreation the world has ever seen."[16] *Right living* was being promoted in Hollywood in 1925.

The film industry was still reeling from a string of lurid scandals which cast a sinister pall over the magic aura of Hollywood. Roscoe "Fatty" Arbuckle, one of Hollywood's great comedians, had been charged with murder in 1921. Virginia Rappe, a minor actress, died several days after an Arbuckle party. The party had been held in a suite on the twelfth floor of the St. Francis Hotel in San Francisco. Bootleg liquor flowed as revelers danced. Rappe, 23, collapsed during the party as the phonograph blared and bottles were emptied. A model named Bambina Maude Delmont told police Rappe had been sexually assaulted. Two Arbuckle trials ended with a hung jury. Although jurors found Arbuckle innocent in the third trial, state censor boards banned his comedies. Will Hays, Postmaster General in the Harding administration, left his government position to assume the leadership of the new Motion Picture Producers and Distributors Association. In the midst of the Arbuckle scandal, handsome screen star Wallace Reid was hospitalized. Millions of fans were shocked to learn their idol was a morphine addict. Even more startling for the nation was the death of William Desmond Taylor. The famous director was shot in an unsolved murder. Within a scant six months, the glitter of the motion picture lifestyle had been exposed in a sinister light. Lasky and his fellow moguls undertook to assure movie fans that the whispered degeneracy of the film industry was unfounded. Wholesome youngsters would be brought to Hollywood, glorious in their shining innocence.

The Todd clan was overjoyed by Thelma's good fortune, as were her friends. However, the fairytale aspect of Lasky's invitation was misleading. Thelma had a single man to thank. Paramount Studio had promoted Lasky's "wholesome youth" plan through film exchanges throughout the nation; exhibitors were asked to assist the search for new faces. Lasky told reporters he wanted educated youngsters with good looks and experience in amateur theatre. An observer of pretty faces knew there was a girl in Lawrence who wanted to be on the silver screen and she had a face that made men stop and stare. Not only pretty, Thelma prepared to be a teacher and had already appeared in two films.

A reporter for the *Boston Evening Tribune* later recounted Thelma's good fortune. Napoleon L. Demara, a partner in Toomey and Demara, a film booking agency for the Merrimack Valley, provided films for the Empire, Broadway, Palace, and Premiere theatres. Demara believed Thelma had a strong chance of being chosen for the new school, so she handed him a portfolio of modeling photographs taken by Lionel G. La Fond. For several years, Demara had conducted business with Famous Players-Lasky and made certain that Thelma's photographs, conveying youthful innocence, reached the right hands.

Thelma, John, and Alice were driven to Boston by excited friends. The trio boarded the Knickerbocker Limited for New York. They were met at Grand Central Station by

Opposite: **The Paramount Junior Stars, date unknown. Front row, left to right: Irving Hartley, Josephine Dunn, Dorothy Nourse, Claud Buchanan. Second row: Thelma Todd, Mona Palma, Ivy Harris, Iris Grey, Thelda Kenvin, Harriet Krauth. Rear: Walter Goss, Jack Luden, Charles Brokaw, Charles "Buddy" Rogers, Greg Blackton, Robert Andrews (courtesy of Don Collins).**

Paramount officials and entrusted to Al Wilkie, a blunt publicist who was tired of the endless stream of hopefuls he escorted into the Astoria studio: "The girl is sent to the studio and it is up to our department to show her a good time and get her back on the train before she drives the stars and directors insane with foolish questions."[17] At Pierce and Sixth Street, Wilkie drove the guests through the gates of the vast Paramount Studios where a luncheon was held in Thelma's honor. She was impressed that Richard Dix and Ricardo Cortez were seated at her table. Though both were pleasant, they hurriedly ate and returned to work. Afterward, Thelma was permitted to watch scenes being filmed in a garden on a small bridge shaded by trees. "Two lovers doing their stuff," Thelma would recall.[18] She watched as the couple blissfully embraced, all the while surrounded by a crew of technicians, sun reflectors, and blinding Kleig lights. The following day, Thelma met Jesse Lasky. Silver-haired, with pince-nez glasses clipped to his nose, he explained the concept of the Paramount School. The calculating eyes surveyed the girl before him. Lasky asked if she would like to enroll. Thelma told him that since childhood she wanted to be a screen actress. Lasky promised her a contract.

As the night train rolled through the darkness, Thelma was overwhelmed with excitement. At the Boston train station enthusiastic Elks cheered the Todds. The exhausted trio was driven to the coastal resort town of Swampscott for the state pageant. Reporters eyed the young contestants and filed accounts with various newspapers. By mid-afternoon, dark clouds rolled in from the steel-gray Atlantic. In the evening a fierce storm swept through the resort, soaking the spectators who arrived at Ocean House, a new convention center. As the crowd huddled under umbrellas, a strong wind toppled three large willow trees that crashed to the pavement. In the ballroom electricity flickered as the storm frazzled the nerves of the lovely contestants.

Thelma nervously waited. Swampscott merchants had furnished the women with expensive gowns and, noted a reporter, each shop hoped to reap the publicity of having dressed the winner. Thelma wore a peach evening dress trimmed with ostrich feathers, chiffon stockings, and paisley slippers with rhinestone buckles. The lights dimmed and the orchestra began an overture. As spotlights swept over each contestant, supporters broke into applause. Thelma, near the end of the line, was greeted with applause, later commented on by her father: "There was more noise and cheering than at any football game I ever attended."[19] The forty women paraded down a runway before the critical gaze of the judges, including Florenz Ziegfeld, a producer famous for his *Follies* show in New York City. Also appraising the young women was Broadway actor Charles Winninger, performing with the *No, No Nanette* company in Boston. As the storm roared, the contestants nervously lined up for the final selection. Thelma was surprised to see the illustrious panel approach her. The audience clapped and cheered wildly. The lovely blonde from South Lawrence stood in the spotlight, chosen as the new Miss Massachusetts. Flashbulbs popped and reporters swarmed and asked questions. "I hate people who are not natural," she told the journalists. "I hate people who are stuck up, and I hate hypocrites. Aside from that I get along with everybody."[20]

The new beauty queen was in demand for civic gatherings, parties, and store openings. In only two weeks Thelma had won two prestigious beauty contests and enrollment in the Paramount School. John and Alice were overwhelmed by their daughter's good fortune. They made arrangements to move. A farewell party was held at the Todd home on Andover

Street. Family and friends crowded into the small rented rooms bearing gifts and good wishes. The summer night was filled with laughter and excited talk of Thelma's success. She was now Lawrence's golden girl. The *Evening Tribune* published the La Fond photograph which had caught the eye of Jesse Lasky. It was the profile of a demure girl, expressing a delicate innocence. The following morning Aunt Edna drove the trio to Boston. Left behind were Jean Campopiano and Carl Eidam; both men had been in love with Thelma, but Lawrence was too small for Thelma Todd. She wanted to see the world, to star in motion pictures, to be famous. At the age of 18, she waved farewell to her hometown.

John and Alice rented an apartment at 190 Twenty-Sixth Street in Jackson Heights. Thelma stayed at the Allerton Hotel for Women at Fifty-Seventh Street and Lexington Avenue. She was introduced to Mrs. J. Walter Taylor, a respectable widow chosen to chaperone the female students. The studio implemented rigid rules; not only were there separate hotels for men and women, but all students were expected to be in bed by 10:30 P.M. The training would last for six months.

On July 20, the Paramount School opened at the studio lot in Astoria. Reporters from around the country covered the event. Speeches were made by Adolph Zukor, president, and Jesse Lasky, vice president of the Famous Players Company; nine men and nine women sat before the studio officials. Their names were released to the press: Josephine Dunn, Robert Andrews, Greg Blackton, Charles Brokaw, Claud Buchanan, Walter J. Goss, Jack Luden, Ethelda Kenvin, Mona Palma, Lorraine Eason, Wilbur Dillon, Laverne Lindsay, Irving Hartley, Marian Ivy Harris, Harriet Krauth, Dorothy Nourse, Charles Rogers, and Thelma Todd.

Lasky delivered a stern warning, wrote a reporter for the *New York Times*: "I have seen players come and go; I have seen extra girls rise to the heights of stardom and I have seen the brightest stars lose their lustre and fade into obscurity. I am going to show you the other side of that great shining light which we call public favor. The public is lavish to its favorites. But while it smiles, it also demands the strictest obedience to its laws, and disobedience brings punishment that is as swift as it is terrible. You must govern yourselves accordingly and let nothing you do bring the slightest smirch upon the profession which today is accepting you as one of its members."[21] The students who succeeded, said Lasky, would be offered a one year contract with Paramount.

Paramount's publicity department informed the nation about Lasky's plan to create new stars. The young performers were watched carefully; a single scandal would bring ridicule to all involved, as *Motion Picture Classic* informed its readers: "If the slightest thing happened to any one of them, the scandal would be terrific. Especially if it should be a girl, and she should attempt to involve some director or executive about the studio."[22]

Thelma found the Astoria studio "a veritable labyrinth."[23] From 9:00 A.M. until late evening, the students were shown how to walk correctly, how to sit, how to cry and laugh. Roles were assigned by instructors for one act plays. Saturday evenings the students were allowed to enjoy the town until midnight. Charles "Buddy" Rogers and Robert Andrews vied for Thelma's attention. Rogers was 21, a native of Olanthe, Kansas, who had studied journalism at the University of Kansas until his father, a prominent newspaper editor, suggested he apply for the Paramount School. During college Buddy Rogers had formed a popular band but felt inadequate as an actor. At one point, he discussed quitting the program, but Thelma encouraged him to remain for the full six months. Robert Andrews, 25, was smitten with Thelma. Andrews had already worked as an extra and advanced to juvenile roles when he was cast in Lasky's *The Warrens of Virginia* in 1924. He had also been an assistant director. Reports circulated that he remained in the school only because Thelma was there.

Lawrence's *Evening Tribune* covered Thelma's activities, especially the rumors of her romance with Andrews. After a New York newspaper published photographs of the couple and announced their engagement, a reporter telephoned John and Alice. Like Thelma, they were shocked and denied the story. Even without romance in her life, Thelma was still big news in her native city. A photograph of Thelma on a horse in Central Park was prominently featured in the local newspaper. Three students rebelled over the monastic atmosphere and were asked to leave. The names of Wilbur Dillon, Lorraine Eason, and Laverne Lindsay disappeared from the school roster. Iris Gray, a runner-up from Kansas, was asked to join. Gray was a professional dancer who had toured on the Orpheum circuit. In fact, many of "the newcomers" had considerable experience in show biz, as verified in a *New York Times* profile entitled "Sixteen Lucky Students."[24]

At eighteen, Josephine Dunn had been a chorus girl, as had Dorothy Nourse, 16, and Harriet Krauth, 17. The girls had danced in Earl Carroll's *Vanities*. Krauth was the sister of actress Marian Marsh. She soon changed her name to Jeanne Morgan. Charles Brokaw, a graduate of Ohio State University, had been a stage actor for five years. At 26 Brokaw was the oldest and elected class president. Greg Blackton, 25, had lived in Cuba and Argentina. He knew the casting director at the Astoria studio and had worked as an extra. Claud Buchanan, 25, was a war veteran. For three years he had appeared in vaudeville, theatre, and films. Irving Hartley, 23, had been a photographer for the *New York World*. While on assignment aboard a cruise liner, he met famous actress Dorothy Gish, who advised him to become a screen actor. He had worked for MGM for a year as a bit player. Jack Luden, 23, was on his way to Hollywood when he was accepted into the school. Luden, a native of Reading, Pennsylvania, was the handsome nephew of William Luden, the wealthy founder of America's famous cough drop company. Of the others, Walter Goss, 24, had worked on the staff of the *New York Herald Tribune*, Mona Palma, 21, had been a fashion model, and Thelda Kenvin, 21, was a runner-up in the 1923 Miss America pageant. Ivy Harris, 18, was from a distinguished Atlanta family. Thelma Todd, 18, was described as "a school teacher — her forte is said to be comedy."

Canon Chase of the Federal Motion Picture Council liked the idea of decent youngsters in Hollywood. The Brooklyn minister led a crusade for "wholesome motion pictures." For years he had complained about gambling, boxing, and horse racing. Chase now demanded film regulation. As he explained, "The whole world is protesting against American pictures right now ... why is the business in the hands of less than a half dozen men: Zukor, Loew, Fox, Laemmle, and Lasky?"[25] Chase denounced *The Thief of Baghdad* because the film "glorified a thief." He disliked *Queen of Sheba* since there was a biblical character "without historical authority," and *The Covered Wagon* had "a shocking drinking scene." The preacher insisted "we must have regulations ... and don't call it censorship."

Jesse Lasky was pleased with the students and praised their "personality galore."[26] The studio made certain that reporters followed the fledgling stars. Paramount executives immediately recognized that Thelma was photogenic and had a flair for comedy. Buddy Rogers was viewed as the likeliest male to succeed. Tom Terris, the director of the school, filmed the students, then evaluated screen performances with the class. Terris was replaced by Sam Wood, a renowned director who had worked with Wallace Reid and Gloria Swanson. Rogers viewed him as "nice but tough." Wood appraised the students for *Fascinating Youth,* a film designed to showcase "the Junior Stars of 1926." Rogers was selected to star as the son of a wealthy hotel owner who falls in love with a working-class girl, Ivy Harris, rather than socialite Josephine Dunn. Thelma was cast in a minor role as the socialite's sister. Interiors were shot at the Astoria studio and finished by Christmas. Although her small role was over, Thelma joined the company at Lake Placid after the holidays where they stayed at the Onondaga Cottage during the three weeks of exterior filming. Paramount's major talent had cameos. They arrived as themselves at a failing mountain resort in the story. On hand were Richard Dix, Clara Bow, Adolphe Menjou, Lois Wilson, Lila Lee, Percy Marmont, Chester Conklin, Thomas Meighan, and directors Lewis Milestone and Malcolm St. Clair. Thelma mingled with the screen luminaries, if not yet an equal, at least a colleague. She organized skiing groups and bobsled races. Thelma accompanied the cast and crew to the North Shrewsbury River, near Red Bank, New Jersey, for the filming of the ice boat races, scenes that were later praised by reviewers as the most exciting in the picture.

The students signed a temporary contract for *Fascinating Youth.* A clause stipulated that Paramount could secure their services, if so desired, within two weeks of the film's completion. Word spread that only Buddy Rogers was assured of a trip to Hollywood. But the *Boston Evening American* recounted how Thelma Todd was also chosen. Lasky and Ben Schulberg, chief of the studio in Los Angeles, huddled in screening rooms, spoke with directors, scrutinized footage, and tried to determine who would set the screen afire. Thelma was summoned to the Astoria studio for a meeting with Walter Wanger, general manager in charge of production. She prepared herself for the worst; after all, she could return to teaching. Wanger greeted her politely and asked if she had seen the completed picture? No, she replied. Wanger picked up a telephone. "I want you to run *Fascinating Youth* in projection room four immediately," he ordered. "Come, Miss Todd, and take a look at yourself."[27] As the lights dimmed, Thelma felt uncomfortable. When the room brightened, she noticed that Wanger was staring at her curiously.

"How did you like it?" he asked.

"I don't know."

Wanger laughed. In his office he showed Thelma a one-year contract to appear exclusively in Paramount films. Startled, she asked if she could use the telephone. Wanger nodded and Thelma called Alice with the news.

Lawrence was soon abuzz with the exciting news that Thelma Todd was going to Hollywood. The *Evening Tribune* confirmed the event, profiling "Thelma of the Screen — Pretty Lawrence Girl Tells of Her First Venture into the Mysteries of Screen Acting." Thelma said that since she was ten years old she had wanted to be an actress and had discussed the dream with her mother: "I expect to put in two or three years of good hard work before I accomplish anything really big. Stars are not made overnight as some people seem to think."[28] Thelma said she would try anything before the camera but preferred dramatic roles, similar to those played by Nazimova and Pauline Frederick. Lawrence's new celebrity was the talk of the town: "She will leave with the best wishes of the home town folks who are ever anxious for the success of their own." Thelma was photographed with her proud parents, aunts, and uncles, the latter dressed in tuxedoes. The Elks, Lions, and other civic groups sponsored a farewell reception at the Winter Garden. Lawrence's golden girl was on her way to stardom, a glowing, exciting life before her, while those left behind faced the mundane. "Big Still Seized In Andover" and "Bold Pyromaniac Terrorizes City" were minor stories compared to Thelma's departure.

On March 2, 1926, the graduates of the Paramount School, those who had won admittance from 25,000 applicants, gathered at the Ritz-Carlton Hotel for a lavish banquet. Adolph Zukor and Jesse Lasky addressed the 300 spectators in the audience, many of whom were newspaper and magazine journalists. The 16 prospective stars were introduced and the first screening of *Fascinating Youth* received applause. Charles Brokaw spoke for the class. He thanked Lasky and handed him a gold cigarette case as a gift. The 16 students were awarded "diplomas," which were actually their studio contracts.

The following morning Lawrencians read that Thelma Todd was assured of future work in Paramount films for the next three months. Thelma's salary would be $75 per week. Paramount scheduled a three month promotional tour. On May 9, 1926, the road show began at the Rivoli Theatre in New York, where the troupe performed before a screening of *Fascinating Youth*. John Murray Anderson, an acclaimed producer of stage revues, created Alice in Movieland, a spoof of the American dream of breaking into the motion picture business. Thelma made a triumphant appearance in her hometown on May 22, hailed as "one of the outstanding events in local theatrical history."[29] While the main company performed in Boston, Thelma and Greg Blackton arrived at the Palace Theatre on South Broadway. The theatre was filled to capacity; a deafening ovation greeted the couple after they danced a tango onstage. Despite three shows, the lobby and entrance were packed with those anxious to see Thelma Todd. The night's attendance numbered 2,300 ticket buyers. Afterward, Thelma and Greg were driven to Boston where they danced again at the new Metropolitan Theatre. Greg Blackton was touched by Thelma's kindness and charm: "Thelma had a heart. She was a beautiful lady in soul and spirit."[30] The troupe remained in each city for a week's engagement. There was usually a local publicity angle. In Chicago the Balaban and Katz movie chain promoted a contest to "Get Into The Movies."[31] After Roland West's mystery, *The Bat*, ended its run at the Chicago Theatre, *Fascinating Youth* followed. There was a splashy advertisement: "See How Film Stars Are Found. Paramount's Junior Stars. Glorious, Young Creatures From Paramount's Picture School In A Smart And Dashing Romance At 17. In Person Singing Young Love Songs, Dancing Strenuous Rhythm Dances, Gamboling All Over The Place. You'll Like These Charming Young People."

A curious incident occurred while the company was in Chicago. "An emissary from a nightclub approached Thelma," recalled Greg Blackton. "He asked her to dance at this place, but she refused to go, asking me, her partner, what we should do. I said, no, since we were under contract to Paramount. They could have found out if we danced somewhere else. We often wondered who the guy was who wanted us to dance. Stories got around that it was Al Capone, but I don't know." The troupe performed night after night, boosting ticket sales and delighting audiences.

In the last week of July, the company arrived in Memphis. They prepared for a performance at the Loew's Palace. The show was promoted as "The Talk of the Town — See Them Make Movie Tests."[32] The humid temperature couldn't dampen the high spirits of the performers. Thelma and Greg Blackton were photographed at the *News Scimitar* operating printing equipment. The next day, July 29, their photograph was on the front page of the newspaper. The day was Thelma's twentieth birthday. In the evening she received a telegram from New York City. The message sent a knife through her heart. Her father was dead. He had been waiting for a bus when he suffered a heart attack. Police officers had observed him staggering but at first mistakenly believed he was drunk. John Todd fell to the pavement unconscious. The officers lifted him into their patrol car and rushed to a hospital, but it was too late. Alice wired her relatives in Lawrence that her husband was dead; frantic with grief, she had failed to provide details. False reports circulated in Lawrence that Todd had been killed in a subway accident. Devastated by her father's sudden death, Thelma boarded a train for New York. Adam and Henry Todd rushed to assist Alice. Tributes for John Todd poured in from hundreds of friends. A wake was held at the Todd family home at 22 Bowdoin Street. Among the dozens of floral offerings were two that were simply inscribed "My John" and "Daddy."[33] Funeral services were at the South Congregational Church. The cortege slowly moved down South Broadway, then turned on Haverhill Street. The procession arrived at Bellevue Cemetery, where John Todd was laid to rest at age 54. Three days after her father's burial, Thelma was stricken with appendicitis. She underwent an emergency operation at Lawrence General Hospital. Thelma slowly regained her health, recuperating from emotional and physical distress at 22 Bowdoin Street. The local press reported her recovery, just as a larger drama was unfolding in newspapers throughout the world.

Rudolph Valentino, 31, was fighting for his life in New York's Polyclinic Hospital. Like Thelma, the screen star had undergone surgery for appendicitis, but complications from gastric ulcers weakened him; food had entered the gastric perforations in the abdominal cavity. Valentino was seriously ill with septic poisoning. "Thelma Todd out of Danger," reported the *Evening Tribune*.[34] But the international film star wasn't as fortunate. "Death Claims Valentino After Valiant Struggle," reported newspapers.[35] Millions of fans were stunned by the sudden death of *the sheik,* the screen lover who had captured women's hearts around the world. Thelma was taken to a summer resort to recover. Valentino was taken to his last appearance — at a New York funeral home. Thousands of mourners lined up for a final tribute. Even in death, Valentino's romantic life elicited a last drama. Fans read about the last days of their idol. According to melodramatic newspaper accounts, beautiful Pola Negri was his last love and fiancée. Negri granted a brief interview in her lavish suite at the Ambassador Hotel in New York. Reporters were searched for cameras and warned not to excite the Polish actress who had been hysterical after Valentino's funeral service. Negri entered the large suite leaning on the arm of a nurse, red-eyed and exhausted. As she sank onto a sofa, a maid placed a footstool under her feet. "If you knew what was in the bottom of my heart," she sighed, "all you would never be so cruel. I haven't eaten; I haven't slept; all I do is cry, cry, cry."[36]

"Will you get over this?" asked a reporter.

"I get over this? I will read you a letter."

The letter was from Harold D. Meeker, a physician who attended the dying actor. Pola read in a soft voice: "Dear Miss Negri, I am asking Miss Pickford, an old friend and patient of mine, to deliver this to you, as I am about to leave for my camp in Maine. Almost four o'clock in the morning on Monday (the day of his death) I was sitting by Rudy's bedside. I was alone in the room. He opened his eyes and put out his hand and said: 'I'm afraid we won't go fishing again. Perhaps we will meet again, but who knows if we will ever go fishing.'

The Todd family celebrates Thelma's new career. Back row, from left: Alexis Raymond; Todd brothers: Charles, David, John, Henry, Adam, and William Todd. Front row: Alice Todd Raymond, Edna Dutton Todd, Elizabeth Todd Henderson, Alice Edward Todd, Thelma, Gertrude Todd, and Frieda S. Todd (date unknown; courtesy of Edna Todd Bixby).

This was the first and only time he realized he would not get well. Then he spoke of you and said: 'Pola, if she does not call in time, tell her that I think of her.' Then Rudy dozed off and began the long sleep from which he never awakened. I feel obliged to get this message to you."

Valentino's death had become sad news for millions. Did Thelma wonder if she would become as famous as Valentino? Would her death have a similar effect? Thelma grieved over the loss of her father and slowly regained her health. Meanwhile, the city was consumed by the scandal of a pretty playground instructor who nearly died from an abortion. The police pressed the girl to reveal the physician's name, as well as the wealthy Harvard student who was her lover. A Chinese doctor was suspected of performing the illegal operation, but the young woman refused to identify anyone. She insisted the trouble was hers alone. Equally compelling was the gruesome murder of the lovely wife of a city official in Springfield. The woman had been strangled to death by her own son. At police headquarters the young man danced the Charleston and sang jazz songs, obviously insane.

John Todd's death had been a tragedy for Thelma and Alice. Afterward, mother and daughter grew even closer. By winter, Thelma was ready to travel. She and Alice returned to New York. Thelma had been cast in *The Popular Sin*, the story of Parisian society and illicit love. Then Paramount Pictures — "the greatest word in entertainment" — beckoned her to Hollywood, the fabled land of dreams.

Two

A Town of Make-Believe

There is a town of makebelieve
Where Hollywoodians live
In seeming something they are not
Their precious time they give ...
A stranger in this funny town
Will think he's had a dream
Until he looks around to find
Things are not what they seem
                    — Edwin O. Palmer[1]

Harvey Henderson Wilcox, a former Michigan farmboy, six feet tall, but crippled by infantile paralysis, arrived in Los Angeles in 1883. Accompanying the wealthy real estate broker was his wife, Daeida, a coachman, and a pair of pinto horses, Duke and Royal. Wilcox opened an office on Spring Street and proceeded to buy property on the city's border. Three years later, the couple purchased a fig orchard; it was a 120 acre tract of land with rich soil in a frostless area that produced exquisite figs, lemons, and oranges. The property was called the Cahuenga Valley Ranch. While on a train trip to her birthplace in Ohio, Mrs. Wilcox met a passenger who described a summer home near Chicago. The name made such an impression that Mrs. Wilcox rechristened her own ranch *Hollywood*. Yet, by the turn of the century, the fruit orchards were vanishing, replaced by banks, hotels, and private residences. A new industry began cropping up in Los Angeles and its suburbs.

Colonel William Selig arrived from Chicago in 1907, impressed with the abundance of sunshine for *movies*. Within a decade, almost the entire motion picture industry relocated to the West Coast. The Nestor Company abandoned Staten Island, led by its famous director, Al Christie; D.W. Griffith opened an office at the Biograph Company on 12th Street; Carl Laemmle started Universal Pictures in 1915; Famous Players–Lasky opened a studio. Dozens of smaller companies were also producing films, creating a powerful new industry, drawing the world's attention to Los Angeles and, more important, to what became known as *Hollywood*. Older residents who remembered the serene past didn't care for the gaudy industry that changed the sleepy city. Hollywood Boulevard, the center of excitement, was filled with theatres, shops, office buildings, and elegant restaurants. The Guaranty Building, located on the northeast corner of Hollywood Boulevard and Ivar Avenue, was the first twelve story building outside of downtown Los Angeles. Built in 1923, the building's most prestigious tenants were to be Charlie Chaplin, Al Jolson, and Cecil B. DeMille.

Everyone wanted to shine in the glow of a screen celebrity. Fans moved to Los Angeles, so there was a demand for more hotels and apartment buildings. Nightclubs and cabarets attracted performers and fans alike. The entrance of Café Montmartre was crowded day and night. As sleek limousines rolled to the curb, screen stars emerged and were ogled by admirers. Parked along the boulevard were rental cars, with drivers awaiting wide-eyed tourists, those ready to gaze at the lavish estates of the stars, directors, and moguls.

Hollywood historian Edwin O. Palmer, a prominent physician and longtime resident, summed up the transformation of his own neighborhood, which he had witnessed with his own eyes: "The name Hollywood became known throughout the world and the footloose came while others planned to come ... on the street were to be seen more than ever all the freaks commonly found in circuses — dwarfs, giants, hunchbacks and trained dogs, million dollar legs, dizzy blondes, and ravishing brunettes...."[2]

If the ornate movie theatres were the temples of the new religion, the altars were in the motion picture studios. Millions of fans believed that the motion picture camera was the sacred instrument that could transform their insignificant lives into meaningful, elevated existences. But to reach the realm of dreams, the pinnacle of all that was desirable in life, the fortress had to be breached, a near impossible task. But Thelma Todd had been chosen, selected to become a screen deity. She couldn't have been happier. On December 1, 1926, Thelma officially signed a one year contract with Paramount Pictures. She would earn the grand sum of $100 per week. Thelma arrived in the Golden State starry-eyed, filled with optimism and excitement. But just as Thelma and the other *fascinating youth* launched their screen careers, a scandal exploded.

On January 10, 1927, Lita Grey Chaplin filed for divorce from her famous husband. The 42 page complaint, prepared by four attorneys, was made public at the Los Angeles Courthouse. Chaplin had married Lita in 1924, when he was 36 and she was 16, after the underage girl had become pregnant. According to the divorce complaint, on their wedding day, Chaplin had told friends, "Well, boys, this is better than the penitentiary, but it won't last long."[3]

Described by George Bernard Shaw as a "genius," Chaplin was the most famous and revered entertainer in the world, but he was about to topple from his pedestal as the lurid allegations of the divorce complaint sent shockwaves through America and beyond. The complaint charged him with "cruel and inhuman treatment ... solicitations and demands that plaintiff commit the act of sex perversion defined by Section 228a of the Penal Code of California. The defendant became enraged at refusal and said to her: 'All married people do those kinds of things. You are my wife and you *have* to do what I want you to do.'" The complaint also alleged that Chaplin had asked his wife to participate in a *ménage a trois* with another woman and himself. There were accusations that he had asked Lita to undergo an abortion and that he had threatened to kill her with a revolver.

Chaplin filed a lengthy cross-complaint denying that he had urged his wife to "submit to, perform, commit or otherwise engage in any act or thing in any way abnormal or unnatural or perverted or degenerate or indecent." He denied everything else in the complaint also, especially requests that his wife violate Section 228a which forbade any persons from engaging in oral sex perversion. The bedroom details of the Chaplins' private life circulated

An early publicity photograph in Hollywood (author's collection).

widely as citizens read the shocking account disclosed in the divorce complaint. When the divorce was finally settled, Lita received $625,000. Chaplin's fall from grace underscored the film industry's worry over scandals.

As Chaplin dangled on the precipice of public popularity, Thelma Todd began her new career. She was assigned a small role in *Mr. Billings Spends His Dime*. For days she sat in makeup, patiently waiting for director Herbert Brenon to call her before the camera. After the success of *Beau Geste*, Brenon was considered a top director. He was hard at work directing Jack Mulhall and Lois Moran in a story about fast living sailors and the girls they leave behind. Thelma took up bridge to pass the time. After the film was released as *God Gave Me Twenty Cents*, her name wasn't even in the credits; nevertheless, studio executives saw a prospective star. The publicity department went to work. The grooming process included less weight, less eyebrows, less accent, and less skirts. Thelma resisted the trend to bob her hair, the current rage sweeping the nation. Independent young women, ridiculed as flappers, asserted their freedom by clipping their maidenly tresses, but not Thelma, noted columnists, even though screen divas like Gloria Swanson, Marion Davies, and Pola Negri shortened their hair. Thelma refused to trim her long blonde hair. The publicity department gave up and launched a plan to introduce her to film fans.

Thelma was photographed above Sunset Boulevard in Moreno Heights where she smiled contentedly in tight-fitting shorts. Other photographs showed her in a swimming pool, kicking a football, romping in the snow with Bruin, a huge black bear, and posing in the Mojave Desert beneath an enormous Joshua tree. Thelma dangled her slim legs from the wing of an airplane. A gag photograph showed her pedaling an enormous tricycle and holding a giant telephone: "Thelma Calling Lawrence." Dozens of photographs were released to newspapers and magazines throughout the nation. Thelma's reluctance to cut her hair made news. Film critic Grace Kingsley was intrigued: "Girls who have bobbed their hair will sigh with regret. Miss Todd's flaxen locks reach almost to her shapely knees."[4]

Only two years earlier, Thelma had been an aspiring teacher; she was now a starlet in Hollywood. *Picture Play* gave Thelma's thoughts on the transformation: "I had always felt so cramped, as if the walls were pressing in upon me. While I had not been conscious of any urge to be wild, I wanted to be where one didn't have to consider the *proper* thing to do."[5] Millions of movie fans avidly read screen magazines each week. They idolized favorite stars and wanted to know everything about them. The national obsession with performers or pretenders disturbed many citizens. What made men and women want to *act*, to be someone else? In 1926, *Photoplay* readers were given the answer by Louis Bisch, a professor of neuropsychiatry. Dr. Bisch sought to solve the riddle of the performer, pondering that a queenly actress or a handsome matinee idol could be suffering from feelings of incompetence and fear of failure. Wrote Dr. Bisch: "I discovered that all actors I analyzed and questioned were built of the same material, pressed out of the same mold ... I soon became convinced that actors belong in a class by themselves and are fundamentally different.... An even greater surprise to them — and I must confess to me also — was to find that it was really such inferiority fears that had obsessed them with wanting to be actors in the first place."[6] Dr. Bisch discussed an actress whose beauty he had admired since he was a boy, but he discovered that she was unhappy, ashamed that she had used her looks to advance in life and "never took the hard road like my father did. I always took the easy way. I can never be sure whether I am competent or not. Sometimes I hate myself." Dr. Bisch had an explanation: "Every actor whose mind I probed had some such similar conflict in childhood.... Acting, in short, is the most likely job that will actually make an individual feel superior as an antidote for any inferiority fears he may suffer deep down inside his emotional self.... Actors are, in reality, children at heart. Their inferiority carries with it what psychoanalysts call 'infantile fixation.' Have you ever noticed how children like to act when at play? Children like to show off, to strut about proudly, to pretend.... Children like to run around nude or with very few clothes on. Cannot that exhibitionist trait be said to exist in many of the female members of the acting profession? Stage people have been noted for marital unsteadiness and boldness in breaking ordinary moral standards for centuries. Rigid observance of codes and customs means emotional control and emotional adjustment. But this latter, it is plain, the actor type of mind specially lacks. The actor is never absolutely sure of himself. He cannot always depend upon himself. He is unable to fix his emotional desires upon any one single object and gain lasting satisfaction from it ... the actor, first and last, is suffering from unconscious inferiority."

The path to fame and fortune in Hollywood was littered with lost souls, once hopefully ambitious, but broken in spirit by constant rejection. Writer Ruth Waterbury sought to give movie fans a taste of backstage reality, as she attempted to find work in the studios by pretending to be an aspiring actress. Over breakfast, the sharp-eyed journalist carefully studied her fellow actresses, boarders of a hotel for women. Some were in makeup, ready for a day of work and cheerful; the unemployed sat downcast. The reporter approached a young woman clad in white sequins who was busy eating oatmeal. Waterbury immediately noticed the fear and distrust; she was surprised since she was hardly a rival. Tall and attractive, the actress did her best to get rid of the newcomer. The elegantly dressed woman was on her way to Goldwyn Studios. She reluctantly agreed to show Waterbury the bus route to Culver City, home of MGM, DeMille, and Hal Roach Studios. As the writer was about to pay the bus fare, a hand shot out. "Never buy the round trip ticket. Try to pick up a ride coming back. It's risky, but it saves you twenty cents," the actress advised.[7] In Culver City, the reluctant guide spoke up: "You get off at DeMille's. Here it is right now." The woman was obviously in a panic that the newcomer would tag along and that would mean unwanted competition. At the DeMille Studio, Waterbury was turned away: "We get everyone through Central Casting." At MGM, the undercover writer joined a group in a bare room, separated from the casting office by a sturdy fence. The guardian to the altar of fame, an excited young man, barked at the desperate faces: "Those of you with paychecks, step forward! The rest of you get out. There's nothing doing. Get out! Get out!" A bearded extra offered fellow losers around him a mint. A gaunt woman rushed forward, snatching the candy, stuffing it in her mouth. Waterbury walked a few blocks to Roach Studios. A switchboard operator gave a familiar piece of advice: "Central Casting," she said. Waterbury hitched a ride with a married carpenter, heading to her next destination, United Artists on Santa Monica Boulevard. When Waterbury declined dinner with the driver, he suddenly stopped and told her to get out. She was forced to walk in the heat, perspiring in her black satin dress. At United Artists she was told to return "in a few months." At Educational, Fine Arts, and Fox she was sent away. The next day she tried Mack Sennett's lot in Glendale.

"Try yourself on the scales," said the man in charge. "You've got to be a shapely mama to get by us." At Universal, she was told to register at Central Casting. At Warner Brothers, a teary-eyed girl sobbed and spoke with bitterness: "You never get in." The same held true at F.B.O., where the assistant casting director claimed he could have used her "the day before." At Famous Players–Lasky, a clerk wrote her name in a ledger. First National Studio in Burbank was her last hope. The weary reporter admitted her identity to Dan Kelly, the man in charge. "Listen, I'm a newspaperwoman. I must break in. Please give me at least a day's work," pleaded Waterbury. "That's a new gag. Why don't you call yourself a countess, too?" said the casting director. After examining her credentials, Kelley recognized a publicity angle. "Come at seven," he said, "and I'll put you on Miss Moore's picture as a streetwalker." Waterbury's article was an eye-opening account for *Photoplay* readers. The studio gates were shut to amateurs. *Stay home* was the unsubtle message. The writer had omitted the seamier aspects of film life. Seduction, blackmail, theft, dope, and suicide were stories that flourished. Despite Waterbury's report, thousands of hopefuls arrived every week, eager to become movie stars.

Unlike the amateurs, Thelma Todd was welcomed through Paramount's gates. Thelma eventually agreed to studio demands to trim her hair. She was cast in a major role, as an impoverished princess in *Rubber Heels*, a comedy starring Ed Wynn. The studio expected the picture to be a hit. Ed Wynn was a successful Broadway stage comedian and *Rubber Heels* was his first motion picture; unfortunately, it was a silent film. Wynn's distinctive comedic voice was useless. He tried to be funny as a novice detective on the trail of jewel thieves. Wrote *Variety:* "If Wynn had a chance at the picture racket, this would have killed it. But he hasn't ... most of the time Wynn doesn't appear to know what he is doing."[8] The scathing review prompted Ed Wynn to return to Broadway. Though the picture was a disappointment for Paramount, it was a big advance for Thelma Todd. Not only was she visually engaging, but she was a fine foil for screen comedy. Thelma was cast in *Fireman, Save My Child,* a comedy starring Wallace Berry. *Nevada*, with Gary Cooper and William Powell, followed. Although a prestige picture, Thelma had little to do except look pretty as a rancher's daughter; all the screen excitement went to Cooper as he fought cattle rustlers. Unknown to Thelma, Eddie Cline, a comedy director at First National Pictures, admired her screen work. Cline was eager to use her in his own projects. Paramount cast Thelma opposite Richard Dix, one of the studio's most popular stars. *The Gay Defender* featured Dix as the son of a Spanish land baron in California. The hero falls in love with the daughter of the U.S. land commissioner. Dix, handsome with dashing sideburns and moustache, fought villains who burned haciendas and threatened Thelma, the commissioner's daughter. Thelma and Dix became friends; both were single and enjoyed a good time. The studio publicity department created a romance that both immediately denied. Though the films in which Thelma appeared were mediocre, she always made an impression with audiences. "Miss Todd is already being featured as a leading woman," wrote Grace Kingsley, "and her work is improving all the time with Paramount officials viewing her favorably for promotion."[9] Thelma had attained national recognition. She corresponded with former students from the class she taught. "I get so many letters from them," she told a magazine writer. "They want to know all the Hollywood secrets and if I have met Mary Pickford."

Ben Schulberg announced that Thelma would again play opposite Richard Dix in *The Traveling Salesman*. After only ten months in Hollywood, her career was taking off. While hundreds of attractive women dreamed of stardom, begging for work as extras or bit players, Thelma was being developed to be a major star. Her friends Buddy Rogers, Jack Luden, and Josephine Dunn were also advancing. Rogers had achieved popularity with his role in *Wings*, William Wellman's aerial masterpiece. Yet, many of "the Junior Stars of 1926" had already boarded trains for home and oblivion. By the fall of 1927, most options had not been renewed. Dorothy Nourse appeared in D.W. Griffith's *The Sorrows of Satan*, then faded from sight. Iris Gray fell in love with vaudeville performer Frank Lynch and retired. Charles Brokaw returned to the stage. Walter Goss changed his name and disappeared. Those who continued became minor actors. But Thelma advanced on the path to fame and fortune. However, one fateful evening, the dream became a nightmare. Thelma received a telephone call from the studio, requesting her immediate presence. She assumed that re-takes were needed for the unreleased *Gay Defender,* which was being rushed to completion. But on her arrival she was escorted to an office rather than a set. "There she recognized familiar executive faces. There were girls, too, young and yielding; drinks, cigarettes, a victrola. The amazing gathering were making merry, to say the least."[10] Thelma turned and walked away, but the executives stopped her and offered a drink. She was urged to "be a good fellow." But Thelma wasn't interested; she knew exactly what was expected. The rebuffed executives became angry. Paramount had the option to keep Thelma or to drop her. She was scheduled to appear in *Hell's Angels* for Howard Hughes. After the incident, whispers circulated that her contract would be sold. Thelma was young, unattached, and considered fair prey for powerful men who "liked to play." She now understood that many "studio conferences," held late at night behind closed doors, were sordid transactions; aspiring actresses exchanged sexual favors for work. Thelma knew about the dreaded blacklist. "The blacklist is denied by the producers," informed *Photoplay,* "and so secret are their meetings, and so closely do they stand together that no victim has ever been able to convict any Hollywood dictator. Yet Hollywood knows what it knows, and the blacklist ranks high in its fears."

Hollywood Secrets

Years later, Thelma discussed the incident with writer Llewellyn Carroll of *Photoplay,* without naming her would-be seducer. By then she was an established actress, unafraid of retaliation. She detested the Paramount officials who publicly lectured the Junior Stars of 1926 to "let nothing you do bring the slightest smirch upon the profession."

"She didn't like Lasky or the other moguls at all," confirms her cousin Bill Todd.[11] She never revealed the person responsible for ending her promising career at Paramount, but it was possibly B.P. Schulberg. Thelma's contemporary, Louise Brooks, ripped the studio chief years later: "His reputation for the sexual abuse of young actresses who worked for him was the worst."[12] Jesse Lasky admitted the truth in his memoirs; the Astoria studio had been a source of party girls: "While the studio was teeming with gorgeous 'ponies,' as chorus dancers liked to be called, and stunning showgirls from the Follies, our Wall Street bankers developed a sudden interest in seeing how pictures were made, and our own business executives gave unstintingly of the time they should have spent in their own offices, to act as guides."[13] Louise Brooks, a free-spirited dancer from the Broadway stage, observed at first hand the parade of chorus girls who were invited to parties for the financiers and influential politicians. According to Brooks, the girls were screened by Paramount production boss Walter Wanger and director Edmund Goulding. The women who pleased the powerful were given minks, jewels, and film jobs, in addition to unsavory reputations. The pastime of selecting women as playthings was soon underway at the West Coast studio.

"They'll never get me on the casting couch," Thelma told the Todds in Lawrence.[14]

Paramount decided that Thelma would be "loaned" to other studios. Paramount charged a steep fee for her services and made a nice profit, but Thelma was only paid the contractual $100. The first assignment was to work for Howard Hughes who was preparing *Hell's Angels,* a million dollar aerial spectacle about fliers in the Great War. Hughes was the wealthy heir to the Hughes Tool Company. His salary was reported to be $5,000 per day. Hughes had already made *Two Arabian Knights, The Racket* and *The Mating Call,* all successful ventures. After six months of preparation, Hughes hired Thelma to co-star with Ben Lyon and James Hall in the story of brothers who leave Oxford University to join the Royal Flying Corps. Marshal "Mickey" Neilan, a director at Paramount, brought Thelma to the attention of Hughes. Neilan, best known for his motion pictures starring Mary Pickford, was a friend of Hughes's father. While shooting *Everybody's Acting* at Paramount, Neilan asked Hughes to become a film investor. This led to the formation of Caddo Productions. Neilan liked Thelma's lively sense of humor. However, the director soon learned, as everyone did, that Hughes was rather eccentric, and he made the final decisions. After Neilan left the production, he was replaced by Luther Reed. While Reed directed interior scenes, Hughes and cinematographer Harry Perry were busy in the clouds filming with practically "every

Starlets. From left: Francis Hamilton, Thelma, Alice White, Yola d'Avril, and Rozella Stillman, secretary at First National Studio (author's collection).

stunt flier and ex-war ace in America."[15] A publicity barrage began immediately. The company released a photograph of Thelma enjoying breakfast in bed on a studio set, while waiting for the cameras to roll. The production got underway at the Metropolitan Studios on Las Palmas. Nearby was the building where Rudolph Valentino had made his famous *Four Horsemen of the Apocalypse* in 1921. Once the crown of the industry, its dingy walls, now faded with cracked plaster, boarded windows, and musty smell made it "a sinister graveyard," wrote Adela Rogers St. Johns.[16] The era of silent films was fading, too. Hughes constantly scrapped footage and story line, and there was speculation he would shoot the film as a *talkie.* Luther Reed left the production. He complained that he was unable to satisfy Hughes. Paramount had contractually loaned Thelma to Universal, and the production date neared. With Hughes behind schedule, Thelma was sent to Universal and replaced by Greta Nissen. Hughes then decided to make *Hell's Angels* as a sound picture featuring Jean Harlow.

Thelma had a small role in *The Shield of Honor* at Universal, seventh billed in a crime drama. Neil Hamilton starred as a police aviator on the trail of diamond thieves. When *Hell's Angels* was finally released at a cost of four million dollars, the film was acclaimed around the world, hailed for its exciting aerial footage. Jean Harlow became an international star. Thelma had come close to stardom.

Thelma was sent to First National Studios for *Vamping Venus*. The film was shot on the same sets used by German actress Maria Corda for *The Private Life of Helen of Troy*. The magnificent and expensive sets in Burbank covered five acres and towered several hundred feet high. There was also a huge wooden horse, built to hold several men. A comedy had been hastily written to utilize the expensive sets, which were incorporated into a dream sequence after Charlie Murray is struck over the head in a nightclub. Eddie Cline chose Thelma to play Venus. The publicity department saw a sex angle and compared Thelma's measurements to those of the Venus de Milo in the Louvre.

	Thelma Todd	Venus de Milo (reduced)
HEIGHT	5 feet 4 inches	5 feet 4 inches
HIPS	36 inches	38 inches
THIGH	21 inches	23 inches
ANKLE	8 inches	8½ inches
CALF	13½ inches	14½ inches
WAIST	27 inches	28½ inches
NECK	18 inches	14 inches
BUST	33 inches	37 inches
WEIGHT	122 pounds	137 pounds

Vamping Venus was a dismal flop. *Variety* reported: "One of dreariest and unfunniest films ever to ever find its way out of the colony. Charlie Murray almost fractures his chin trying to mug some comedy into it and Thelma Todd's beauty and scant wardrobe, revealing a streamline chassis, help a lot but not enough."[17]

Paramount declined to renew her contract. Thelma could have returned home, just as the other junior stars had done, but she was determined to pursue a screen career. First National offered her a contract that she signed on February 16, 1928. Though legally able to sign her own contracts, Alice Todd's signature was penned on the document, attesting to the obvious interest she showed in her daughter's career. The contract contained the standard morals clause which must have brought a cynical smile to Thelma's lips. Paragraph Five stated: "The artist agrees to conduct herself with due regard to public conventions and morals, and agrees that she will not commit any act or thing that will tend to degrade her in society or bring her into public hatred, contempt, scorn or ridicule or that will tend to shock, insult or offend the community or ridicule morals or decency or prejudice the producer or the motion picture industry in general."[18] Jesse Lasky had lectured the Paramount students about right behavior while his executives took advantage of the young actresses.

There was another stern paragraph in the contract. Thelma had to fill in the weight spaces herself: "The artist accordingly represents and warrants to the producer that the weight of the artist at the date executed is 122 pounds, and the artist agrees that she will maintain said weight at all times thereof. In the event that the weight of the artist should at any time vary more than three pounds above, or six pounds below said weight of 122 pounds, the producers may forewith cancel the employment of the artist hereunder." To lose your career over a few pounds was an unnerving thought, for Thelma enjoyed good food and had a natural tendency to plumpness, like her mother. In fact, while filming *The Gay Defender*, Richard Dix made a crack that touched a nerve. "If you want to be my leading lady you'll have to reduce," said Dix.[19]

Thelma later admitted to a magazine writer, "I was-er-broad." She lost thirty pounds in a month by a strict diet. The new contract boosted her salary to $250 per week during each film production, a nice sum for 1928. She was cast in *The Noose*, an underworld drama starring Richard Barthelmess as a rum runner in love with Thelma, a high class society girl. Also in the cast was Lina Basquette, a sultry, dark-eyed brunette who played a cabaret dancer, a rival for the handsome gangster's affections. Though a year younger than Thelma, Basquette had lived quite a life by age 21. A talented child dancer, known on stage as "California's Little Ray of Sunshine," Lina had grown up in the spotlight. At age eight, she danced in Universal featurettes. Florenz Ziegfeld starred her in the Follies as "America's Prima Ballerina" in 1923, when she was only 16. Two years later, a chance meeting in an elevator with Sam Warner led to marriage and a child. Her husband was the visionary who realized the potential of sound pictures. But Warner never saw his dream fulfilled. The day before the premiere of *The Jazz Singer*, the motion picture that revolutionized the industry, Warner died of a brain abscess. His death altered the course of Basquette's life. She allowed Harry Warner to become the guardian of Lita, her daughter. She later sued to regain custody of Lita and a larger portion of her late husband's estate. Despite the lawsuits, she failed.

Noah Berry and Lina Basquette in Cecil B. DeMille's *The Godless Girl* (1929).

Basquette blamed "crooked lawyers who were paid off by the other side."[20] As time passed, Lina was caught in a net of mounting personal problems. For the moment though, she was allowed to work at the Warners' First National Studio, but she was told to abandon the custody case over her daughter; if not, her films would be unwelcome in any theatre where Warner Bros. had influence.

As time passed, Thelma observed that the social fabric of Hollywood life was riddled with unhappiness. But on the surface it was a glamorous world, especially at night, when spotlights swept across the sky, as films premiered and stars basked in the adulation of the adoring multitudes. The rich elite whooped it up in nightclubs across the city. Abe and Mike Lyman's dance orchestra was popular with the movie crowd. The Lymans drew the famous to the Sunset Inn, one of the dozen beachside cafés that brightened the coast at night. There was a $5.00 cover charge to get in, but patrons could see screen luminaries and dine on "Shrimp Cocktail a la Buster Keaton."

Despite Prohibition, illicit booze was consumed from silver flasks, neatly tucked in hip pockets and handbags. Stargazers at the Sunset Inn were wide-eyed as they pointed to Chaplin, Lloyd, Keaton, Mix, Fairbanks, Swanson, Normand, and Nazimova. Impromptu clowning by Chaplin, wrapped in a tablecloth, made the cover charge worthwhile. Thelma became a familiar face in nightclubs, often in the company of Lina Basquette: "Thelma and I were very close friends. She was one of the most naturally beautiful gals who was out there at the time. She had skin like alabaster."[21] Thelma endeared herself to everyone, exuding warmth and laughter. She was slim and chic. She dazzled men with her blue eyes and marcelled hair, puffing smoke from an expensive cigarette holder. She came alive at night. She loved fine restaurants, ballrooms, and nightclubs. She was in demand as a date and escorted to elegant parties. She acquired a fondness for champagne and dancing till dawn. She had caught the tail end of the Roaring Twenties, and she made the most of it. Motion pictures reflected the times, as well as America's flaming youth, like Madge Bellamy's *Mother Knows Best* — But Who Cares — quipped the advertisements — *step on the gas!*

Newspapers around the country printed the story of the luncheon Thelma hosted for Otto Kahn, a wealthy New York financier and philanthropist. Kahn, an early investor in Paramount, asked to meet Thelma in Los Angeles. Thelma agreed and decided to bring her friends. At the fashionable Montmartre Café on Hollywood Boulevard, Kahn was greeted by his hostess, alluring in a black frock with a camellia shoulder corsage. The black dress enhanced Thelma's golden hair. Patrons watched as she introduced the famous Wall Street banker to her friends who sat at a table adorned with roses. Among the guests were Jeanne Morgan, Seena Owen, Kathleen Key, Shirley Dorman, Prince Francisco Ruspoli, David Gray, and James I. Bush, Kahn's wealthy associate, a younger man who was immediately attracted to Thelma. James Bush and Thelma were seen together at several parties. Newspapers reported they were engaged, a story Thelma denied. Bush had indeed proposed, but Thelma felt he simply wanted a plaything, as she told the press. Soon after, newspapers reported she was engaged to James Ford, an actor and Lawrence native. Thelma denied the reports. Ford was only a childhood friend, she insisted. Gossip columnists claimed she would wed writer Charles Furthmann. Thelma denied that she was engaged to anyone. Three false engagements in three months, she laughed.

Thelma made news again. As usual, men were involved, but this time there was a scandalous brawl. While on location for *The Crash* in Truckee, a town on the border of California and Nevada, Thelma, Ned Sparks, Barbara Kent, and Percy Westmore, hair and makeup artist at First National, drove to nearby Reno. The revelers saw everything there was to see in "The Biggest Little Town in the World."[22] In the Calneva Club, made famous as the casino where Clara Bow lost $12,000 because she thought the chips she played were worth a nickel, instead of a dollar, the group gambled at blackjack, then moved to a roulette wheel. Suddenly, a drunk staggered into Thelma and made a rude remark. Percy Westmore hit the drunk and a melee broke out. By the time the police arrived, Westmore had a black eye and split lip. News accounts hailed him as the hero, fighting for lovely Thelma Todd. The brawl was amusing for everyone but Thelma and Westmore. Virginia "Tommy" Westmore was told of her husband's gallantry, along with rumors that Thelma was having an affair with her husband. Tommy Westmore denied the gossip. In Truckee, the company went to work in the beautiful countryside of the High Sierras. Most of the picture was filmed outdoors. Thelma played a singer in a theatrical troupe who marries a jealous, two-fisted railroad man. Milton Sills was the suspicious, hard-drinking husband who loses his wife, only to rescue her in a dramatic train crash. Sills, a former college professor and stage actor, coached Thelma to improve her speaking voice. Movie theatres around the nation were converting to talkies, despite Chaplin's belief that sound was only a fad. Silent era screen performers were suddenly afraid. *The Crash* was shot as a silent, but before its release a desperate attempt was made to keep step with the sound trend, so sound effects and dialogue were added. The effort failed and the film died at the box office.

Thelma's next picture was also a disaster. *The Haunted House* was a mystery drama that incorporated sound effects but no dialogue. The story had a dying millionaire testing the loyalty of his heirs as they encounter a mad doctor, sleepwalkers, ghosts, and a beautiful nurse, played by Thelma. In a futile attempt to salvage the production two songs were added, but the picture flopped. "Synchonization of the song stuff was badly handled with the player and the sound always out of kilter and neither starting nor finishing together," complained *Variety*.[23] The real mystery, quipped Thelma was "how it was ever made in the first place."[24] Thelma was admitted to Good Samaritan Hospital for a tonsillectomy in October. The event was reported in newspapers. Though cast in minor films, Thelma's popularity with fans was solid. Mervyn LeRoy directed her in *Naughty Baby,* a comedy featuring Alice White and Jack Mulhall. White had gone from a stenographer's desk to screen acting. Mulhall had successfully teamed with Dorothy Mackaill in several films and didn't think much of White, resulting in considerable tension on the set. But Thelma, playing a gold-digger, avoided trouble, as she explained, "By saying nothing, smiling at everyone and listening to everyone." The picture was released with sound effects and music; it was another disaster.

The sound revolution left many stars bewildered. Chaplin refused to acknowledge sound and kept making silents. Douglas Fairbanks disliked sound but admitted he had to adapt: "The public is demanding dialogue with its motion pictures these days, which gives us practically no choice as to whether or not we want to use it."[25] Fairbanks was filming *The Iron Mask*, a sequel to his successful *Three Musketeers*. "My plan is to have all of the talking done before the picture actually starts. I will come on the screen and invite the audience to come with me to France back in the Seventeenth Century.... By using this plan the audience will have its dialogue and we can look directly at them while speaking, thus making our words convincing — a thing that is difficult to do when talking to one another in a picture." Paramount reopened its Long Island studio for "all-dialogue pictures" and said it would film the latest stage successes of Broadway with the actual players. First National announced its future pictures would be "in dialogue," but silent and talking versions would be made and distributed according to the ability of the theatres to project them.

First National cast Thelma in *Seven Footprints to Satan,* her first real sound picture, though with limited dialogue. Thelma and Creighton Hale were youngsters in search of a lost gem at the spooky mansion of a gruesome, wolfish-looking creature called Satan. A witchlike housekeeper shows the first of seven steps the youngsters must take to solve the mystery. The film was a succession of bizarre sights, freakish characters, disappearing walls, trick bookcases, and what seems to be a secret society devoted to orgies. Filmed at a cost

Seven Footprints to Satan (1929). Left to right: Thelma, Creighton Hale, and Kamiyama Sojin.

of $129,950 the studio released a theatre trailer featuring Creighton Hale: "Honest, I've been scared to death ever since I started to rehearse *The Seven Footprints of Satan*. This is a First National-Vitaphone picture that is coming to this theatre in the very near future. I had the pleasure of playing with Thelma Todd, Sheldon Lewis, William V. Mong, Dewitt Jennings, Sojin, and a very fine cast. Now we've had the movies for a very long time and then we got the talkies. While now we've got the squeakies, I can guarantee you that this is the snappiest, zippiest melodrama that ever played this theatre."

Though not yet a star like Gloria Swanson or Pola Negri, Thelma Todd was a recognizable face. As she put it: "I haven't done anything big and exciting, but I'm always working."[26] With her appearance in *Trial Marriage,* a melodrama of a woman's affair with a doctor, reviewers took notice: "Thelma Todd is the choicest addition to the picture. The girl looks like big time."[27] Although she was climbing the ladder of success, Thelma still maintained her small town manners, as Greg Blackton was to discover. While walking across the First National lot he encountered Thelma near a sound stage. There was a pained, serious expression on her face. "You never visited my mother," she said sadly.[28]

Discontent surfaced in a revealing interview with writer Dorothy Lubou. The girl who had bubbled with enthusiasm in 1926 was no longer cheerfully naïve. The women met at the Russian Eagle, a fashionable restaurant on Sunset Boulevard. Theodor Lodijensky, a former White Russian general, greeted them with a low bow and a kiss on the hand. Thelma was chic in a stylish black dress with an enticing *decollete*, matching wide-brimmed hat, and pearl earrings. Lubou described Thelma as "Fifth Avenue, rather than Hollywood Boulevard." The sophisticated diners who sipped illegal vodka and consumed Beluga caviar paused when Thelma breezed through the dining room, past the far right corner table where Greta Garbo liked to sit.

"Men in Hollywood are very rude creatures," said Thelma, as she dipped into her borsch soup.[29] "Perhaps meeting men as a school teacher and later on as an actress, I've gotten different reactions.... You know, teachers are supposed to be dried up old maids, sort of sexless beings but, of course, there are very many attractive, modern young women teaching.... Men have a more familiar attitude toward actresses." A gypsy violinist serenaded from table to table playing romantic music as Thelma answered questions.

"It isn't the actors who are at fault," she continued. "I've found them to be clever, amusing, a lot of fun. They may try to get you to play around, but they'll drop you if you don't encourage them. But the businessmen, the outsiders who smirk suggestively when they learn that your work is acting. A movie actress. Well, not so long ago I had an appointment with a well known photographer. After the sitting he invited me to stay for tea, and of all things he chose to talk about — degeneracy. Do you think he would have dared if I had come to him as a schoolmarm, instead of an actress?" Then she expressed a comment shared by desperate working women anxious to maintain a job: "You can't be openly offended. You need the good will of everybody in the game." She lashed out at those who took shortcuts. "Girls out here have cheapened themselves by permitting too much familiarity. Girls who can't get anywhere by their own merits, who'll be nice to anybody, if it will advance them the slightest bit. I guess men get cynical and hard-boiled. Maybe they shouldn't be blamed for holding us in such poor esteem. I'm too thoroughly New England to get away from the fundamentals of life. I like to play, to make eyes at the boyfriends. Youth has the right to play. But things are so extreme here. I can't quite get Hollywood.

Alice and Thelma, date unknown (author's collection).

People have no sense of values. They don't know how to live. Everything is done for effect. There's no sincerity, no balance — twenty-year-old girls with the experience of forty." She shook her head in disapproval of such behavior but laughed. "Gosh, I'm being serious," she said, "but you wanted to know, didn't you?"

Thelma had expected Hollywood to be a magic land. Paramount had groomed her to be a major star, but executives lost interest when she wouldn't sell herself. "I think we're all a bit crazy," said Thelma. "Picture people, I mean. Too much of a strain on the nervous system, too much parading of emotions. It's bad. We get so that everything that happens to us away from the studio is dramatized — we exaggerate our personal emotions." When the women finished their custard at the Russian Eagle, the violinist and singer performed for them. Thelma offered the singer a tip, but he refused: "No, for you I sing anytime. Ten times as many songs. For one as you who knows music it is a pleasure. You are an artist too, understand." His admiration was evident. Thelma had such an effect on men. Lubou asked about her six months at the Paramount School. "I don't think the school helped us very much," she answered. "Learning to swim, fence, dance, and ride horseback doesn't add to one's histrionics. And we were made to do the most ridiculous things. Imagine Buddy Rogers with a long beard and distorted face. If one of the directors wanted us for a bit part, our school director would say. 'What! Those kids? Don't be silly.' We would have been helped more definitely by doing extra work."

By the beginning of 1929, Thelma's salary was raised to $300 per week. Alice hired attorney Jack Sherril, whose office was at 6675½ Sunset Boulevard, to supervise her daughter's contracts. With her comfortable income, Thelma and Alice rented Room 20 for $150 a month at the Highbourne Garden Apartments, located at 1922 N. Highland. Thelma's perseverance was about to pay off.

At the Hal Roach Studios in Culver City, plans were underway for Laurel and Hardy's first talking picture. Elmer Raguse, head of the new sound department, supervised the drastic and complex overhaul of the art of filmmaking. Sound cameras were housed in a boxlike enclosure, so the noise of the motor was muffled. Laurel and Hardy, the greatest comedy team in silents, worried if their voices were adequate for sound pictures. Stan Laurel, the creative genius of the team, was fearful that his English accent and slight lisp would end his career.

Hal Roach liked Thelma's comedic talent. He hired her for *Unaccustomed As We Are,* along with actress Mae Busch, a former Max Sennett bathing beauty. Busch had starred in many silent era classics, including Lon Chaney's *Unholy Three* and Eric Von Stroheim's *Foolish Husbands.* Busch excelled at playing the shrewish wife for laughs. The script had Thelma as the wife of tough policeman Edgar Kennedy. After an explosion in the Hardy apartment, when Stan attempts to light the oven, pretty Thelma offers her help with the cooking. Suddenly, her dress is in flames. She bolts from the apartment, clad in her underclothes. She is fleeing when a policeman arrives to investigate; it is her husband and the equally suspicious Mae Busch, as Mrs. Hardy.

Although the Roach Studios was known as "the lot of fun," there was tension on the set. Warning signs were placed at all stage entrances: "Do not enter when the red light is on." Thelma found the transition to sound difficult, especially the moments of dead silence, before the sound crew lit the red warning light. After each take Stan Laurel wanted to hear a playback, to make certain his voice registered properly. Edgar Kennedy had already adjusted his voice during *Hurdy Gurdy,* the studio's first *talkie.* Kennedy was stung by Hal Roach's crack that he "sounded like a fairy."[30] Kennedy, a former boxer, added a gruff tone to his voice. Most of the two-reeler was shot at night. There was only limited equipment and Our Gang's first sound film, *Small Talk,* was being filmed during the day. After three years of hard work, Thelma proved to be a fine actress. She demonstrated skill in comedy timing, camera angles, and slapstick. Hal Roach was so pleased with the production that he rushed it to theatres.

On April 25, 1929, the *Los Angeles Times* reported that Thelma had signed "a significant contract" with Hal Roach and the Victor Talking Machine Company. Roach immediately cast her in Harry Langdon's *Hotter Than Hot.* This was followed by *Snappy Sneezer* with Charlie Chase. Thelma made *Her Private Affair* at First National, as a flashy card cheat. Afterward, Thelma made her singing debut. She recorded "Let Me Call You Sweetheart," "If I Had You," and "Honey" for RCA. Thelma was perfect for Roach films. Directors found she had the courage to try anything, from jumping off a bridge into a river or driving a breakaway automobile. By day, Thelma was a familiar face on the Roach lot; by night, she was spotted at the most elegant restaurants favored by the movie crowd. She socialized at the cafés, nightclubs, and Sunday afternoon parties where colleagues relaxed. She was a regular at the nearby Brown Derby on Vine Street and Al Levy's.

Though prim, Thelma was certainly no prude. While she attended Sunday services at the Hollywood First Baptist Church on Selma Avenue, she enjoyed a good time. She partied with the gaudy showbiz crowd. Despite the Eighteenth Amendment ban on the sale of liquor, it was readily available. Speakeasies were numerous and "private clubs" catered to the elite, offering not only illegal booze but gambling. Thelma indulged in the carefree lifestyle, drinking nightly, to her mother's disappointment. As a devout churchgoer, Alice frowned on alcohol, as well as the antics of Hollywood's rowdy set, who cavorted without restraint.

Thelma loved to dance. She was often at the Cocoanut Grove Ballroom in the Ambassador Hotel or the Blossom Room in the Hollywood Roosevelt, where the rich and famous whirled across the dance floor, the gentlemen in black tie and tux, the ladies in strapless gowns and long gloves. Columnists often mentioned her in their articles. Thelma was seen in expensive nightspots with wealthy insurance broker Harvey Priester who wanted to marry her. He had made news when he paid $2,300 for Valentino's yacht, the *Phoenix.* But Thelma's most serious romance was with Ivan Lebedeff, a handsome Russian aristocrat. Lebedeff was in love with Thelma. The romance was followed by gossip columnists. Charming and suave, sporting a monocle and exquisite manners, Lebedeff pursued Thelma. According to his studio biography, Lebedeff had lived quite a life. Born on the family estate in Lithuania, Lebedeff had been educated and trained for the diplomatic service but, at the outbreak of the Great War, he enlisted in the Corps of Pages, a privileged military school for future guard officers. He fought against the Germans and was decorated. In the revolution he fought against the Bolshevists but was captured and imprisoned. He escaped to Paris where he survived as a stockbroker, playwright, and actor. After making pictures in Vienna and Paris, he attracted the attention of D.W. Griffith, who hired him for *The Sorrows of Satan.* Though charmed by Lebedeff, Thelma told him that she wasn't ready to settle down.

Thelma had not been to Lawrence in three years. The previous Christmas she wanted to visit, but her busy film schedule prevailed. Thelma and Alice had gone for a ride Christmas

Day, lamenting the absence of snow. They managed a trip to Lawrence in August. Despite her wish for a quiet holiday, word of her presence spread fast. While shopping on Essex Street, Thelma drew excited crowds and snarled traffic. Everyone wanted to see the hometown girl who had achieved fame. A reporter for the *Lawrence Telegram* followed her closely and captured her visit in print. In response to the tremendous adulation of the city, Thelma agreed to make three personal appearances at the Broadway Theatre. On the marquee her name was emblazoned in electric lights. Each night she walked onstage to thunderous applause and addressed the adoring spectators. After her speech the theatre darkened and *Careers,* her new film, was shown. Each night hundreds were turned away. Traffic jams formed on South Broadway, as the disappointed stood outside hoping to catch a glimpse of their idol. The night of her farewell speech, Thelma spoke to another capacity crowd. White-haired Jim Carney, the theatre manager, introduced "Lawrence's own Thelma Todd." As Thelma walked to center stage, applause broke forth, lasting several minutes. Thelma graciously thanked her fans. She told the audience of 1,300 admirers that they were her strength. Then she spoke of Hollywood: "There are thousands of beautiful women and attractive men from all parts of the world in Hollywood and anyone starting in the movies has got to have a lot of courage and determination. The work is by no means easy. On the contrary, it is very hard. There have been many times when I have felt discouraged and thought of giving it up, but when I thought of your faith in me, the implicit trust which you have placed in me has been the means of helping me to continue my fight for success. In my discouraging moments I think of the people back home and it gives me renewed strength ... I love my work. It takes a lot of grit to carry on. At times I have cried, but I soon get over it and keep on fighting." The audience sat enthralled, as Thelma spoke from the heart.[31] "I can assure you that I will always claim Lawrence as my home." Turning, she said, "Let's all give a hand to Jim Carney, the man with the silvery hair and twinkling eyes, who used to greet me on Saturday afternoons in front of this theatre when I used to come here regularly. Those days are pleasant memories to me. I used to come up to the front of the theatre and say, 'Oh, Mr. Carney, can I go into the show?' And he would say, 'Why certainly, if you've been a good girl. Pay your nickel.' But I got in tonight without paying my nickel."

The vacation in Lawrence brought back memories. "During my stay here I have enjoyed it wonderfully. It seems like old times again to walk up by the high school and recall the days that I went there. Visiting the stores here and shopping at Woolworths is a treat which I never get in Hollywood. When I see the old familiar faces of my friends the greatest feeling in the world comes to me. I was walking along Essex Street the other day when a little boy, accompanied by his mother, hailed me and said, 'Hello, Thelma,' and then he began to tell me how much he enjoyed my pictures."

Discussing the new phenomenon of sound pictures, Thelma said she had been in 14 or 15, explaining how absolute quiet was needed, that even a dropped pencil could spoil a scene. Thelma attributed a great deal of her success to her mother, counseling young people that "their parents were their best friends." She asked that the spotlight be turned on her mother, who was sitting in an orchestra seat. Alice rose amidst applause. Thelma expressed her belief that it would be several more years before she again returned to Lawrence and that she was fortunate to arrange a brief vacation. She thanked the Broadway management for allowing her to appear. After speaking for 30 minutes, Thelma left the theatre for the

Roseland Ballroom. As she entered the waiting automobile, fans surged forward; police officers had to push the crowd back. At the ballroom, over a thousand dancers at the pavilion gave Thelma an ovation which echoed through the cavernous building. Ushered inside the manager's office, Thelma flashed a warm smile and extended her hand to the reporter for the *Evening Tribune*. Thelma sat for a brief interview.

✗ "Do you really like to work in pictures?" came the first question.[32]

"I am crazy over the work," responded Thelma, "and I do not think I could be happier in any other work."

"What feature in the work do you enjoy the most?" asked the reporter.

"To be honest, I do like the character work." When asked what type of picture she preferred, she quickly replied, "I like the comedies." She explained that they allowed for more training. "What picture you worked in do you think showed to the best advantage?"

"None," she said, without a second's delay. "I don't believe I am good in any of the pictures. By that I mean I am not as good as I want to be, for if I were satisfied with my work at this stage of the game I would never progress in the picture world, there would be no opportunities for me, and instead of progressing, I would slowly but surely fade out of the picture. Don't misunderstand me. When I say none, I simply mean that in all those pictures that I have worked in to date I have not shown to the advantage that I hope to show when I have had more training."

"What is your ultimate ambition in pictures?"

"I have no ambition to be a star, nor do I ever hope or want to have my own company. I would like to be a good feature player."

And what about her free time?

"There is little time for recreation, for in pictures you have to work hard to keep in condition for the work. You know it is not so much the physical work, it is the mental work you do, and sometimes you get so nervous that when you hear a noise you want to jump. My evenings are quiet and they are happily spent with my mother at home."

Thelma said she would leave for Hollywood in a few days, "to put the war paint on and go to work. I am under contract for five years with Hal Roach, and really he's a wonderful man."

"Is there something you want to say to all the people in the city?" asked the reporter. Before Thelma could answer, a knock interrupted the conversation, and she was told the crowd was anxious. "Everything I will say now is intended for all the people," said Thelma. Passing through a corridor of fans, Thelma made her way to the ballroom stage. Her first words were drowned in applause. Then she recounted her arrival in Hollywood "in a strange land with no friends." At times, she admitted, she wondered if it was all worthwhile. Perhaps she should return home. But through each difficult period her mother urged her to stay. "She is the one who is entitled to a great deal of my success, if I have been successful, and I want you to meet my little mother. I call her little. She is not little this way or that," said Thelma, measuring her own height and width, "but I have gotten into the habit of calling her my little mother. I want her to come up here with me and meet you and I want you to know her." Alice ascended the stage to lively applause. In closing, Thelma again thanked those who were solidly behind her: "I only hope that I shall be able to make the place in the sun that you all hope I will make." As she made her way to the exit, Thelma stopped to shake hands with former classmates and friends. After three years away, she had returned in magnificent triumph.

A few days before her departure, in a last flurry of dinner parties, reunions and dances, a reporter from the *Boston Globe* tried to track her down. Reaching Alice by phone, he was told to arrive promptly at one in the afternoon at 160 Parker Street, where Thelma had a luncheon date with Uncle Charles and Aunt Edna. The reporter arrived on time, but his subject was missing. She was still out shopping. "It's one now," fretted Alice, "and she's got to eat and be in Boston at three."[33] As everyone waited, Alice apologized for her daughter's tardiness. "You know," she explained, "one of Thelma's failings is that she's never on time. She always gets there, but usually she's a few minutes late." Ten minutes later, Thelma appeared. "She'll scold me," said Alice. Thelma only expected family members. But Thelma graciously agreed to an interview.

"How do you like so many people making a fuss over you?" she was asked.

"I don't like it," she replied. Then smiling, she said, "I don't and I do. It's all wonderful, but when a girl likes to be alone, well, it's quite an ordeal to go through."

Did she mind standing before large audiences?

"Nothing seems to bother Thelma," interjected Alice. "Three years ago, when she was home, they asked her to speak in one of the theatres, and she accepted. I did a lot of worrying about it, but Thelma didn't seem to. Finally on the night she was to speak she took a pencil and paper, after supper, and told me she was going out to the piazza to jot down a few notes about what she was going to say. I went out there half an hour later and Thelma was sound asleep in a chair. She had written just three words on that paper. I had to wake her up so she'd get to the theatre in time. That's how much talking bothers her." Then Thelma spoke up: "But there is a time when I'm afraid of my own voice, and the same can be said of a lot other 'talkie' actors and actresses. It's in the zero hour just before they begin to shoot us." Thelma explained how, with sound pictures, everyone had to be letter perfect, as no prompter's voice could be heard. "You can't see the little red light until it lights. And it doesn't light until the cameras and sound recording are all running. Sometimes you wait for what seems like two or three hours. It is the most terrible two or three minutes I have ever spent."

"Is there any short cut to become a movie actress?"

"You mean how can a movie struck girl get into the game? There are several ways. She can go out to Hollywood and hang around, hoping day after day that somebody will take notice of her or she can get in through her acquaintances — especially if she knows an author, or director or anyone else who is a position to help her, but they can't do anything more. She makes good or she doesn't, solely on her own ability. And what's more, one picture doesn't secure a life's job for an actress. She's got to keep on making good all the time, and in every picture.... There's no short cut to stardom. Once in a while you read of this or that actress who has become a star overnight, but don't believe it. A woman who has been acting several years may be suddenly elevated to stardom ... that doesn't take into consideration the long time the actress spent on the lots trying to get small parts wherever and whenever she could. No, sir, all stars have to rise gradually."

What about all the engagement reports?

"All I can say is that I'm sorry," said Thelma.

"Sorry in what way?" asked the reporter.

Exuding charm, date unknown (author's collection).

"Well, I come home and find my school friends married, some of them two years, some three years. And some have children! It makes me wonder if I'm going to be left. You know I'm getting older every year!"

"She's just 22," reminded Alice. Either Alice had shaved off a year to suit herself or she had forgotten Thelma's true age was actually 23. Perhaps Alice wanted to keep Thelma forever young. The interview, although unplanned, showed a gracious side of Thelma that her friends and family recognized. She didn't have to do the interview but kindly did so. Bill Todd, 16, knew his vivacious cousin was famous, but never saw Thelma exude any pretensions: "Thelma never had any celebrity status with us. When she came home, she was just family — one of us, which I think she appreciated and gave her a chance to relax."[34]

Back in Los Angeles, Thelma announced she hadn't gained weight during her month in Lawrence: " I left Hollywood weighing 120 and I'm back again with that identical poundage."[35] Thelma resumed her career, playing in Roach comedies and outside feature pictures, an arrangement that was part of her contract. Unexpectedly, the film industry was reeling from the collapse of Wall Street. On Black Friday, October 21, 1929, the stock market crashed, taking the American economy with it. The ranks of the unemployed swelled, as desperate men and women searched for work. Every city reported terrible tragedies. In Los Angeles, the secretary of the Guaranty Building and Loan Association confessed to bank directors that he had written an overdraft of $7,630,000, explaining, "I thought I could quickly return it. I wish I could have another week to work this thing out."[36] The prosperity of the twenties had vanished overnight. Banks closed around the nation; prominent citizens suddenly found themselves destitute.

Thelma's friend Lina Basquette was still riding the wave that had yet to crash. But Lina's marriage to J. Peverill Marley, a cinematographer for Cecil B. DeMille, was unraveling. They had met on the set of *The Godless Girl*, a film that featured Lina as a teenage atheist who rebels but finds religion in a reformatory. Married only a few months, Lina discovered her husband had a roving eye. When they separated, Lina handed Pev Marley $10,000 and continued her romance with a married stockbroker. Basquette, like her friends Clara Bow and Jean Harlow, was indeed running wild. Lina's lavish apartment at 3925 Wilshire Boulevard, decorated in black, white, orange, and turquoise, was always filled with partying sycophants. But the high society crowd had fallen after the financial crash. They now let Lina pick up the tab. Basquette had a chauffeur on call, ready to bring her twelve-cylinder Packard limousine, the avocado Cadillac, or the red roadster. Lina preferred the Cadillac; she liked to drive at 110 miles per hour.

Thelma often came to Lina Basquette's apartment and joined the merrymaking. As Thelma had admitted in Lawrence, the mental stress of being an actress was tremendous: "Sometimes you get so nervous that when you hear a noise you want to jump." A shot of alcohol helped to calm frazzled nerves. As for her beauty, when men raved over her, "I feel absurd. I never think about it."[37] Beneath the delicate features and porcelain skin was an intelligent woman who preferred qualities "in the old beano." Men chased her, but she felt strangely uncomfortable with her good looks: "It makes life difficult. It must be like having too much money. You see, I can't trust anyone. Especially, I can't trust men." She related how a millionaire had recently proposed. "He would have surrounded me with Rolls Royces, sables, personal maids, and trips to the Riviera and homes like Buckingham Palace ... but I would have been another museum piece for his collection, something to exhibit. That's the way it is. I never believe a man really loves me — me — for whatever qualities I may possess in the old beano or for that quaint, old-fashioned thing, a soul, if any."

Lina observed that Thelma was trying to assert her independence, trying to break away from Alice's critical eye. "She drank when she was depressed," says Basquette.[38] "Her mother always felt that Thelma was far above the scum of Hollywood. Thelma used to come to my apartment constantly. Her mother didn't realize that I was a good, honest friend to Thelma, trying to help her. Sometimes when Thelma would come to my house her mother would call and read the riot act to me. Thelma used to bring her own flask because I didn't keep liquor in the house. Sometimes she was in very bad shape. I would have to drive her home. Her mother, of course, hated me because I had been divorced and there were a lot of bad stories about me floating around, just as there was about everybody." Like her mother, Thelma liked to boast of her *Mayflower* heritage which grated on Lina. "For chrissakes," exclaimed Basquette, "would you stop talking about the *Mayflower*? My dear, you must remember that there were a lot of convicts and political enemies that were thrown on those boats. Don't brag about it so much. My family came over before the *Mayflower* and *they* were on convict ships." Lina was often approached by Thelma's suitors, to exert her influence. "She was very popular with the bachelor crowd. Harvey Priester, a wealthy guy who insured a lot of stars, was very much in love with her, but she didn't care for him. He used to come to me and say, 'I'm in love with her but I'm just worried about this weakness she has with liquor.'"

Lina had troubles of her own. People kept asking when she was going to get her baby back. She smiled, holding her head high, but inside she was unraveling, angry over her lost child and philandering husband. Temporarily reconciled, Lina and Pev Marley were at the Embassy Club when Pev seemed to nod at a woman on the dance floor. Lina became enraged and threatened to slap his face. Thelma, seated at an adjoining table, jumped up and calmed her distraught friend. After her husband finally left for good, Lina Basquette's world crumbled. On a hot August night in 1930, driven by loneliness for her child in New York, thinking she would never see her four-year-old daughter again, Basquette drank poison after a rowdy party. Wan and exhausted, she spoke with reporters from her bed at the Georgia Street Hospital: "I can't do anything about the estate Sam Warner left. I was only nineteen years old when he died.... When the other Warners offered to settle $300,000 upon her I agreed to their being appointed her guardians ... I consented and now I don't know what she is doing. That's why I drank poison."[39]

A month later, Thelma was a witness at the Marley's divorce hearing. She admitted Lina's jealousy at the Embassy Club. Basquette's second marriage was over. Lina was pursued by passionate Harry Cohn, the vulgar but generous head of Columbia pictures, who showered her with diamond bracelets and solitaires. Her next lover was song and dance man Harry Richman. But Lina married Ray Hallam, a sensitive young actor she knew was dying. Basquette seemed to find happiness, at least for a while.

Thelma, too, had found the great love of her life.

THREE

Roland and Jewel

Thelma was soon one of the most popular players on the Roach lot. "We all loved her," reminisced Joe Cobb, one of the Our Gang stars.[1] "We kids would try to sit next to her in the studio commissary. She was so friendly. We all had a crush on her." Thelma's cheery personality endeared her to Dorothy Granger, who appeared with her in *The Pip From Pittsburgh*, a Charlie Chase comedy. "She'd get the giggles easily," says Granger, "especially when she was with ZaSu Pitts. They'd break up laughing and have to do a dozen takes. Thelma was always smiling, not at all bitchy. The scuttlebutt going around at the time was that she was carrying on with Charlie. I didn't see anything, but when you're working at a studio you hear all the lowdown. I was just a teenager and really didn't care."[2] Granger remembers that there was no drinking on the Roach lot, just hard work and laughs. Anita Garvin, famous for her harridan roles with Laurel and Hardy, knew Thelma well, and viewed her as a "very intelligent" person who loved to laugh.[3] While making *Show Business,* Garvin never forgot what happened. "Oh, my God, they strapped this monkey around my neck, and all of a sudden I feel this hot thing running down my back. The monkey's owner said, 'Oh, Josephine, she just wet a little.' Boy, it was horrible. Thelma and ZaSu laughed their heads off."

Harry Mines, drama editor for the *Daily News,* interviewed Thelma in his office, where he wrote his column, Raps and Raves. The critic was impressed: "She sparkled. She was just so vivacious and exuded warmth."[4] Mines often saw her in nightclubs, always surrounded by a group of admirers. Thelma revealed her goal to Mines: "I'm going to be a dramatic actress. People respect you as an artist, rather than a clown."

On June 5, 1931, Thelma's agent, Jerry Mayer, drafted a letter. Mayer wrote to Warren Doane, general manager of Roach Studios, that his client would not be available until the end of July for Roach projects. Thelma was busy on the set of *Corsair,* an adventure film about rum runners. Hal Roach became concerned as stories circulated that Thelma was going to change her name and become a dramatic actress. Moreover, there was also talk that she had fallen in love with Roland West, the picture's director. Based on a serial in *Liberty Magazine,* West brought to life the story of Johnny Hawks, a football hero who accepts a position with a Wall Street brokerage firm. Alison, the financier's daughter, is attracted to him, but when he is ordered to take an elderly woman's savings in exchange

Billed as Alison Loyd in *Corsair* (1931), the film that changed her life.

for worthless bonds, he refuses and is fired. Johnny becomes a bootlegger. Chester Morris played Johnny. Morris was a handsome, dark-haired actor under contract to West. The talk that Thelma had fallen in love with West was true. She was under the spell of the noted director. Thelma was grateful that Roland had selected her for the dramatic role. She wanted to distance herself from comedy. Thelma and Morris spent days on the deck of the *Invader*, an old sailing ship moored off Catalina Island. A strong ocean breeze swept the wooden deck and whistled through the rigging as West positioned smugglers in navy jackets and bell bottom trousers around the lead characters.

West was master of the production, both producer and director of *Corsair*. At his request, Thelma had agreed to screen billing as Alison Loyd. West demanded that the cast and crew call her by her new screen name. West, 46, was short and plain, but he had a forceful personality and a brilliant, creative mind. Dressed in a charcoal gray coat with white flannel trousers, West held sway over the production with a quiet but definite authority. Roland gave Thelma a sense of artistic confidence; she believed she could achieve her dream of becoming a dramatic actress. West's wife, Jewel Carmen, occasionally visited the set, but she disliked ships and the ocean. Roland was all business on the set, pensive and isolated. Performers found him aloof. "Roland was an odd, taciturn, enigmatic man," says William Bakewell, who appeared in West's *The Bat Whispers* in 1930.[5] Actor Regis Toomey also found West peculiar: "He was a very odd man; a nice pleasant man — nothing *weird* about him, but he was a difficult man to get to know. He was rather shy, very reticent, a very retiring man. He had little to say."[6]

During a break from filming, Thelma went to a beach on Catalina Island for a swim. She donned a bathing suit and enjoyed the foaming green surf, but she became faint, staggered, and collapsed. Rescued from the ocean, news of the incident spread quickly. Later, Thelma told Roland that she had a heart murmur. West was emotionally torn between Thelma and his wife. Thelma came to Lina Basquette's apartment, pouring out her heart that West wasn't available when she needed him. "It was a very tempestuous love affair. It was probably the most serious one she ever had," says Basquette.[7] "She was madly in love with Roland. But he had told her he wouldn't marry her." Lina witnessed Thelma's depression over her failure to capture West's full affection. Lina was upset seeing her friend in such a sad state. And what was it that drew Thelma to Roland West? Who was this brilliant, yet enigmatic man?

There was an aura of mystery about Roland West. His motion pictures were dark dramas like *The Unknown Purple, The Bat, The Bat Whispers, The Monster,* and *Alibi.* Roland West and Jewel Carmen were theatrical names. West's real name was Roland Van Ziemer. Born in Cleveland, Ohio, in 1885, he came from a stage family. Albert Ziemer, his father, was an actor and writer. Margaret Van Tassel, his mother, was an actress who achieved acclaim on the stage. Cora Van Tassel, his aunt, was not only an actress but one of the first women to produce her own productions. At the age of ten, Roland had worked in a broker's office but abandoned stocks and bonds for the magic of the theatre. His aunt hired him for *The Volunteer,* produced at the Cleveland Theatre. Over the next four years, Roland learned his craft in stock productions. As a teenager, he was sent to St. Joseph's School in Cleveland, but left school and returned to the stage. At age 17, Roland won recognition in *Jockey Jones.* He made a living as a vaudeville actor and writer. He performed his own sketches on the Loew's circuit. West produced 53 stage acts which were successfully performed in theatres around the country. At age 18, West was a smash in *The Criminal,* his own one act drama. He played eight roles, ranging from an eighty-year-old man, to a fourteen-year-old boy, a gunman, an Englishman, a German, and a Jewish comedian. He toured in the play for eight years on the Keith Circuit. He wrote "When Women Rule," an act that toured England.[8] However, the theatre became less interesting to him.

West was drawn to the new form of entertainment that entranced audiences around the world: *the flickers.* In New York he had the good fortune to meet Joseph M. Schenck, a Russian-born immigrant and businessman. Schenck started his career as a delivery boy in a New York ghetto, delivering packages for a shady drugstore where illegal drugs were sold. According to Anita Loos, Schenck and his friend Irving Berlin, "made their first dimes as messengers for the underworld."[9] Joe and his brother, Nicholas, had become enormously wealthy with the Palisades Amusement Park in Fort Lee, New Jersey, a business that brought in daily revenues of $100,000. When Marcus Lowe installed penny arcades in amusement parks, the Schenck brothers invested and later became fascinated by *movies.* Joe Schenck later managed the Marcus Lowe theatre chain and was a member of the Sixty Club, a social group of Broadway titans, founded by Florenz Ziegfeld, Sam Harris, George M. Cohan, Billy Rose, and Sam Goldwyn. Parties were held every two weeks in a ballroom at the Ritz Hotel at 54th and Madison Avenue where "a galaxy of crystal chandeliers shone down on the pick of the Broadway beauties."[10] At a party in Long Beach, California, Schenck met Norma Talmadge. He abandoned his longtime mistress, Peggy Hopkins Joyce, and married Talmadge in October 1916, just two months after meeting her. The new bride called her balding, portly husband "daddy." Joe Schenck would remain a lifelong friend of Roland West.

In 1918, at the height of his stage fame, West was introduced to Jewel Carmen, a pretty blonde who had appeared in several films, including D.W. Griffith's *Intolerance*. Born Florence Lavina Quick in Oregon, the petite blonde and her mother arrived in Los Angeles in February 1912, where they lived at 150 North Hill Street. Vina, as she was known in her family, wanted to be an actress. Two weeks after she arrived, she found work as an extra with the De Mille Company. Since minors under 16 could not work, Vina said she was 17. She was active as an extra on the movie lots of Keystone, Pathe, and Fine Arts. Vina's siblings soon came to Los Angeles: Allie, Edna, Fred, Henry, and Alberta; two sisters, Luella and Florence Evelyn, had died. The Quick family had struggled to evade poverty. Florence Lavina Quick's success was amazing in light of her humble birth.

Her parents, Amos and Minerva Quick, had wed in Arkansas in 1882. Minerva, born in 1862, grew up in Danville, Arkansas; her father died in the Civil War. Amos worked as a carpenter and farmer. The couple soon had children and moved to Texas and Colorado. By 1890, they were on a farm in Blaine, Oregon, 26 miles from Tillamook City, where they moved in 1900. The next year they were in Portland, where Vina attended Mount Tabor School. Amos left his wife and children in 1911 and found work in Los Angeles. The family followed the next year.

Vina Quick was involved in Hollywood's first major scandal in 1913. A grand jury investigating white slavery had indicted William La Casse, 35, a prominent and wealthy auto dealer, on a charge of statutory rape. "Child Testifies In Vice Inquiry" was the headline. "I am fifteen years old," she insisted.[11] The press portrayed her as "a beautiful moving picture actress," an innocent girl led astray by fast cars, the nightlife, and an older man. The age of sexual consent was 16, so La Casse found himself in deep legal trouble. If convicted, he faced life imprisonment. However, if he could prove that she was 16 or older, he would escape prison. Vina told reporters she didn't like her first name, so she used the name Evelyn Lavina Quick, a curious change, since it was her dead sister's name, a name she preferred, or so she claimed.

In January, she had been a guest at the Vernon Country Club in Pasadena when La Casse approached her table. A few weeks later, La Casse hired her to pose for auto advertisements. The couple shared outings to the beach communities of Venice and Playa de Rey. One evening La Casse took her to his room at the Raphael Apartments on South Hill Street. She remained there all night. Her sister Allie, also known as Alice, discovered her with La Casse. Minerva Quick was furious and called police. She filed a complaint and insisted her underage daughter had been victimized. La Casse denied any sexual intimacy took place. He told investigators that they had dined together; afterward, they went to his apartment with another couple and talked, but the girls went home early. Despite his pleas, La Casse was arrested and later released on $5,000 bail. A hearing was held in Juvenile Court before Justice Sidney M. Reeve. Evelyn, as the press called her, insisted she was 15; her birthday was July 13, 1897. However, she had no proof, since there was no birth certificate.

The scandal filled the newspapers. The district attorney requested a closed door hearing but defense attorney LeCompte Davis objected, complaining "there had been so much printed about this case that I want the public to get the facts as they are legally presented in court."[12] Minors were banned from the courtroom due to the sensational testimony. Yet, the alleged victim smiled for photographers and appeared to enjoy the publicity. Reporters interviewed her before the hearing. She expressed sympathy for La Casse and was sorry he was in court. She hoped that he would not be punished but made it clear she didn't love him.

Evelyn was the first witness, elegantly dressed in a blue gown and a black hat with red roses. She recounted her story and testified that she would not be 16 until July 13. But defense attorney Davis argued that her birthday had been changed in the family Bible and charged that she lied about her age. She admitted that she was guilty of "white lies" but, she smiled, "they never amount to anything."[13] When Davis casually asked if she had told others her age was more than 15, she replied, "Yes, because I am large for my age, and anyway, who wants to go out with a 15 year old girl?" It was a damaging admission. In addition, she acknowledged that La Casse had put a $10 gold piece in her stocking. Defense lawyers raised eyebrows when reporters were told about spicy letters between Evelyn and a man identified as "Abie." The letters "burned with affection."

Davis carefully questioned Alice Quick, who testified that she had seen La Casse give her sister a coin after he drove her home. Davis got Alice to admit that her sister was 18, before she withdrew the answer in confusion. Officer Bert Cowan testified that Alice had given him the family Bible as evidence of her sister's age. The entry proved that her daughter was a minor, said her mother. But the officer observed that the date after "Evelyn Quick" had been changed from 1890 to 1896. The Quicks insisted Evelyn had died as an infant in 1896. Below her name, after "Lavina Quick," the date had been changed from 1895 to 1897. The entries in the Bible failed to conclusively prove Lavina Quick's age but raised suspicion that she was older than 15. Since Vina had admitted giving an older age, Justice Reeve dropped the most serious charge. Justice Reeve held La Casse for trial and charged him with contributing to the delinquency of a minor. The case brought more sensational articles: "La Casse Faces Girl Accuser" and "Girl Names Clubman."

The second trial began in July in a packed courtroom. Evelyn, now dressed demurely in black, testified that she had visited La Casse at his apartment, where she was served liquor. On July 18, she took the stand. LaCompte Davis asked if she drank soda pop and lemonade. "Not on joy rides," she smiled.

When the intimate details of the night were mentioned, she became embarrassed, ill at ease, and blushed. Davis probed her contradictions. He pointed out that earlier she could not recall her first meeting with La Casse, but now it was different. The defense attorney probed deeper.

"Did he make any proposals to you first?" asked Davis.[14]

"Not that I remember."

"Did he hug or kiss you?"

"Not that I remember."

"Did he ask you to go into the room with him or did you invite him to go in with you?"

"I don't remember that." But she did remember intimate relations with La Casse. Davis fired back; she had previously been unable to recall details of their sexual intimacy.

Los Angeles Record
NIGHT EDITION

Eighteenth Year   FRIDAY, JULY 18, 1913.   Number 10995

EVELYN QUICK ARTFUL

TELLS OF JOY RIDES

FIGURES IN DELINQUENCY TRIAL

Upper picture, Wm. La Casse, on left, entering the Hall of Justice Friday to appear at his trial. Lower, Evelyn Quick, who is being questioned regarding her alleged joy rides with the rich automobile man.

Sharp questions penetrated the delicate armor of Evelyn Quick in Judge Wilbur's court Friday.

Pilloried before a sea of grinning faces, the beautiful moving picture actress blushed and fidgeted in her chair as lawyers for Wm. La Casse, who is charged with contributing to her delinquency, harried her with a cross-fire of searching queries.

During the proceedings Judge Wilbur was accused by Defense Counsel LeCompte Davis of shielding the girl witness from the rapid volleys of inquiries which were fired at her. Davis charged that Wilbur was aiding Asst. Dist. Atty. McCartney to protect the girl.

Judge Wilbur replied that Davis' remarks were uncalled for, and stated that he would not permit a witness to be insulted in his court.

Starting with the meeting between La Casse, a wealthy automobile agent, and Evelyn Quick at the Vernon Country club, Davis went carefully into every incident to the finish. Getting down to the incident of the "joy ride" which preceded the alleged midnight orgy at La Casse's bunga-

"Weren't you introduced to her?"

"I don't remember."

"What did she look like?"

"Well, I rather think she was a blonde."

"Young or old?"

"She was rather young."

"What happened on the ride?"

Davis then demanded if she was accustomed to drinking soft drinks when on larks.

DOES NOT DRINK POP

"Do you drink lemonade and soda pop and such stuff?" asked Davis.

"Not on joy rides," smiled the witness.

Getting down to the incident at La Casse's bungalow, Davis ascertained that Hollingsworth and his girl ragged for some time and then went into a bedroom. A few minutes later La Casse and Evelyn Quick went into another private room, according to the girl.

"Did he make any proposals to you first?" asked Davis.

"Not that I remember."

"Did he hug you or kiss you?"

"I don't remember."

"Well, did he ask you to go into the room with him or did you invite him to go in with you?"

"I don't remember that," replied the actress.

She was on the witness stand most of the day.

Hollywood's first scandal. Evelyn Quick changed her name to Jewel Carmen (author's collection).

"You seem to have a convenient memory," he said sarcastically.

The following day, the *Los Angeles Record* described Evelyn Quick as "artful." On July 25, after six hours deliberation, the jury was deadlocked eight to four for conviction. La Casse walked from the courtroom a free man. The court accepted the girl's word that she was a minor. She was assigned to a probation officer and allowed to work as an extra, but Evelyn Vina Quick vanished. In her place emerged Jewel Carmen, a name she used on the Triangle lot, where she earned $50 a week. Jewel stayed with Triangle for a year and three months, without a contract. Good fortune came her way.

On October 17, 1916, a contract was signed between Jewel and the Fox Film Corporation for a salary of $100 per week. Minerva Quick signed the contract, which Jewel acknowledged with her initials: "J.C. a minor." Jewel later complained she had initialed two blank contracts with Fox and Fox Vaudeville. In August 1917, after she was sent to New York to appear in *Les Miserables*, she saw the contracts and discovered the blanks had been filled in. Jewel believed she had been tricked.

"Who is Jewel Carmen?" asked *Photoplay* in 1917.[15]

Readers were informed that Jewel was "The Girl Who Photographs Like a Million Dollars." According to the article, during the filming of *Intolerance*, D.W. Griffith saw an attractive blonde. The director was preparing a shot on the massive Babylonian set, dominated by the mammoth steps and towering elephants along the giant wall, as hundreds of extras milled about. During a break, Griffith's voice rang out: "Where is that young lady who can act?"[16] Assistant director George Seigmann shouted for Jewel Carmen. Griffith liked the blonde with the angelic face and gave her a chance before the camera. Jewel appeared in *A Tale of Two Cities* with William Farnum and *Manhattan Madness* with screen idol Douglas Fairbanks. After signing with the Fox Company, she was acclaimed for her performance in *Les Miserables*.

Although she earned $125 per week, Jewel was dissatisfied. On July 13, 1918, when she reached 21, she informed Fox the contracts she had signed were invalid because she was a minor at the time. Two days later, she signed a new contract with Frank A. Keeney Pictures for $450 a week. Fox denied her claim and responded that Jewel had agreed to California contracts, and age 18 was sufficient. However, to her surprise, both companies agreed not to hire her. Jewel believed she would have earned $190,000 under the Keeney contract if options had been taken. Jewel decided to sue the Fox Corporation.

Jewel grew close to Roland West after they met in 1918. West introduced her to the elite entertainment circles of Broadway where he was recognized and respected. West was wealthy. The first floor of the American Theatre Building at 260 West 42nd Street was occupied by the Roland West Producing Company, the Roland West Film Corporation, Roland West Enterprises, and Roland West Bookings. His array of companies was headed by Charles H. Smith, who handled the money that poured into West's pockets. West and his father lived in the building. Roland West turned his back on the theatre for motion pictures. West acquired film expertise when he worked for William Fox, directing Valeska Suratt. Captivated by Jewel, he directed her in *Nobody,* a drama about a murdered financier who, it is later revealed in court, had drugged and seduced another man's wife while on a yachting trip. Blackmailed and shamed into silence, the victim later shoots her attacker in revenge. The victim confesses her crime in court; the stunned jury declares her innocent and agrees never to divulge her tragic story. The film was made on location in West Palm

Beach and other fashionable Florida resorts. West asked his friends, Florenz Ziegfeld and Lee Shubert, to make cameo appearances. Filled with lurid sex and violence, *Nobody* was a smash in 1921. The same year, Jewel had her day in court. She obtained a verdict granting an injunction against Fox and awarding her damages of $43,721, but an appeal was made by Fox Corporation. In July 1924, during the pre-trial interrogatories, attorneys for Fox questioned Minerva and her daughter Allie, or Alice Carmen, a name Jewel's eldest sister now used. They had discovered Jewel's "criminal proceeding" that had taken place in Los Angeles in 1913. Exactly how old was Jewel Carmen? Perhaps Jewel was not a minor when she initialed the Fox contract. When William La Casse had been charged with the crime of statutory rape, both Minerva and Alice insisted Jewel was only 15. The Fox attorneys discovered corrections in a family Bible had been noticed during the statutory rape trial, thereby making it appear Jewel was younger. The birthday was originally written as 1895, but someone had crossed out the 5 and inserted 7. When Amos Quick gave his deposition, he insisted that 1895 was a mistake, and he had corrected it. Sarah Dillow, a resident of Blaine, verified Jewel's birth occurred in 1897.

The Fox attorneys revealed that Jewel had admitted she had lied about her age to support her family. During the trial Jewel acknowledged that she, though only 15, "usually tell them that I am 18 or 19, and in the second place, who wants to go out with a 15 year-old girl?" But in her Fox deposition, when asked about the La Casse trial, she said, "I can't remember what I said at that trial, it is so long ago."

In the spring of 1925, Jewel was in court, represented by attorney Nathan Burkan. She claimed that Fox had conspired to make the Frank A. Keeney Picture Corporation break a contract with her. The lawsuit asserted that she had been underage when she signed the Fox contract. The outcome of the litigation hinged on Jewel's true age. Amos Quick testified that his daughter had been born in an obscure town in Oregon. Her correct birthday had been inscribed in a family Bible which was later "destroyed in a fire."[17] A second Bible replaced it, he explained to the court, and the children's birthdates were again recorded. "A mistake was made" in entering the birthday of Florence, said her father, "in which she appeared to have been born in 1895, but was corrected to 1897, immediately after it had been noticed." Despite the mystery over her birthday, the jury accepted that Jewel had indeed been the victim of a conspiracy. William Fox was furious over the decision. Fox appealed to a higher court but, two years later, Carmen's victory was upheld, and she was awarded $59,000. Although she won the case, the notoriety did not help her motion picture career. Joe Schenck advised his friend Roland West to move to Los Angeles. Roland and Jewel decided to leave New York City. Hollywood would be the couple's new home.

Schenck moved his company to Los Angeles in 1921, where he and Marcus Lowe bought the Metropolitan Studio. Schenck was accompanied by Norma, his wife, and sisters-in-law, actresses Natalie and Constance. Natalie was married to comedy star Buster Keaton, whose pictures Schenck controlled. Schenck had big plans for West.

In 1925, Schenck was elected the board chairman of United Artists, a distribution company formed in 1919 by Charles Chaplin, Douglas Fairbanks, Mary Pickford, and D.W. Griffith. United Artists allowed the stars creative independence and high incomes. Schenck began expanding. He brought to UA Norma Talmadge, John Barrymore, Sam Goldwyn, Gloria Swanson, Corrine Griffith, in addition to West. In July 1925, West became an associate producer at United Artists. The following year, Schenck formed the Art Cinema Corporation with headquarters at the Pickford-Fairbanks Studio in Hollywood. Schenck had the Midas touch and knew how to invest in motion pictures and make sure United Artists and Art Cinema made money; his close friend West invested in stocks, bonds, and land, just like his friend Schenck. Schenck was a lavish host who liked to entertain and knew everyone; he was also a gambler who lost high sums at cards.

West's first Hollywood picture was *The Monster*, starring the master of disguises, Lon Chaney. The mystery tale was about an amateur detective trying to solve the disappearance of a small town's prominent citizens. Amidst shadows, clutching hands, and corpses awaiting reanimation, a young detective discovers madman Chaney conducting bizarre experiments in an institution for the insane. *The Monster* was another successful film by Roland West, a director whose reputation was growing with each picture.

The Wests lived in a home at 6662 Whitley Heights, a two story residence on a steep street. Though located in an exclusive neighborhood, the home was peculiar, since the roof was practically level with the street. Visitors had to use a descending walkway to enter. Roland and Jewel took a special interest in their garden which was filled with plants and exotic flowers. They paid a gardener $32.50 a month to tend it. A chauffeur-driven Hup-mobile took Jewel to shopping sprees in downtown Los Angeles or to nearby Hollywood Boulevard. She easily spent the $80 check her husband wrote weekly. Jewel shopped at chic stores like the House of Exquisite Short Vamp Footwear, while Roland picked up a box of 50 Corona Perfectos for $14.50 at Clubbs Cigars on Hollywood Boulevard. Life was sweet.

All bills were duly forwarded to United Artists Studio at 1951 N. Formosa Avenue, where Roland kept an office, and managed his company, Feature Productions, a part of the Art Cinema Corporation. Schenck had taken full control of United Artists. Although an independent producer, West's films were financed and distributed by UA. West's goal was to release a single motion picture a year, but the single film would be an expensive production, carefully planned in advance.

Roland bought the rights to *The Bat*, a successful stage play by Mary Roberts Rinehart and Avery Hopwood. He adapted for the screen the successful thriller about a criminal who disguises himself as a bat. Though Jewel was in the film, her career was fading. She was practically forgotten, to the point that *Variety* proclaimed, "There's not a star in the cast but one man, an Italian actor named Tullio Carminati."[18] The lavish production utilized enormous sets, miniatures, as well as an ominous shadow of a bat projected by a spotlight, signifying the murderous bat's presence. At the start of the picture audiences read a plea: "Can you keep a secret? Don't reveal the ending of *The Bat*. Future audiences will enjoy this mystery play if left to find for themselves." The profits were enormous from *The Bat*, and Roland and Jewel spent lavishly. Jewel wore a platinum bracelet, a gift from Roland. Their high income allowed them a life of luxury. The Wests relaxed at the Casa Del Mar Club, situated on the beach in Santa Monica. The golden California sun shone on a parade of Rolls Royces, shiny limousines, and bright colored roadsters, as the wealthy arrived in style at the club's main entrance on Ocean Avenue. A doorman in gold epaulettes welcomed Roland and Jewel to beach fun and lavish dinner parties. The building had an enormous swimming pool, card rooms, indoor gyms, a handball court, and a large dining room which could accommodate seven hundred guests. There was a spacious sun parlor where the gentlemen discussed business and the ladies chatted. Gaily striped beach umbrellas dotted the beach; beautiful women strolled in the latest swimwear of chic Jacquard design. West was

Roland West's silent *The Bat* (1926), featured the bat symbol, an iconic image in motion picture history (courtesy of Scott MacQueen).

drawn to the white sand and blue water. He decided he would live near the Pacific, with a yacht to sail the sea. But first, there was more money to be made.

Schenck chose Roland to direct *The Dove,* an expensive production with Norma Talmadge as an enticing dance hall queen, enamored by handsome gambler Gilbert Roland. The torrid romance before the camera ignited off-screen. The Schencks were to remain married but lived apart. A rumor swept through the film community that Schenck had been so enraged by his wife's affair that he had thugs emasculate Gilbert Roland. To quell the gossip, the actor assembled male reporters at a tennis club and displayed his genitalia, to prove that he was intact and not a castrato.

Roland and Jewel witnessed the wreckage of the Schenck marriage. They lived quietly, without children. They enjoyed the Club Casa Del Mar, where Roland met the city's elite and puffed his Corona Perfecto cigars. Roland endorsed his friend, Harry A. Hollzer, Judge of Superior Court, for appointment to U.S. District Court. The Wests avoided the flamboyance of glittery nightclubs, wild parties, and fashionable restaurants. Roland's only eccentric habit, noted columnists, was his dislike of neckties. They wrote that he preferred expensive blazers, open-collared shirts, and white flannel trousers. His $165 custom suits were made at Eddie Schmidt's Shop, at 714 W. 7th Street. UA publicity wrote that West's youthful ambition was to be a stockbroker, until he discovered the stage, and the money that came with it. The studio biography was on the mark. Roland's main passion in life

Roland West has the cast of *The Bat* (1926) swear not to reveal the ending. From left: Jewel Carmen, Jack Pickford, Emily Fitzroy, Kamiyama Sojin, Louise Fazenda (courtesy of Scott MacQueen).

was directing his yearly film and making money. He established Roland West, Inc., a corporation organized under the laws of the state of Nevada but a company whose principal business was in the city of Los Angeles. Vice presidents were A.M. Brentinger, a film associate, and Helen Hallett, West's secretary, who was paid $75 a month. Roland and Jewel registered as Republicans.

The success of *The Bat* brought more fame and fortune. Relatives who had lost track of "cousin Roland" and Margaret, his mother, suddenly found him. West brought them up to date: "My dear cousin Minnie, I received your letter of September 1, and I was glad to hear from you. At present, my mother is in London, England, so I do not think you can go to see her right away. However, you can drop her a line, and know she will be very glad to hear from you, although she is a very hard hand at writing, in fact, she has not written a letter to me in a couple of years, but I hear from B — her husband, regularly."[19]

Although Roland had once been a dynamic stage actor, he disdained the spotlight as time passed. West seems to have inherited his reclusive nature from his mother, the wife of Elmer E. Bellamy, known as "B," an executive with the Decalcomania Company of Canada, an international manufacturing firm. The company, headquartered in King Street in Toronto, made decorations, signs, and name plates. Bellamy established the London office, then offices in Bombay, Calcutta, and Sydney. Roland and his stepfather corresponded frequently, with Roland sending gifts of money to his mother who had retired from the stage. Roland wrote to another cousin that his mother would be glad to receive a letter "but to get an answer out of her is almost impossible, although I hear from B — If I get a letter from her every two years I am lucky."

In the fall of 1928, Roland and Jewel purchased a magnificent Spanish-style residence at 17531 Posetano Road in the exclusive Castellammare neighborhood. The large home had eight bedrooms and overlooked the Pacific Ocean, high above the Malibu State Highway, later known as the Roosevelt Highway. The Frank Meline Company had developed the property and advertised the area as a picturesque reflection of the famous French and Italian rivieras. The homes, priced at $5,000 and up, dotted the hillside and resembled Mediterranean residences with white stucco walls and red tile roofs. Each home boasted a panoramic view of the ocean, mountains, and evening sunset. The nearby Mesa Unit, started in 1925, was located on property of the former Ince Studio, near Santa Inez Canyon. Residents of the Castellammare and Mesa neighborhoods shopped at a community center that housed a drug store, grocery, market, and café. Homeowners were allowed the use of a private beach reached by a pedestrian bridge over the highway. In October, the company sent the Wests the title and a certificate of stock ownership in the Castellammare Beach Corporation. Roland's reply was rather testy: "I do not care so much about having the deed as I did for the plants and trees I asked for...."[20] Roland and Jewel began furnishing their new home, never paying cash for anything. The smallest items were billed to Roland's office. He kept a meticulous account of every penny spent and exerted special care with his bookkeeping, since many purchases were deducted as "business expenditures." Many checks were paid to A.B. Carmen, identified as "a special writer," but possibly one of Jewel's siblings. The home on Whitley Terrace was sold to actor Chester Morris.

Ledda Bauer of Joe Schenck's office in New York was constantly searching for literary properties for Roland. She found *Nightstick,* a successful play. Retitled as *Alibi,* the play became the first sound picture for United Artists and featured Chester Morris as a sly criminal wed to the daughter of a police sergeant. The hoodlum uses his innocent wife as an alibi for his secret robberies and murders. Regis Toomey, hired to play a detective, argued with West on the set about how a drunken man should talk. West was dissatisfied with Toomey's performance. West emerged from the glass sound booth, high above the set, to argue: "He had some sort of screwy idea of something mechanical that had to be done with the tongue in order to sound drunk. I said, 'Well, hell, Mr. West, the audience won't understand what I'm talking about. This is a talking picture.' He didn't like my attitude. The assistant director stepped in, and he risked his job, and said, 'He's right, Mr. West.' ... So he sulked a little and finally that was the end of it."[21] West disliked any display of temperament on the set, either from himself or from his cast. Toomey never felt that West was a good director, but *Alibi* won praise. "If Roland West never makes another picture it doesn't matter. He has made one that has burned the ears off a couple of producing companies," proclaimed *Exhibitor's Herald World*[22] "Jolt packed drama," hailed *Variety.*[23] Morris was lauded for portraying "a clever young rodent" in a story filled with third degrees, brutal crooks, and heroic detectives, exposing the young hoodlum as a groveling coward when, as blank cartridges are fired, he faints. *Alibi* was a smash; within three months of its release, West had earned $37,000 for himself.

Despite his success, some critics viewed Roland West as a talented but self-indulgent director. They asked why he had made only seven pictures in 13 years. West responded,

"Producers usually play a pretty good game of golf. With about two exceptions that is all I can say for any of them. The only business they have in the motion picture industry is to furnish the money with which to make pictures."[24] The day of "the dummy" was over, said West, and the beautiful "dumbbells" who starred in silents were finished. "It is personality that counts on the talking screen," he proclaimed. "The dummies can go home and the plain little vaudevileans who have had to live on their wits, and so developed a natural intelligence and personality, can come into the spotlight. The stage, rather than Hollywood, will supply most of the talking picture actors. Intelligence is the chief requisite for the talking screen and I can state it as a fact that intelligence is at a premium among the film stars." West enhanced his stature with *Alibi,* recognized as "the cream of the talking product." He told an interviewer the praise for his pictures was usually for the photography, ignoring the artistic innovations he created. "All the shadows in my pictures are painted, every one of them," West boasted. When a listener commented that the UFA Studio in Germany had been painting shadows for years, West was miffed: "Young man, I painted in the shadows on my sets before the UFA was born or thought of." He told the interviewer that "he got his biggest kick out of life doing things differently." Roland's comments indicated a strong sense of self-worth, at least artistically.

The Wests enjoyed their lavish life in the Castillo del Mar, as they called their sumptuous home, which had a $1,000 a year insurance policy and was valued at $80,000 in 1930. The residence had a library, a piano, and Nibs, a white bull terrier. The home was looked after by Cecil Olsen, a British butler-chauffeur, and Anne Jones, a cook. Roland and Jewel bought several undeveloped lots in the exclusive Castellammare area, where Victor McLaglen and other wealthy neighbors resided. They also bought parcels of land in the adjoining Castle Rock development and property in the Rancho La Ballona region, the original Spanish land grant territory. Roland fulfilled a dream when he bought the *Joyita,* a yacht he moored at the Watchorn Yacht Basin in San Pedro. He subscribed to *Pacific Coast Yachting* and made plans for a world cruise. He relaxed on the yacht, accompanied by friends Joe Schenck, producer Ned Marin, and Harry Brand, UA's publicity director. Jewel disliked the sea. She preferred to remain at home, where she read or designed clothes, including brassieres that she had patented. In January 1928, Roland sued businessman E.H. Cronenweth for $10,000, then attempted to seize Cronenweth's Castellammare land. Cronenweth countersued Roland West Productions for $27,000, and placed an attachment on the Wests' home. Fearful of losing the lawsuit, Roland transferred the home to "Jewel West (a married woman) ... as her separate property." Jewel was also given parcels in the Castle Rock development. Roland and Cronenweth resolved their dispute, but the home and property remained in Jewel's name. Although the Wall Street crash ruined many investors, the Wests avoided major losses. They received income from CalMex Oil, Sun Life of Canada, and stock in Famous Players–Lasky, as well as income from Agua Caliente racetrack, the Mexican playground of the Hollywood crowd, whose major investor was Joe Schenck. West watched his money closely. As Roland Van Ziemer, he was a Mason of the New York order, a member of the Mecca Temple of the Ancient Arabs Order of the Mystic Shrine. But West resigned his membership "to remain permanently" in California.[25] He refused all brotherly pleas to pay back dues, despite a stream of letters. In January 1930, Roland was appointed to the producers' motion picture fund, selected as a member of the Advance Gifts Committee, whose goal was to raise $75,000. Frequent pleas for money arrived at his office: "Dear Cousin

Roland, possibly you don't remember me ... I have always wanted to know you personally. I have often heard mother or some of my relatives speak of you. I am twenty years old now. For the past two years I have been an aeroplane mechanic. I have been out of work for the past two months ... if you would loan me $150 until I can get some work...."[26] "Dear friend Roland, Agnes and John have wondered what had become of you.... His two baby girls have grown to be beautiful big girls of sixteen and eighteen. I think they ought to be movie queens...."[27] Actor Dwight Frye asked for a job, as did Charlotte Kay, a desperate actress: "There is no place for a middle-age woman since I am 'fat, fair and forty,' my ability means nothing and I cannot just simply find a position...."[28]

Some received handouts and jobs, most didn't, but all were sent courteous replies. To an engineer aboard his yacht, West wrote that no loan could be given "on account of the stock market and a loan I have to meet for $25,000 on the 25th of this month." Those who did obtain help were grateful. "Dear Roland, I want to thank you for what you have done for our mother during her recent illness.... If it were not for your generosity I do not know what would have happened, Ollie."[29] West sent frequent checks to relatives who were ill. He even paid funeral expenses of $800 to transport a body to Philadelphia. But West could be tight with his money. The Academy of Motion Picture Arts and Sciences offered West a foundation membership for a fee of $100. The invitation went unanswered. Jewel also kept a close eye on expenses. "Dear Allie: Sorry I missed you but cannot come back today. Tell K.K. that she had better plan on coming down to my house Friday as I am going to San Pedro on Thursday. I think you can pay your share of the gasoline and expenses out of this. Stay sober and have a good time. Jewel."[30]

When United Artists announced that Roland West would make *The Bat Whispers,* a sound version of *The Bat,* actors and crew contacted West's office with requests for work. To Frederick Wallace, former stage director for the road show of *The Bat,* Roland wrote: "Be glad to keep you in mind." But to Jerry Storm, assistant on *The Dove,* he stated: "There really isn't a thing on this picture for you." Emmett Corrigan wrote from his booking office on Vine Street where he provided "Everything Theatrical–Plays–Players–Productions. We Specialize In Screen Artists With Voices."[31] Corrigan made a personal plea: "My dear Roland West: I have given up my office and am in the market for acting or dialog directing. Have you anything for me? Just finished a picture for Columbia in which I had a corking comedy part. I also did the dialog direction on the first talking picture made, *The Lion and the Mouse* for Warner Brothers...." West filed Corrigan's request. Others, such as actor Dwight Frye, were given hope: "I received your letter and will keep you in mind when casting, I will be glad to do what I can."

＼ Roland faithfully corresponded with his mother and stepfather: "Dear mother and B., Enclosed find pictures which I photographed; there are some missing which, if they are any good, I will send to you. Trust that you had a nice trip east and that the weather there is satisfactory and I don't want you two to get the colds again that you lost in California. All my love to you both. Your son."[32] E.E. Bellamy answered Roland, his stepson: "We received the pictures you sent us for which we thank you. Some of them were not so bad but in many cases you didn't have your camera properly focussed on your subject."[33] In the summer, Bellamy had to apologize for an incident over money: "I recently learned from your mother that I kept the $200 you sent her when we were in London and I do not want you to believe I would be guilty of an act like this. The check you sent her was your personal check, which had to be sent back for collection and I suggested that I put it in the bank, rather than have her carry it in her stocking which she was in the habit of doing and which was risky ... I do not consider this money as belonging to me, but I doubt that she told you that when we sold our home in Lakewood, that the entire amount was put in the bank in her name.... This is a little shabby on mother's part I am sure, but just like her at times, and she thinks everyone is trying to rob her, or cheat her, and this is not so.... E.E. Bellamy."[34] Elmer and Margaret Bellamy moved to Los Angeles in 1930, when he changed jobs.

Roland's patched-up relationship with businessman H.E. Cronenweth again became strained. Wrote West: "Dear H.E., I have at last located the CalMex Oil and Refining Company stock certificate for 12,500 shares, dated December 7, 1923. I have forgotten whether or not you asked me to send the certificate to you, but will do what is the most advantageous. Would have attended this before but could not locate the certificate. Best wishes to you and Eloise."[35] Cronenweth's acerbic response: "...with reference to the CalMex Oil and Refining Company stock certificates. I think you were standing closer to that quarter bottle of beer when I was talking to you at Agua Caliente and had a better understanding of it than you did with me on the CalMex Oil and Refining Company stock...." Litigation was avoided, to West's relief, as he prepared to make *The Bat Whispers*. West first considered filming *The Loon*, a story he penned with Henry Leverage, a magazine writer and author of *Whispering Wires*. *The Loon* was another mystery drama: "Again the loon's long cry, as the bird of evil omen trailed a line across the lake...." But West cast aside *The Loon*, just as he declined *Man-Beast*, a horror tale by radio dramatist W.H. "Bill" Clifford who, like H.E. Cronenweth, discovered that West was a shrewd dealmaker. Wrote Clifford: "I don't know whether you ever think of me, but often know I often think of you, and wonder if you are *happy* making money.... No one can hurt me but my friends, and you hurt me once *deeply*. Every day brings both of us nearer to the 'end of the lane' and I'd like to go out realizing your friendship ... I never had my day and I believe that the big strike is to come...."[36]

William Bakewell had just completed *All Quiet on the Western Front* when he landed a role in *The Bat Whispers*. Bakewell was told all filming was to be done at night. "Una Merkel and I were the juvenile romance and Chester Morris played the Bat. Roland would work only at night. For about three weeks, from seven o'clock at night to seven in the morning, we filmed at United Artists. An interesting thing was that he would say, 'Cameras! Action!' then he would walk away, and not watch the scene. He just listened to the dialogue, then he would say, 'O.K., print it,' which was very odd."[37] According to Bakewell, West chose night production to avoid the prying eyes of studio executives. West shot the picture with two cameras, a 35mm camera, and a 65mm camera for widescreen format, which he believed would revolutionize the industry, just as sound had done. West and his crew invented a special zoom device which could send a heavy camera a distance of eighteen feet in a fraction of a second. The dynamic camera effects and special low-key lights created an eerie atmosphere. A startling visual effect had the camera rocketing forward, through an open second story window, to a desk, just like a bat in flight. Another scene transformed a dwarfish, sinister shadow into a large, menacing figure. Chester Morris was captivating as the clever thief, finally unmasked but unrepentant: "I've got the greatest brain that ever existed. You think you've got me, don't you? Well, let me tell you this — there was never a jail strong enough to hold the Bat and after I've paid my respects to your cheap lockup, I shall return at night. The Bat always flies at night and in a straight line." Word of Morris' fine performance spread fast. E.M. Asher, a Universal producer, wrote to West: "We will start *Dracula* in about three weeks. Is there any possibility of getting Chester Morris to play Dracula?" Responded West: "Dear Efe, Don't think I'd care for that part for Chester as we are looking for romance."[38] The role of Dracula went to Bela Lugosi, who achieved international acclaim.

Instead, *Corsair* would be the ideal picture for Chester Morris. West offered Morris $50,000 and ten percent of the net profits. West would earn 35 percent of the net profits. To protect his investment, West purchased a $50,000 insurance policy from Lloyd's of London on Morris, paying a premium of $1,300. Joe Schenck owned 25 percent of the policy. West followed the example of Schenck, who had collected large sums in insurance money when Valentino unexpectedly died at a young age. West spent considerable time making tests of various actresses to play the female lead. Thelma Todd was perfect. Despite her comedic flair, West believed Thelma had great dramatic potential. The selection was risky. West owned stock in Jesse Lasky's company, so it is likely he had been following Thelma's steady rise in screen status. However, West didn't want audiences to expect a comedy, so he suggested that she change her name. The sensational name switch made nationwide news. "The changing of Thelma Todd's name to Alison Loyd is in the nature of an experiment," West told the press. "It goes far beyond her name. It is an attempt to change her personality and psychological outlook as well. I have instructed everyone connected with the picture to always address her as Alison Loyd. Thelma Todd is dead as far as we are concerned and there is to be no mention of her as long as this picture is in production. In this way we hope to make Miss Loyd forget that she ever was a comedienne. I had hoped to keep the identity of Miss Loyd a secret until *Corsair* was released and then spring her upon the film world as an entirely new actress — which she is, having never done a role of this nature before. But I have discovered that a goldfish has more privacy than an actress in Hollywood. Nothing can be kept secret as long as you newshounds are around."[39] And how did Thelma feel about her new name?

"I have always wanted to play dramatic roles," she said. "But you know how it is out here. Casting directors have a way of keeping players in certain grooves and never letting them out. Once you make a good impression in a certain type of role, there is practically no chance of getting away from it. Everyone has always thought of Thelma Todd as a rowdy comedienne. She never could get an opportunity to do anything else, but as Alison Loyd I at least have a chance of being disassociated from my past roles. Yet, even after establishing myself as a dramatic actress, should a comedy role come along that I want to play, I at least will be able to get some consideration because of all the years I spent as a comedienne."[40]

Hal Roach was angry over the news. In the spring he had launched Thelma and ZaSu Pitts as a comedy team, a female version of Laurel and Hardy. Roach had even directed their first episode, *Let's Do Things*. Thelma's classic blonde beauty made her an excellent comedy foil for Pitt's plain looks, wide-eyed stare, and fluttery hands, noted critics. Before signing for the series, Thelma had thought long and hard over what direction her career should take. Thelma received a long letter from Frank Green, general manager of Filmophone, Ltd., a British company. Green offered to star her in a series of feature films. Thelma showed the letter to her friend Mickey Neilan, who worked for Roach Studios. Neilan said to stay in Hollywood, so Thelma stayed with Roach. Neilan directed Thelma and ZaSu Pitts in *Catch as Catch Can* and *War Mammas,* popular comedies that sold tickets. However,

With Chester Morris in *Corsair* (1931).

Thelma told Roach she wasn't happy making comedies. He was stunned. Thelma was perfect for comedy. Her performance as Lady Plumtree in Laurel and Hardy's *Another Fine Mess* had brought praise, not only from audiences, but from Stan and Ollie, who adored her. Thelma played Oliver Hardy's wife in *Chicken Come Home,* another hit. Her comedic ability was so perfect that Sam Wood, the former director of the Junior Stars, cast her opposite the Marx Brothers in *Monkey Business.* When Thelma again told Roach of her discontent with comedy, he was amazed. He showed her letters from exhibitors throughout the country asking for more Thelma Todd comedies. *Pajama Party* was scheduled for release; now he faced a reluctant actress. Roach seethed over Thelma's career turn.

"Hal Roach is pretty burned up," reported columnist Louella Parsons.[41] "When director Roland West put her in a dramatic role in *Corsair* he rechristened her 'in order that no taint of comedy might cling to her skirts.' Roach says that when she starts her next comedy with ZaSu Pitts he's going to change her name to Susie Dinkleberry, so that no taint of drama will cling to her pajamas." Fumed Roach: "I don't want to cause any unnecessary trouble for anyone, but if at any time I find Thelma's use of the name Alison Loyd becoming detrimental to her future in my comedies, I will take the necessary legal steps to prevent her from using it."[42]

Thelma's dual screen identity was peculiar. The uproar became more intriguing when Thelma said that a numerologist had been consulted in selecting "Alison Loyd." The name was derived by combining the first name of Alison Corning, the character she played in

Corsair, and the last name of Rollo Lloyd, an assistant director on the picture. The numerologist decided that "Loyd" would be preferable to "Lloyd," since it gave the new name the key number of *nine.* Movie writer Dan Thomas explained numerology for Thelma's fans: "By a process of numerology the name Thelma Todd resolves itself into the co-efficient *three.* This is known as a success number, but it is 'under the influence of easy success and general happiness and its vibration is one of gayety.' On the other hand, the name Alison Loyd reduces itself in final calculation to the number *nine.* This, according to numerologists, is the number of material success, wealth, and power in the fields of the arts. The various implications of the name are mystic, sensitive, and psychic and the vibration is an emotional one. Numerology therefore predicts a stormier, more fiery, but still more successful career for Alison Loyd."[43]

The publicity surrounding the name change generated curiosity. On the *Corsair* set at United Artists, on a scorching summer day, the new Alison Loyd sat with an interviewer. Dressed in a beige wool suit on a humid sound stage, resembling a Wall Street office, she answered questions between scenes. "I think it is every woman's duty to look as attractive as she can, to make loveliness an art and to take advantage of all aids to nature that offer themselves, and I also believe it is fatal to consider beauty an end in itself ... I never heard of a beauty contest winner getting very far in any other line ... building on beauty seems to me to be the worst thing any girl can do. I like real people who are sincerely what they appear to be, and since I am not unique, I believe that most people rate sincerity above looks. Did you ever see an emotional scene wherein the actress remained beautiful? No, and neither did I. People aren't beautiful under the stress of terror or grief or pain. Such scenes only get over when the actress forgets how she looks and simply feels the emotion and so reflects it."[44] A propman swept through an office door on the set, holding an electric fan, offering to take it to her dressing room. "Oh, I'd rather you put it where everyone could get the benefit of it," she said, then continued: "Sincerity shows in voices even more than it does in looks. I'm fortunate in coming from a part of the country where women's voices are usually low-pitched and rather sweet, and where we naturally use good diction. I've never had a voice lesson in my life and have no intention of taking any. But I watch my voice more carefully than I watch my facial expression. People used to say that truth could be seen in a person's eyes, but I know I could look anyone in the face and tell the biggest kind of lie without a blink. It's the voice that betrays you. Spontaneous sincerity is the necessary thing."

"Alison!" called out an assistant director. She went on the set for a scene. When she returned, Chester Morris was crossing the large sound stage.

"Hello, sweet one!" he called out.

"Hello, darling!" she answered.

She grew thoughtful, then spoke: "At first, when I was making a picture and men hailed me as 'honey' or 'sweetheart,' or came up and put an arm around me when they wanted to tell me something, I was insulted. We don't take familiarities from men in New England! That's one reason why I think I'd hesitate to marry a man who wasn't in this business. A lawyer husband, or a doctor or banker, happening to visit me on the set, might very well hear Chester Morris or another actor speak to me as 'dear,' and in spite of explanations he'd probably say to himself: 'There's more in this than meets the eye!' Which would make married life most uncomfortable.

"I've never been married. Like every girl, I think I shall marry some day — though Hollywood is the worst place in the world to keep illusions about matrimony. According to my observation, second marriages are usually more successful than first ones. When people marry very young, they are often so terribly in love with each other that they refuse to look facts in the face. They won't take account of her quick temper or his extravagance, his indolence or her excitability. They both expect too much. The other is the embodiment of great and thrilling romance and altogether perfect! Naturally, the awakening is not so good. Tolerance is necessary in all relationships, but seldom is reckoned on except in a second marriage. In that venture, the experienced party realizes that allowances must be made, too much cannot be expected of any partner, and so no impossible ideal is smashed because human nature is human and not divine."

When the first marriage faded, there was only one choice.

"I believe in divorce if it is a case of severing marital relations or living together in eternal warfare. It seems more honest to me to make a clean break than to stay together, hating each other, living a lie, making life bitter. But always back in my mind, I think, as probably all girls do, that when I marry I'll be quite sure, so that it will last with us. Perhaps if two people are good companions and good sports, if they are willing to pull together and believe the best of one another, they can win through. I hope so. I like to think I'm the sort of big person who would always play fair in marriage but of course no one really knows until they've had the experience. It's like believing that if we were held up by a bandit, we'd be cool and brave and resourceful; or if a fire broke out, we'd keep our heads. You don't know until you meet the bandit or see the flames."

Then came a reference to the eternal triangle.

"I like to think that if I were married to a man I loved, and he and I were friends besides being husband and wife, I'd stand by in crises. Say that he met another girl and fell madly in love with her, he was in love with her, not that he loved her, I hope I'd be wise enough to say to him: 'I see how it is. You go on and get her out of your system and then come back to me. If you find you really prefer her to me, after you've had time to know your own mind, come and tell me and I'll step out. Only tell me yourself, and don't let me find it out.' But the trouble with the noble-wife attitude is that, unless the man is particularly worthwhile, he may eventually say to himself: 'I needn't worry about my wife. She doesn't mind.' And because you give him a little rope, he'll take all there is."

In a rather wistful reference to her personal life, she said: "It would be great to be able to depend absolutely on someone. But so far as I can see, the only person you know you can depend on is yourself and it's up to you to see you don't let yourself down." But there was no room for self-pity. "I am a fighter. I have made my way alone and can stand up for myself. I think I am the sort of person who can take a great deal from one I care for and forget it, but there is a limit; beyond that, and it's all over...."

The interview was revealing. Thelma was involved in the eternal triangle, but Roland would not leave Jewel. Perhaps it was West's fatherly demeanor that attracted Thelma. Though only in his mid-forties, West seemed older. His appearance, like his personality, was sedate; the eyes were calm below a wide forehead, which in turn dominated a stocky physique. The square-jawed director seemed to wear an expression of unhappiness. Clothed in expensive hand-tailored suits, West observed the world with a pensive and morose face. As West directed his cast in scenes aboard a yacht, speedboats, and docks, curious eyes noticed that he was strongly attracted to the lovely blonde he had named Alison Loyd. Jewel was no longer the pretty, golden-haired girl of years past. She had aged in a rather unflattering way. Jewel appeared thin faced, pale, tense, and nervous. The extent of West's intimacy with Thelma became evident when, besides changing her name, he offered financial advice, which she readily accepted. An officer of the Farmers and Merchants National Bank wrote West on September 11, 1931, at his UA office: "I have noticed the changes which you suggested in the proposed trust indenture for Thelma A. Todd, and they are agreeable to us, with the exception of the portion relating to trustee's compensation. The fees set forth in the trust indenture follow the schedule adopted in Los Angeles and we would not care to deviate from it. If this is approved by your client, please advise us, and we shall have a new indenture drawn."[45]

Thelma was now West's protégé, just like Chester Morris. But Thelma wanted more than a business manager, more than a friend. She was the other woman and Jewel was the noble wife. Once *Corsair* was underway, a romance had flamed. Thelma's affair with Roland was apparent to cast members during the production. However, Jewel was confident Roland would not leave her. They had worked hard to achieve careers, wealth, and a mansion that towered high above the ocean. Jewel slipped off her platinum bracelet, donned her voile pajamas, and pulled back the rose satin bedcover. Roland was hers.

After the incident at the beach, when Thelma fainted, rumors circulated that she had a serious heart condition, and her life would be a short one. Thelma told Lina Basquette she was in love with Roland, but he would not leave Jewel; moreover, he was supporting her family. By the time insiders had tipped off Louella Parsons, it was over. Roland admitted his strong infatuation with Thelma but said he was going to put her out of his mind, for he did not believe that she returned his feelings. But most important, he told Louella Parsons, he did not want to hurt his companion of 15 years. "I'll take a trip around the world," Roland said, "and get it out of my system. I wouldn't hurt Jewel for anything in the world. She's too fine."[46]

West's confession to the columnist about his personal life was not printed until four years later. But she did print his dissatisfaction with his professional life. Dramatically gesturing, waving his hand, Roland said he would never make another film in a studio: "I only had four interior scenes in *Corsair,* and it was the best picture I ever made. My next picture will be made outdoors."[47] Was it true, asked Parsons, that he was leaving United Artists? West responded he had been with his friend Joe Schenck for 25 years and had no plans to leave, but he would no longer work inside a studio.

Parsons wrote that West was sailing on a long cruise "to rest his nerves." Before his departure, West prepared *Corsair* for release. He sent a message to Joe Schenck at the Park Central Hotel in New York: "Have laid the *Invader* up. Keeping two men that are necessary. Will be cutting in ten days to two weeks, Love, Roland."[48] Roland planned another film with a sea theme and considered *The Blue Lagoon,* by Henry de Vere Stacpoole, and *The Adventures of Captain Kettle,* by C.J. Cutliffe Hine, books he wanted to read before his sea cruise.

Thelma was left behind, heartbroken. She was emotionally wounded over Roland's decision to stay with Jewel. She was also stung by the whispers, reported *Photoplay:* "Thelma found, too, that Hollywood gossiped viciously. No person was safe from *the pack.* It was smart for women or men to launder an absentee's linen and to strip the victim of his or her reputation. It was smart to be familiar or to assume familiarity with private lives. Thelma was appalled at the cheapness which with Hollywood treated its own ... Thelma was rumored to have been quite fond of a man who directed her in a recent picture. Hollywood never knew for sure, but the community gossiped.... She'll find her escape from Hollywood and its petty treacheries. It may be marriage...."[49]

As the summer slipped away, the crisp cool fragrance of fall filled the chilly nights above Hollywood Boulevard, where Thelma brooded in her apartment. Alice was aware of the romance. Unable to forget Roland, Thelma drank. She disclosed her unhappiness and tears to Lina Basquette. Thelma had experienced love, a deep passion that overwhelmed her. Now she was left behind with only lonely nights ... and a new name.

West expected a smash picture. His unbounded confidence led to plans for a cruise to Mexico, reporters noted. By day he edited the footage with Hal Kern at United Artists. In the late afternoon, he returned to his mansion on Posetano Road, greeted by Jewel and Nibs. The romance lingered in his thoughts, but he was determined not to desert his wife. From their home, perched high above the ocean, Roland could view the deep blue of the distant sea, green and silver waves rolling to the shore, crashing in the surf, the coastline red with the glow of the fading sun. As night fell, Roland planned his cruise to Mexico aboard the *Joyita*. But his sedate existence masked an unhappy man. Alison lingered in his thoughts.

The spotlights beamed skyward above Grauman's Chinese Theatre as Thelma and Alice left their apartment at the Highbourne Gardens. Within minutes their chauffeured limousine rolled to a stop before Grauman's Chinese Theatre. Hundreds of fans surrounded the entrance. They were thrilled to see Alison Loyd in person. The gala world premiere of *Corsair* would be the pinnacle of her career, thought Thelma. She had attended many openings and, as she stood on stage, her arms filled with flowers, applause engulfed her and she experienced one of the most enthralling moments in her life. *Corsair* marked an important turning point in her career, she believed. The usually sedate Roland West beamed with pleasure also. He, too, believed *Corsair* would sweep the nation. But it was not to be. Across the country, audiences stayed away. The excitement of the premiere died fast.

"Not impressive," sniffed *Variety*.[50] "It's really rather old-fashioned at this time, with neither the playing, dialog, or action unfolding other than much worn material. And none of the characters make a pertinent bid for audience sympathy." West was shocked and angered by the poor reviews. He had publicly announced that this would be his greatest picture. *Variety* sliced deeper: "Thelma Todd, who here inaugurates her new professional name of Alison Loyd, continues to register like cold marble...." As the spoiled heiress, Thelma was visually glamorous, dressed in a gold lame gown which clung to her rounded, full-bodied figure, but she had little to do, other than to tease Johnny Hawks in a snooty way. The critics were right. The film and Alison Loyd lacked emotional impact. Despite all the hoopla over her new transformation to dramatic actress, Alison Loyd was a dismal failure but, ironically, Thelma Todd was a screen smash.

In fact, Thelma's popularity had grown; moviegoers around the nation lined up for *Monkey Business*. Thelma played beautifully opposite the mad Marx Brothers. Their outrageous comedy was already sweeping the world. Thelma portrayed a gangster's girlfriend. Groucho flirts with her aboard a cruise ship. Thelma was alluring in satin pajamas in a memorable scene with stowaway Groucho.

THELMA: "Come here, brown eyes."
GROUCHO: "Oh, no, you're not going to get me off this bed."
THELMA: "I didn't know you were a lawyer. You're awfully shy for a lawyer."
GROUCHO: "You bet I'm shy. I'm a shyster lawyer."

As Groucho strums a guitar, Thelma performs a lively, impromptu dance, kicks her heels, ecstatically shouting: "I want life! I want laughter! I want gaiety! I want to ha-cha-cha-cha-cha-cha!" Alison Loyd vanished. Thelma Todd was back and triumphant.

Roland sailed for Mexico aboard the *Joyita* in December, along with five crewmen and $3,250 in gold and cash. The crew salaries would total $500 per month. Left behind was his motion picture career. Jewel later boarded a train and met the yacht, but she soon abandoned the cruise. She couldn't endure the hardships of a ship at sea and retreated to Los Angeles, "a physical wreck."[51] Though pampered by servants and luxury, Jewel told friends she now detested the sound of the ocean. The tranquility of the Wests' quiet life had been irrevocably shattered. Roland was now more isolated than ever, estranged from Jewel and Thelma. Three lives were set adrift by the ill-fated *Corsair*.

In the heart of Hollywood, Thelma was lonely. She hoped to fill her life with someone who loved her. Thelma and Alice moved to the Knickerbocker Hotel. Often she was escorted on the town by a handsome star or wealthy businessman. Thelma once called Hollywood "the port of missing men."[52] She was unimpressed by the males in the film industry for three reasons: "First, they are more egotistical; second, they think money can buy anything; third, they have very little self-respect." Deep in her heart she still loved Roland West.

Four

Pasquale

For the first time in 50 years, two inches of snow fell in Los Angeles in January 1932, a rare event. From her apartment in the Knickerbocker Hotel, Thelma could see the white flakes swirl on Ivar Avenue. She hoped the new year would bring a new romance. Thelma had matured and sought her freedom.

She became intrigued with numerology and was encouraged by a prediction: "Numerology shows, through the dates of birth who will walk the path alone ... 1931 is a 5 year. And under its restless, changeful vibration, few people will want to take the responsibility that marriage entails. If you expect *him* to come on bended knee and propose this year, you are doomed to disappointment.... There will be a return to stability and domesticity under the vibration of 1932, which will be a 6 year. This is the number of domestic harmony, and statistics will show an increase in the marriage rate during this period."[1]

Thelma did not want to walk the path alone; she socialized in the exciting nightclubs, eager to meet someone special. Columnists followed her nightly outings. When friends visited from Lawrence, she took them to her favorite spot, George Olsen's in Culver City. Thelma was a familiar face in chic clubs, especially the Cocoanut Grove, where she enjoyed dancing and watching entertainers like Al Jolson. Thelma laughed at the antics of film stars whooping it up. At the Garden Room in the Biltmore Hotel, she stole the show at a charity ball. Photographers snapped Billy Bakewell and Polly Ann Young dancing on the ballroom floor. Jack Oakie and Pat Wing whirled by. Claudette Colbert arrived on the arm of Norman Foster, her husband. But Thelma's entrance dazzled everyone. She wore a tight-fitting gown of Alencon lace over a flesh covered slip, with a wide bow of bright red in the back. Thelma was a sensation, as she greeted friends and introduced her escort, Schuyler Van Rennsselaer of New York.

— Thelma had an array of nightspots to enjoy, including the private clubs that offered gambling. Baron Long, a hotel owner from Santa Monica, popularized high-stake gambling with his Sunset Inn in 1916. Gambling was offered in country clubs, private nightclubs, and dives alike. In July 1932, an effort was launched to rid the city of gambling before the Olympic Games began. Newspapers reported that deputies raided fashionable "gambling clubs," arrested employees and seized expensive equipment used for roulette, craps, and poker. The proprietors insisted they operated private clubs. When Club Richelieu at 8477

Sunset Boulevard was raided, the elegant clients were allowed to leave. The site soon reopened as the Clover Club. Despite the raids, gambling was widespread. Film stars frequented the private clubs along Sunset Boulevard: the Old Colony Club, at 1131 Alta Loma Drive, could hold as many as 500 patrons; Club La Boheme, at 8614 Sunset Boulevard, was popular, just as the nearby Clover Club at 8477, operated by Al and Lou Wertheimer, friends of studio mogul Joe Schenck. Howard Hughes, an aspiring film mogul, frequented the Clover Club.

Each night Thelma sparkled like a brilliant diamond, aglow with an inner charm that brought men to her door. "Austin Parker and Todd are very hot cha cha," informed the *Hollywood Reporter*.[2] When Thelma and Ronald Colman were seen together in nightspots, rumors of romance circulated. The handsome actor fell for Thelma when he starred in *Arrowsmith* at United Artists. Colman had arrived from England five years earlier but avoided the night life, columnists reported; reports circulated that an engagement was near. However, Thelma insisted that she had no intention of marrying until she retired from the screen. When Thelma dated bandleader Abe Lyman, there was more speculation: "The papers say they are going to do it. But Abe is a long way away, but Todd or Alison Loyd, as she is known at UA, is right here in Hollywood where she has weathered so many engagement rumors before. This one rates three stars because the bandleader comes right out and admits he's that way about Thelma. One hopes she will say *yes*." But she never did.

The array of escorts seemed to be a desperate attempt to provoke Roland West into returning, but their romance came and went, as did *Corsair* and Alison Loyd. West remained on his yacht, moored off the coast of Mexico, where he fished by day and read by night, more interested in his next film project than the press stories that followed the nightclub dates of Thelma Todd.

During the day Thelma often lunched at the Brown Derby on Vine Street, a trendy restaurant close to the Knickerbocker Hotel. The Derby was the place to meet, eat, conduct business, romances, and divorces. Beneath the bronze derby lights which lit the large booths, the wealthy and famous held court. Owner Herbert Somborn, husband of Gloria Swanson, kept a watchful eye on business. *Motion Picture Magazine* sent a reporter to write about the exclusive restaurant. Herbert Somborn's droll sense of humor was noted; whenever Swanson's former husbands came to dine he would greet Wallace Berry and the Marquis de la Falaise with a hearty, "How are you, brother-in-law?"[3] The silk cord of admittance was guarded by Nick, the headwaiter. As tourists waited patiently for a table, they gaped at stars who were led to semi-circular booths with leather cushions. Reserved tables were held for a mere five minutes, then late arrivals were excluded. The Derby was famous for its bouillabaisse and onion soup, but the movie crowd had special tastes. Gary Cooper enjoyed broiled Eastern lobster; Wallace Berry preferred a simple hamburger, brought to the table in a sizzling copper frying pan; Gloria Swanson liked creamed chicken hash; Bebe Daniels ordered lamb chops and spinach, while her husband, Ben Lyons, ate spaghetti. Late at night, Chaplin arrived, ordering steamed clams. Performers who watched their weight sipped iced tomato juice and ordered a salad of finely chopped ham, hard-boiled eggs, and watercress. Nick the headwaiter confirmed that "stars do eat a lot of bran, bran muffins, bran cereal, bran bread...." Thelma lunched on avocado salad. She tried to keep her waistline trim, aware that once an actress approached 30, she had better look good, or else it was mother roles or retirement.

Thelma and her new husband, Pasquale De Cicco, 1932 (author's collection).

After her screen career faded, then what? Thelma had a warm personality; she enjoyed good food and social gatherings. Why not open a place like the Derby? The fateful day when her career would end would surely come. A restaurant was a business to consider. Yet, despite the *Corsair* fiasco, her career was going strong.

The Todd–Pitts comedies, produced by Hal Roach, had a solid audience. Her popularity sold products: "Thelma Todd Knows Bread Is One of Her Best Friends," heralded a Betty Crocker advertisement. Thelma wrote an article praising chilled honey for a clear complexion. She endorsed Maybelline Cosmetics. On the town almost every night, escorted by the most handsome bachelors in Hollywood, the jealous and rejected were bitter. Behind her back, they called her "Hot Toddy," a nickname she detested. There was a long list of men who had been given a chance to win her heart but failed. Then she was seen everywhere with a new escort.

Thelma fell into the arms of Pasquale "Pat" De Cicco, a tall, handsome playboy with a wide smile and wavy black hair, slicked back in a sculptured pompadour. De Cicco became Thelma's escort to nightclubs, polo matches, and baseball games. There was talk that Thelma was in love. And who was her new man, asked columnists? Newspaper accounts described De Cicco as "a New York sportsman," with reports, later shown to be false, that he had been the Italian vice-consul in New Haven, Connecticut. De Cicco once had theatrical ambitions and had appeared onstage for a while, wrote columnists; his grandfather was identified as a wealthy horticulturalist who had developed broccoli. But what was the truth about Thelma's new boyfriend?

De Cicco, born in 1906 in Astoria, was the child of immigrants from Cosenza in Calabria. He had been brought up on Long Island, where his parents, Pasquale and Luigina, raised a large family. Pasquale senior had cultivated a rented farm outside Astoria. Pat's cousin, Albert "Cubby" Broccoli, later described his uncle as "a domineering roughneck ... an overbearing Calabrese."[4] Although the tough farmer was crude and fast with his fists, he was also hard working. He sold the family's crops at the Harlem Market at 166th and First Avenue. From his native Calabria, he had brought broccoli seeds that would make him wealthy; the seeds crossed two Italian vegetables, cauliflower and rabe, to produce broccoli. Where others had failed to cultivate the vegetable in America, the immigrant farmer had the magic touch. He bought his own farm in Smithtown and eventually made a fortune. Though domineering, the elderly Pasquale allowed his namesake to live a privileged life. The eldest son enjoyed a lifestyle of nightclubs and beautiful women. Pat grew up spoiled and self-assured. He was a smooth talker who drove a La Salle roadster. The young man knew what he wanted and went after it. Pat liked to play polo and impress wealthy women that he was a member of their social set. In New York City and Long Island, he became known as an eligible playboy. Handsome and suave, Pat was successful with women. His seductive power melted them. He had dark, penetrating eyes, a dazzling smile, and a zest for laughter and pleasure. Throughout his life, De Cicco had a knack for making useful friends. At opportune moments, he escorted well-connected women as a career move. However, women soon discovered that beneath his smooth urbanity was a hothead inclined to shouting tantrums. After his father's death, the family fortune soon vanished. According to "Cubby" Broccoli, Pat came to Los Angeles in pursuit of actress Claudette Colbert, one of the highest paid screen stars in the world. The romance didn't last, but it allowed Pat entry into the elite circles of Hollywood. Just as *papa* had cultivated the fields, Pat harvested introductions. One night at the Clover Club, he met Howard Hughes and they became fast friends. He also became a close friend of Cary Grant. Somewhere along the way he met Thelma Todd, most likely at a nightspot. Thelma was soon in love. And so was Pasquale — or so it seemed. Thelma Todd was lovely and famous. She drove a sleek 1932 Lincoln Phaeton touring car, a vehicle with a starting price of $4,300. The chocolate-colored automobile had a twelve cylinder motor and plush rear passenger seats. She was quite a catch. Alice liked Pat and thought he was handsome.

Thelma was not only beautiful, rich, and famous, she was also lonely. Yet, Pat's handsome exterior masked a surly side. He was capable of sudden fits of anger. William Bakewell saw it erupt: "I used to play tennis with him at Ginger Roger's home. I remember his temper. Once he lost a point and was furious. He went over and smashed his racket on a post."[5] Thelma and Pat made a stunning couple: the tall, dark, handsome Italian and the petite New England beauty. But they were hopelessly mismatched. Friends like Lina Basquette felt that Pat was merely a social climber. "De Cicco was a lounge lizard," thought Lina Basquette. "He was young, good-looking, and a playboy. A lot of those guys had reputations, deserved or not, as gigolos."

Thelma's circle viewed the swift affair as a hasty response to the failure of her romance with Roland West. Thelma had chosen a man totally different from Roland. They had barely known each other for four months when they eloped. On July 16, 1932, newspapers reported that Thelma had been married in a brief ceremony before a justice of the peace in Prescott, Arizona. Yet, Thelma had doubts. The marriage was so sudden that she consulted attorney Bert Irving, who suggested a prenuptial contract before she became Mrs. Pasquale De Cicco. The agreement was presented to Pat, and he signed it. The film community was surprised by the unexpected marriage. After a short honeymoon, Thelma returned to finish *Alum and Eve* at Roach Studios. They were soon once again in the nightly spotlight.

Thelma and Pat were congratulated on their marriage by Jimmy Manus, manager of the Cocoanut Grove. Thelma was photographed in a white mink cape that draped her shoulders. She wore a tight dark dress that accentuated her shapely figure; on her bosom were two gardenias. Pat posed regally, dressed in a dark tux with a white bow tie. *Movie Mirror* reported that "Hot Toddy Thelma Todd" had found a husband. The trade magazine tagged Thelma with a nickname she detested. Her sexy image had always

Thelma and Pat, date unknown (collection of the Lawrence History Center, Lawrence, Massachusetts).

brought such remarks, but she shrugged her shoulders; after all, she was in show business. Beauty and sex sold movie tickets. Soon after her marriage, Thelma was asked to join the prestigious welcoming committee for the International Olympic Ball. Louis B. Mayer announced a list of 26 film favorites who would greet guests in the Shrine Auditorium. Thelma was honored to welcome the athletic contingent from Massachusetts.

Pat drove his wife to the studio. He picked her up after work, and they returned to their apartment at 1207 North La Brea. De Cicco's temper soon began to erode the relationship. Thelma remained close to her mother and spoke with her every day on the telephone. Alice was disappointed by news of the souring marriage. But Thelma did her best to balance matrimony and a skyrocketing career.

Thelma in her Lincoln Phaeton (courtesy of Roy Windham).

Thelma's increasing fame was the result of successful films. Director Frank Tuttle brought to the screen *This Is The Night,* a bedroom farce. The film cleverly blended satire and sex. Thelma played the wife of javelin thrower Cary Grant, who appeared in his first major screen role. The opening had Thelma emerging from a limousine and losing her dress in a slammed door. In *Speak Easily,* her blonde good looks made her a perfect foil for deadpan Buster Keaton, an absent-minded professor. Thelma and Keaton made audiences sit up when they engaged in a risqué sofa scene. Noted *Variety:* "Her stripping down to her undies doesn't harm the scene at all, for Miss Todd is an eyeful of lines and curves."[6] She made a sizzling impression in *Horse Feathers* in scenes with Groucho Marx. Their dialogue had audiences roaring with laughter:

GROUCHO: "Who was that?"
THELMA: "The iceman."
GROUCHO: "Is that so? Well you can't pull the wool over my ice."
THELMA: "Oh?"
GROUCHO: "That iceman stuff leaves me pretty cold. And if I leave you cold I'm not the man I used to be."

The Roach comedies with co-star ZaSu Pitts made money. The 22 minute shorts were zany comedies like *Seal Skins.* Thelma and ZaSu played bumbling reporters in search of

With Cary Grant in *This Is the Night* (1932).

stolen property. The girls enter a boarding house and encounter Clifford Thompson, the tallest man in the world, at six feet, eight inches; then they met Major Mite, the smallest human in existence, a man who measured only 22 inches. They discover they have located not the missing Royal Seal but a barking trained seal.

In August, while lunching at the Brown Derby, a fire started in the kitchen. Thelma and other patrons scurried into Vine Street. The Derby fire was a strange omen of danger, for a brush with death was soon to follow. Thelma and Pat spent many evenings at elegant night spots on Sunset Boulevard, private clubs, where they liked to dance and gamble. They made a stylish couple but marital problems started fast. After only a month, Thelma regretted the hasty marriage, as Bill Todd recalls: "She told my mother, 'I made a big mistake marrying Pat De Cicco.'"[7] Pat's dark side frightened Thelma. He had a domineering streak that brought violent arguments. From the start, Thelma's friends disliked him. Pat borrowed $300 from Buddy Rogers. A year later, Rogers asked for repayment. "What the hell do you want it for?" sneered Pat. "You're rich."[8]

Thelma became seriously ill in October, suffering from a painful abdominal abscess. Dr. Edwin Larson, her personal physician, treated her for several weeks, but the condition worsened. Thelma was rushed to California Lutheran Hospital, suffering from peritonitis, the abdominal inflammation that had killed Valentino. Newspapers reported her grave condition. Though she was bedridden, audiences flocked to *Speak Easily* and *Horse Feathers*,

With Buster Keaton in *Speak Easily* (1932).

laughing wildly as she played scenes with the Marx Brothers and Buster Keaton. Thelma was acclaimed by reviewers as "the blonde menace, one of the best comedy menaces we have."[9] Her popularity was also growing abroad. Offers to perform in British productions were frequent, since the Roach comedies attracted huge audiences in England. Despite her career success, Thelma was very unhappy.

On the night of January 23, 1933, the De Ciccos were returning home in the pre-dawn hours when Pat lost control of the car at the intersection of Hollywood Boulevard and Nicholas Canyon. Skidding wildly, the auto slammed into a curb and crashed into a palm tree. Her face bloodied, Thelma was rushed to California Lutheran Hospital in agonizing pain. Dr. Larson issued a statement about her serious injuries: "She suffered three broken ribs on the left side, a broken shoulder and internal injuries."[10] The fact that her husband was driving, nearly killing her, did little to improve the failing marriage.

While recuperating, word came from Roach Studios that her next project would be *The Devil's Brother*, a comic opera starring Laurel and Hardy. The news cheered Thelma. The film would be an expensive musical. A month later, she had recovered and reported for duty at the "Lot O' Fun." Thelma was cast as Lady Pamela, a married flirt who is loved by Diavolo, a singing bandit, portrayed by opera star Dennis King. The film was a smash, especially in England where Laurel and Hardy were idolized. Hal Roach arranged for personal

With Groucho Marx in *Horse Feathers* (1932).

appearances in London for Thelma, Dennis King, and James Finlayson. She applied for a passport in April. Thelma informed the press that she would be abroad for a few months, to promote *The Devil's Brother*, and to co-star in a British film. Thelma was sought by every studio, recalled comedian Bert Wheeler: "We'd all fight to get Thelma Todd. She used to laugh about it ... she was such a beautiful girl, and she would do anything. She just loved to be with us. See, that was her life, doing comedy. She was such a wonderful person to get along with. We loved her."[11]

Thelma's traveling companion for the trip to England was Sally Eilers, the wife of cowboy actor Hoot Gibson. Left behind was Pat De Cicco. He had become an agent for cameramen and wanted to manage his wife's career. But Thelma still retained Jerry Mayer, her long-time agent, who had negotiated the British film. Director Monty Banks was elated to have Thelma for *You Made Me Love You*, a modern adaptation of Shakespeare's *Taming of the Shrew*. Thelma signed a contract to co-star with Stanley Lupino, a famous stage and screen comedian.

One morning in May, fifteen-year-old Ida Lupino awoke in the family mansion on Leigham Court Road in Streatham, curious at the tone of her father's voice, exchanging shouts with someone. She peeked into the lounge to see her father rehearsing dialogue with a lovely blonde. She watched the lively rehearsal until her father glimpsed Ida's curious face peering through the doorway. "Ida, dear, come meet Miss Todd," he said.[12] Though only 15, Ida Lupino was already a film actress. Ida was part of the famous Lupino theatrical

With Stanley Lupino in *You Made Me Love You* (1934; courtesy of Don Collins).

dynasty. She was enthralled to meet a star from Hollywood, where she longed to work, in hopes of meeting her idol Gary Cooper. Thelma became a close friend of Stanley and his wife, Connie. She regaled Ida with stories of the fabled land of cinema dreams. Ida listened wide-eyed, impressed that Thelma knew everyone, from Gary Cooper to Charlie Chaplin. Near the end of production, Stanley returned home one evening quite distraught. He related how Thelma had collapsed on the set and was carried unconscious to her dressing room. The studio doctor suspected a heart condition. Stanley had telephoned a prominent physician,

Dr. Eric Wornum of Guys Hospital, a specialist with offices in posh Harley Street. After an examination, Dr. Wornum asked Stanley if they had filmed everything with Miss Todd that was important. Stanley replied that they had, except for some long shots. Dr. Wornum suggested a double be used, explaining that, in his opinion, Thelma was suffering from valvular disease of the heart. "She will never live to be an elderly woman," said Dr. Wornum. The tragic news devastated the Lupinos, all of whom were fond of Thelma. "She was booked," says Ida, "and it broke our hearts." Dr. Wornum said he would inform his patient before she returned to America.

Unknown to Thelma, another personal drama was unfolding. Pat De Cicco read of his wife's adventures in the *Hollywood Reporter* and he wasn't happy. The *Reporter* was published by flamboyant entrepreneur Billy Wilkerson. The trade paper had a penchant for colorful innuendo and biting gossip, as found in its Rambling Reporter column: "Now that the fact that Hitler is a homosexual has been printed without causing a murmur from diplomatic circles, or any libel suits, the latest and funniest crack around Manhattan is that Hitler is praying for the Kaiser's return, so he can be Queen ... Marlene Dietrich made a complete assess of herself in the few hours she spent in New York and the papers gave her the well-earned panning ... Peggy Blumenthal may come to Hollywood for pictures, she's had plenty of offers and is getting all the sympathy around, we hear tell, Blumey has been nourishing his social complex with Beth Leary, but she just leaped off to Europe by herself."[13] Wilkerson's Rambling Reporter liked to relate alleged marital peccadilloes, such as the reference to Broadway actress Peggy Fears and A.C. "Blumey" Blumenthal, her wealthy spouse. The De Ciccos were in for the same treatment. When Pat saw the June 1 edition, his Italian blood boiled. The column stated: "After Thelma Todd got over being robbed of five hundred dollars at the Dorchester, she set out to have herself a grand time. Dennis King and Jerry Horwin getting her divided attention...."[14]

A few days later, Thelma made a personal appearance at the Empire Theatre, to the delight of her British fans. Far away, her husband was irate again, incensed with Wilkerson's latest column: "Thelma Todd and Dennis King billing and cooing in London...."[15] Pat, who would curse violently in Italian when angered, went through the roof over the titillating but unfounded gossip column. Rumors of impending divorce swept through the Hollywood grapevine. As the *S.S. Europa* approached New York harbor, a launch filled with reporters clambered aboard ship. Thelma was startled by questions about her marital future. Thelma posed for photographs and smiled graciously, but she was upset by the unexpected onslaught. Once ashore, she booked a flight to Boston, then rushed to her Uncle Alexis's home at 22 Bowdoin Street, the safe haven where her grandparents had once lived. She sat up most of the night. She admitted to family members that the marriage had been a mistake but that she would try to keep it together. The fretful husband telephoned his wife at 3:00 A.M.; afterward, Thelma telephoned her mother in Los Angeles.

By morning, word had spread that Thelma was in town. Friends and admirers flocked to Bowdoin Street. They expected to get a warm hug from Thelma. Instead, no one even answered knocks on the door. The local press finally cornered Thelma in Lowell, as she sat with friends in the Idle Hour Tearoom. When asked questions about her personal life, she denied the reports of a failed marriage. She had spoken with her husband the previous night and insisted that rumors of a divorce were absurd. Thelma disappeared from public view. A local reporter wrote that she was trying to "do a Garbo" by remaining in seclusion.

Thelma attended the Fourth of July holiday at Foster Pond, where her Uncle Alexis kept a summer home. Bill Todd recalls Thelma's excitement over the fireworks in the sky. However, by the next day, she had packed her suitcase and was on her way to Boston, quite upset that even the hometown press was prying into her personal life. Lawrence, once regarded as a sanctuary, was left in the dust. In her suite at the Statler Hotel in Boston, Thelma met with reporters, determined to quell the gossip that wounded her pride. As she sipped coffee, she bravely insisted that she was too happy to think of a divorce. Perturbed that her crumbling marriage was being dissected under intense scrutiny, she lashed out in uncharacteristic fashion: "Poor Pat. He was so worried over the rumors that he telephoned me at 3:00 A.M. to find if I had stopped loving him. If I was a man the person that started the rumor would get a punch in the jaw."[16] She added that her haste to return was prompted by a wish to celebrate her first wedding anniversary with her husband, who she still loved, proclaiming that there would be a little party on July 10, just for the two of them. Her husband had let her go to London to fulfill career ambitions, she explained. Separate spousal vacations were wise, she added. Thelma indignantly protested that the gossip columnists were mistaken in any talk of divorce; someone's imagination was simply working overtime.

When her limousine rolled to a stop at the East Boston Airport, Thelma made a final statement to a Boston reporter: "I'm still Thelma Todd to all my old friends in the Merrimack Valley, and the report that I've been avoiding them while on my brief visit is a lot of bosh."[17] On July 10, Thelma stepped from the United Air Lines plane into her husband's arms. Before a throng of reporters and photographers she gave her husband a little peck on the cheek. "Is that the best kiss you have for me, dear?" asked De Cicco.[18]

"Certainly, darling, you don't expect me to make a scene here," responded Thelma with embarrassment; nevertheless, to please her husband and reporters, Thelma gave Pat a kiss. The couple attempted to salvage the marriage. They were seen in the most elegant nightclubs and restaurants. One evening they posed with boxer Max Baer and his ex-mate, Dorothy Dunbar. The champion towered over the trio and flashed a toothy smile, as Thelma and Pat also grinned for the camera, but the former Mrs. Baer had an unsmiling face, neither forgiving nor forgetting, noted a reporter. Despite the image of marital bliss, whispers of the death throes of the De Ciccos' marriage persisted in Hollywood.

By mid–July, Thelma had a new screen partner at the Roach Studio. ZaSu Pitts had left to remarry and to advance her screen career. She had divorced her first husband, fight promoter Tom Gallery, and was ready to marry Edward "Woody" Woodall, a former tennis champion. Thelma had grown close to Pitts and wondered if she could continue with a different partner. The Pitts-Todd comedies had been a great success, praised by the San Diego Better Films Conference, a group whose motto was: "Keep all worthwhile plots wholesome and we shall make the best film pay best."[19] Hal Roach's comedies were in demand, as civic organizations clamored for morally uplifting pictures, devoid of sex and alcohol. The Hays Office was constantly bombarded with a variety of complaints, especially about drinking, which had crept back into scenes, since it was apparent to Hollywood that the repeal of Prohibition was imminent. Will Hays opened angry letters: "When did the motion pictures sell out to the liquor interests, and how much are they paying? The public has a right to know."[20] There were other offenses: "The smoking done in those pictures was really nothing but advertising for the cigarette manufacturers." And ethnic protests as well: "Stop using

Italian names for all your disgusting gangster pictures. Stop biting the hand that has given the world everything that is worthwhile."

Hal Roach chose Patsy Kelly, a New York stage actress, to be Thelma's new partner. Kelly was honored to play opposite "the great Miss Todd." Kelly's first week at work was difficult. In a set, resembling a theatre, Kelly was handed a tiny piece of paper. "I was supposed to come in the door," Kelly recalled, "hit my head on the seat, and then I win the raffle...."[21] Gus Meins, the director, had her play the scene, then told her to fall off the stage into a drum, which she did. Thelma began laughing at the prank. "You know, we have doubles," said Thelma. The pair became fast friends. "It was a shame to take the money," Kelly later reminisced, "because we laughed all the time." Kelly liked the informality of the Roach lot, where anyone could contribute an idea and, if it was funny, it would be used. Laurel and Hardy would stop by and make suggestions. Thelma and Patsy liked to watch them work, learning all the while.

In the midst of Thelma's effort to patch together her marriage, the Raymond family arrived from Lawrence. Uncle Alexis, Aunt Alice, and their daughter, Shirley, were enjoying a tour of the West. Thelma graciously entertained her relatives. She arranged for her young cousin to swim at the exclusive Deauville Club and escorted her to the Roach Studios for a visit to the set of *Babes in Toyland*. Thelma introduced Shirley to Laurel and Hardy. Thelma personally drove the Raymonds to Agua Caliente in her plush Lincoln Phaeton. Baron Long's lavish Sunset Inn had once been the favorite nightspot of the movie crowd, but it had been surpassed by the magnificent Agua Caliente Hotel and Race Track, three miles across the border in Tijuana. Thelma pulled up to a white Spanish-style building with tall bell towers. On the patio guests were greeted by white macaws and screaming cockatoos. Thelma had reserved a private bungalow, near the central building. The following morning, she showed the Raymonds the famous race track with the richest purse in the world. Joe Schenck was the racetrack president and the person responsible for featuring thoroughbreds from the world's best stables. Everyone bathed in the famous mineral waters, then had lunch in the casino where waiters in crimson cummerbunds rushed from the kitchen amidst the tinkle of cocktail glasses and lively music. During lunch a dancer in a lace mantilla whirled to castanets and strumming guitars; afterwards, the party went into the Gold Room where, reported *Motion Picture Magazine,* director Raoul Walsh had won $77,000 on his honeymoon. Once again in Los Angeles, before the Raymonds' departure, Thelma presented her young cousin with a surprise gift. She had collected the autographs of Shirley's favorite stars, including the signature of Charlie Chaplin. Thelma's kindness to her relatives made the hometown newspaper. But Thelma's gracious and gentle heart was unable to soothe her husband. The De Ciccos rented an apartment at the classy Villa Celia, a chateau-style building, located at 8320 Fountain Avenue, where the halls echoed with the couple's fiery arguments. Pat wanted to control his wife's life as if he were lord and master. Pat's tirades forced Thelma into hysterical fits, as her maid observed.

Their latest marital rift made The Lowdown in Billy Wilkerson's *Hollywood Reporter:* "Husbands, it appears, step in where others fear to tread, and don't always do so well. Thelma Todd y' know, has been under contract to Jerry Mayer, who has gotten her some swell jobs, wot with taking her out of shorts, sending her to London and landing her the lead in the new Wheeler–Woolsey feature. But when her contract with this agency expired recently, her husband, Pat De Cicco (who up to now has been handling cameramen), stepped in and argued that he could get her more money, bigger jobs and a lot of other things that took Todd right out of Mayer's office. Only so far, we hear that Thelma had been denied two possible jobs because Pat asked for too much gold for the services of the former slapstick comedienne, but maybe love will find a way into the big money!"[22] The scathing article infuriated Pat and embarrassed Thelma, who had a great deal of personal dignity. She hated having her private life paraded in trade publications. But she knew all too well that her husband was a manipulating bully. Pat tried to control her career with devastating results. His attitude had become intolerable. Thelma became nervous and irritable. The day after The Lowdown column appeared, Thelma wrote a Last Will and Testament in the office of attorney A. Ronald Button. Her husband was left one dollar, as a nominal beneficiary, so he could not contest the document. Thelma's Last Will and Testament reflected the depth of her disillusion with Pasquale J. De Cicco.

By now, Thelma knew all too well that her childhood version of a star's life, fantasized in a darkened theatre, was the stuff of dreams. Thelma's unhappiness was drowned in cocktails. On November 7, 1933, revelers in Hollywood celebrated the death of Prohibition. The attempt to ban alcohol had spawned crime czars who quenched the public thirst with illegal brew. Citizens finally admitted that Prohibition had failed miserably. At the Biltmore Ballroom and the Cocoanut Grove, the elite of Hollywood society came for the legal alcohol. Palates that had been satisfied with 3.2 near-beer now downed the real thing. Over 500 celebrants crowded the Beverly Wilshire's Gold Room for a lavish party that Thelma and Chester Morris hosted from the stage as dancers whirled and the ballroom filled with laughter and song. Whatever troubles plagued film stars by day, the booze lifted depressed spirits at night. Thelma Todd was no exception.

On December 6, Thelma joined a crowd of several hundred in honoring Hal Roach. The studio was the scene of an elaborate party that celebrated the twentieth anniversary of Roach's career as a producer. A large building was transformed into a nightclub with three bands, a vaudeville review, and lavish dinner. Speakers toasted and congratulated Roach, led by Will Rogers, who spoke over nationwide radio. Rogers recounted Roach's rise from a $5.00 a day cowboy for Universal, to his phenomenal success with the Lot O' Fun. Additional accolades were given by Harold Lloyd, Jean Harlow, Laurel and Hardy, Bebe Daniels, and others, including Thelma, resplendent in a tight white sequin dress which accentuated her shapely figure. She posed for photographers with Roach and her chums Stan and Ollie. All smiled warmly before an enormous cake. But Pat no longer escorted her to parties. The marriage was over.

Thelma was now seen alone at nightclubs, including the Colony Club, where everyone was upstaged one evening by Clara Bow, outrageously attired in a bright green dress with orange gloves. On February 20, 1934, the couple officially separated. Three days later, attorney A. Ronald Button filed for divorce on Thelma's behalf, stating that Pasquale J. De Cicco had consistently quarreled with her, calling her "harsh and opprobrious names."[23] Thelma charged that her husband was not only rude and unpleasant toward her, but Pat had inflicted grievous mental and physical suffering by his conduct, embarrassing her in front of guests, nagging and arguing for no reason whatsoever. The divorce complaint further asserted that she was "a highly nervous woman of extremely refined and delicate temperament" who had been subjected to "surliness and temper on the part of the defendant." As a result she had become ill and suffered great mental anguish and physical pain.

At some point in the downward slide in her marriage, Thelma had turned to Roland West, the man she never stopped loving; it is likely that Roland referred her to A. Ronald Button for legal advice. Button was a successful lawyer, the first president of the Hollywood Bar Association, and Roland's friend. Button had an office at 6331 Hollywood Boulevard and owned property in the Castellammare neighborhood. The denouement of the marital drama was reached when a downcast Thelma came to Department 38 of Superior Court. She wore a taffeta blue hat, matching blue dress, white coat and scarf, which had a cameo pinned to it. Thelma sat before the judge. Button asked if her husband had treated her in a rude manner, called her names, and was surly toward her. She acknowledged he did. Mae Whitehead, Thelma's maid, testified that she had found her employer in a hysterical condition several times, after arguments with her husband.[24] Yet, it was Thelma's testimony that brought a rapid court decision. "As a result of this treatment, the effect on your refined and delicate temperament was profound, was it not?" enquired her attorney. Thelma nodded in agreement. "Decree granted," said Judge White.[25]

Thelma had been Mrs. Pasquale J. De Cicco a scant one year, seven months, and ten days. In the city of cinema dreams, Thelma became another divorced Hollywood star, with a failed marriage dissected in public. But there was more to come. Thelma was soon back in court to answer charges in a civil suit filed by the widow of attorney Bert L. Irvin. The widow demanded $600 in legal fees. Thelma had consulted with Levin before her marriage to discuss a will, as well as a prenuptial agreement with Pat De Cicco. The public disclosure of a prenuptial contract was a devastating humiliation. Of all the exceptional men who had courted Thelma, she had married a toad, and the prenuptial agreement clearly indicated she had doubts about Pat De Cicco from the beginning. Why she chose him as a spouse baffled friends and family. However, the hasty marriage could have been motivated by the thought that her life would be a short one. The prenuptial agreement removed Pat De Cicco from any claims of community property and verified her misgivings about her prospective husband. Thelma's will made certain that the main recipient of her estate, Alice Todd, would be well provided for in the event of her death. She likely believed Dr. Wornum's diagnosis was accurate and that her life would be brief, so she gave marriage a try.

The lawsuit with Mrs. Irvin was settled; the court agreed with Thelma that a fee of $600 was too steep and ruled that $75 was reasonable. Thelma suffered a final indignity when she and her ex-mate were sued by the owners of the Villa Celia. The lawsuit claimed that the last month's rent had not been paid and rugs and furniture had been damaged. After tortuous months of having her marriage discussed in public, the fanfare eventually faded.

For a while, Thelma shared a modest bungalow at 7274½ Fountain Avenue with her close friend Catherine Hunter, a former actress, who was Charlie Chaplin's secretary, script supervisor, and publicity representative. Alice Todd occupied a nearby bungalow at 7272½ Fountain, just a few yards from her daughter's temporary residence. In a year, the divorce would be final and she would be free to marry. Thelma's spirits soared. Thelma and Roland West had big plans for the future. They would open Thelma Todd's Sidewalk Café.

FIVE

Shimmering Blue

Hollywood in 1934 was an enticing paradise. Fans devoured movie magazines to read about the incredible salaries, mansions, and sleek automobiles of screen stars. The entertainers who succeeded enjoyed a hedonistic existence. Nightly carousing conveyed the impression of a carefree life, but there was also another side to the film capital, another life beside the glamorous one, a dark undercurrent of fear. The luxurious lifestyle made celebrities targets for crime, as *New Movie* revealed in 1933. Mae West had been robbed of $16,000 in jewels and $34,000 in cash; Helene Costello's home was ransacked and $55,000 in jewelry stolen; burglars robbed the palatial home of Mae Murray and her titled husband, Prince David Mdivani, of property valued at $10,000. A plot to kidnap Mary Pickford, though thwarted, shocked the world, and sent stark fear into the lives of film stars. There were threats to kidnap the children of Chaplin and Ann Harding. Ruth Chatterton and Ann Sothern were also mailed demands by kidnappers. Many threats were never made public. Screen stars were left to their private lives, unless they were unfortunate enough to be led into the courtroom or police headquarters. Thelma Todd did not escape the threats. According to Bill Todd, the family learned that Thelma was disillusioned with Hollywood: "When Thelma came home many times, toward the last, many people said she didn't seem as friendly, that she didn't go to places where we could see her. But she wanted to get away. She'd go up to my aunt's cabin at Forest Lake, at Little Alice's camp. She told my mother many times the Mafia was always after her, always wanting money. She was scared all the time. They were trying to get money out of her for protection."

The most notable divorce in 1934 occurred when Norma Talmadge divorced Joe Schenck in Juarez, Mexico; a week later, she married entertainer George Jessel. Joe Schenck had few words about the long separation and hurried divorce in a Mexican court. Schenck was too busy searching for studio sites in Florida, fearful that Upton Sinclair would be elected Governor of California and initiate a heavy taxation program. "He is a Socialist," said Schenck.[1] Sinclair lost the race for governor and studio heads breathed a sigh of relief, but they were still worried about organized labor.

Lina Basquette's romance with mobster Johnny Roselli allowed her to see the growing influence of organized crime in union activities. Harry Cohn and other studio heads hired Roselli as "a labor conciliator."

Hollywood Glamour: Thelma enjoys an elegant party at Claire Windsor's home. Biographers depend on every scrap of information to document a subject's life, whether a newspaper article, letter, or memory. Photographs are just as important. Thelma Todd brightened every picture. Don Collins was especially helpful by bringing to my attention unique photographs from his collection. Especially interesting is this photograph, taken by Hyman Fink at Claire Windsor's home on South Orange Drive in Los Angeles in May 1932. In an unknown hand, the partygoers are identified on the reverse, from left to right: "Polan Banks (popular writer with Universal), Thelma Todd (popular with everyone), Phillis Clare (popular to start with, but not popular with wives), Claire Windsor (popular with alienation suits) [penciled out], [J. Parker] Read Jr. (popular with Claire), Vivienne Osborne (always has been popular [not identified]), Ivan Lebedeff (popular with bands). Just a quiet evening at Claire Windsors. Yes, some parties are quiet." The photograph was taken while Thelma dated Ivan Lebedeff. The men are handsome in tuxedos; the women are lovely and stylishly elegant; another fun night in Hollywood. If only walls could talk (courtesy of Don Collins).

Though the Hollywood elite feared Upton Sinclair, some embraced Italy's Benito Mussolini. After a trip to Europe, MGM's acclaimed director Clarence Brown voiced his admiration: "We didn't meet Il Duce personally, but we could feel his presence. He has done so much for his people that they worship him."[2] When Donna Margherita Sarfatti, journalist and biographer of Mussolini, came to Hollywood a luncheon was held in her honor at MGM, hosted by Louis B. Mayer, who turned out a distinguished crowd. He spoke of "America's admiration" of Mussolini and his achievement.[3] Madame Sarfatti defended fascism and the role of Italian women: "True they cannot vote, but we place little importance on voting in Italy."[4] If support for Mussolini was respectable, those who were viewed as leftists had their careers threatened. When detectives of the police Red Squad raided Communist Headquarters, the district attorney announced that the names of James Cagney, Dolores Del Rio, Ramon Novarro, and Lupe Velez had been discovered. All denied that they were Reds.

"I deny ever giving Communists any aid," said an indignant James Cagney.[5]

"I need my own dough," answered Mexican actress Lupe Velez.[6]

Most performers kept their political views to themselves, realizing their livelihood depended on one thing alone — popularity. And everyone wanted to be popular. Any scent of scandal or controversy could jeopardize careers. But people loved to read about scandals, so the newspapers were eager to discover anything shocking.

After blue-eyed blonde Anita Page wed Nacio Brown, a prolific and talented black songwriter and composer, eyebrows across the nation were raised by the interracial marriage. Matters were made worse when it was revealed the bridegroom's divorce wasn't final yet, thereby making the Tijuana marriage suspect, noted reporters. Jean Harlow's short-lived third marriage to cinematographer Hal Rosson ended after a brief eight months, an attempt to end the loneliness created by the suicide of her previous husband, Paul Bern. Cary Grant was rushed to a hospital after a drinking bout, despondent over the end of his marriage to Virginia Cherrill. Mae Clarke, famous for her scene in *Public Enemy,* where James Cagney pushed a grapefruit in her face, suffered a nervous breakdown. She blamed overwork and a failed romance. Director Al Rogell made news when he followed his wife to the home of a wealthy attorney and staged a midnight raid. He found his wife hiding in a closet, though she insisted she was there merely for legal advice. As silent era film star Lew Cody was being laid to rest, his private effects, ranging from saffron-hued pajamas to bath towels and framed autographs, were being sold at auction. The home went begging for a buyer, but fans bid on Cody's copy of *Science and Health* and an autographed portrait of Rudy Vallee, which sold for sixty cents. Actress Dorothy Dell, a nineteen-year-old Mississippi beauty, barely established in Hollywood, died in a Pasadena auto accident. Crooner Russ Columbo, whose voice rivaled that of Bing Crosby, was struck in the brain by a bullet from an antique pistol, fired by a friend who thought it was unloaded. Lovely Sigrun Solvason, known as "Greta Garbo's double," due to her resemblance to the famous star, took her own life. She left a note filled with anguish at her failure to attain stardom. Police found the Nordic actress, who had just completed a bit role in *Cleopatra,* clad in green pajamas, surrounded by photographs of herself and Garbo. She was dead of an overdose of sleeping pills.

Depression-era Americans, many of whom barely managed a living, marveled at the reported wealth of Chaplin, the richest man in Hollywood. Reports stated that Chaplin was worth three million dollars. Yet, Chaplin lived surrounded by bodyguards who protected his sons from kidnappers. Newspapers daily reported the trials and agonies of the screen deities, but still the star-struck flocked to Hollywood, not unlike the clever girl named Velma, a native of Memphis, who incorporated herself, offering stock sales in her screen career, before she faded into obscurity.

However, the seductive, mad whirl of fame and fortune no longer interested Thelma. Once, returning to the coast by train, people flocked around her, ignoring fellow passenger Albert Einstein. She thought it a shame that someone so brilliant was ignored, she told Bill Todd. During the hard times of the Depression, Thelma always remembered her family, he recalls: "In 1931, my father was out of work. She was forever sending things home, bundles of clothes, money ... she was very generous." Yet, despite the fame and fortune, Thelma wasn't happy. "She wanted out," says Bill Todd. "She figured her time was up. She realized that the life of an actress was limited, then it's all downhill. She made a lot of money in pictures, but she didn't like the Hollywood lifestyle."[7] Thelma was fast approaching the dreaded age of 30. She reunited with Roland West, and they had big plans. Thelma had long thought of a reliable business, something to depend on when her screen career faded. Mary Pickford had started miniature golf courses; Charles Bickford owned a fashionable dress shop; Conrad Nagel owned markets. Many stars bought and sold real estate. Thelma had considered opening a movie theatre in Lawrence, but the ideal business was a restaurant. Since her early days in Hollywood, Thelma entertained friends with her cooking; she liked to prepare lamb chops over a charcoal broiler. She missed Boston-style seafood. Thelma and Roland decided to open a restaurant that would cater to the film elite, many of whom lived in nearby Malibu, an exclusive colony where wealthy film stars enjoyed expensive beach homes. Gloria Swanson, Barbara Bennett, Ronald Colman, Barbara Stanwyck, Dolores del Rio, Chico Marx, Clara Bow, and others, kept homes on the beach. The planned restaurant would be located in the Castellammare neighborhood, on the ground level of the large, three story, Spanish-style building that was the community shopping center for wealthy residents. In April 1934, West bought the building from attorney A. Ronald Button and his wife, Gladys. Situated on the coast highway, the building was renamed Thelma Todd's Sidewalk Café. The Wests' home was nearby, but they were estranged. Jewel suffered emotional distress over Roland's renewed attachment with Thelma and moved out of their mansion.

West hired his brother-in-law, Rudolph H.W. Schafer, to manage the restaurant. Schafer had operated a meat company and was married to Alberta, Jewel's sister. Roland provided the capital for the business project. A façade was constructed over the open-air portico. Roland bought the latest restaurant equipment and paid for the expensive décor, including plush booths, and tables. They hoped that Thelma's friends and associates in the motion picture industry would come to dine. West had plans to make the second floor a private dining room. By summer, the restaurant was open, accompanied by considerable fanfare. Newspaper advertisements invited patrons to savor the fine cuisine: "Thelma Todd's Sidewalk Cafe, three miles north of Santa Monica, on the ocean road, at the arch, serving a Long Island shore dinner, fish with Alison Sauce, unequaled, French-Italian dinner, pancakes suzette, unsurpassed ... the reason ... from the Savoy-London, Crillons-Paris comes our chef." The café had a modern bar and a liquor license, a good business move because in April police squads had raided celebrity cafés that illegally served hard liquor. The raids were made at Sardi's, Al Levy's, and the Russian Eagle. Not only were the waiters arrested, but the prominent proprietors were taken into custody, too. In July, the county grand jury summoned five members of the Los Angeles Police Commission and warned them of their responsibility to stop liquor and gambling violations in the city.

The same month, Thelma hosted a party honoring British writer Margaret Chute. Among the guests were Harry Langdon, Bert Wheeler, Robert Woolsey, Patsy Kelly, Dorothy Lee, Lyle Talbot, Joe E. Brown, Walt Disney, Jeanette MacDonald, and Pat O'Brien. She never missed an opportunity to mention the restaurant in interviews. Thelma told Louella Parsons she wanted to restore fine dining: "I have heard so much about the choice foods of those days preceding prohibition when eating was still a fine art. Always I read with great interest about the Bon Vivants of the Gay Nineties, when people dined with pomp and

Thelma Todd's Sidewalk Café (courtesy of Jim Heimann).

ceremony and before they became addicted to grabbing a sandwich, a slab of pie and call it a meal." The private dining area, called Joya's Room, was upstairs; guests could choose gourmet cuisine — aged beef steaks, Eastern seafood, grouse, partridge, and frog legs, as well as expensive wines. Joya's advertised itself as "California's finest, where Epicureans dine in seclusion, private rooms and chef service by appointment only. Tea Dansant in the Sunset Room, from 3 to 8 P.M."

Months later, British writer Nora Laing interviewed Thelma and asked why she undertook a business enterprise when she was so busy acting. "I realized long ago that it is only a case of a few years for an actress, before she gradually, sometimes almost imperceptibly, loses popularity, and younger ones start to take her place," said Thelma. "Look at some of the one-time famous stars of a few years ago. Who ever hears of them now? Most of them are unhappy and rather bewildered. It's pretty hard to have your lifelong career at an end. They're left with nothing but a past — no future. So I decided long ago that I wasn't going to be one of them.... The years are not going to bother me as they do so many of my colleagues; wrinkles won't worry me, neither will increasing weight, because as long as I can use my head, it won't matter how I look."[8] When the interview was published in *Film Pictorial,* the accompanying photograph showed Thelma regally dressed, proudly posing in the kitchen, amidst plates and refrigerators.

The Bar (courtesy of Jim Heimann).

Thelma had Roland West to thank for making her a businesswoman. She and Roland both loved the ocean and spent time together on the *Joyita*. She was very happy in her personal life. Thelma was often at the café, especially on weekends, when the movie crowd drove down to the beach. She liked to sit at the cashier's booth and make change for customers. Roland was content to watch. He gave ideas that Thelma accepted. Though he and Jewel Carmen lived separate lives, neither filed for a divorce. Thelma rented a home nearby, at 17925 Tramonto Drive, just minutes from the restaurant. She was close to her business venture and the man she loved. If they could not be united in marriage, at least they were business partners. Thelma celebrated her 28th birthday at the café in August. A photograph showed her stylishly dressed, smiling before a cake.

Thelma Todd was a prominent name in the society register of newspaper columns, a welcome guest everywhere. She was among the Hollywood elite who were invited to attend the premiere of George Gershwin's *An American in Paris*. Thelma was so popular that she was chosen by the beauty industry as a spokeswoman. She invited Mayor Frank Shaw to the industry's annual convention. In addition to her business and social life, Thelma stayed busy before the camera. Her brief scene in *Palooka*, as a woman with designs on Robert Armstrong, brought increased pulse rates in male viewers, who were wide-eyed over Thelma's racy cleavage. *Cockeyed Cavaliers*, a Wheeler-Woolsey comedy, also featured a risqué scene when idiot kleptomaniac Woolsey steals a powderpuff from Thelma's bosom.

Thelma liked to wear a good luck necklace that contained a small diamond ring, a gold elephant, an enameled four leaf clover, a cross, a crown, and other odds and ends. Although 1934 was a year that began dismally with her humiliating divorce, good fortune came her way. The Sidewalk Café was a labor of love, a dream made possible by Roland West. Financially, she was well off. In 1934 the Roach comedies alone earned her nearly $30,000. Her fee per picture was now $2,500 a week. For her role in *Cockeyed Cavaliers*, she earned $8,000. By year's end, Thelma and Roland were reunited. Above the restaurant, on the third level, they shared adjoining apartments. Life was sweet.

Thelma celebrates her 28th birthday at the Sidewalk Café (by permission of Hearst Communications, Inc., Hearst Newspapers Division. Hearst Newspaper Collection, Special Collections, University of Southern California Library. Courtesy of University of Southern California, on behalf of the USC Special Collections).

As 1934 passed into 1935, everything was going her way. But Thelma's life changed on February 26. After a week of studio work, the telephone rang at her home on Tramonto Drive. She was instructed to immediately come to the studio. There was a letter she had to see. Unlike the usual fan letters she received, this one was different. At the studio she was shown an envelope addressed to "Thelma Todd, Hal Roach Studio, Culver City, California." A note warned: "Pay $10,000 to Abe Lyman in New York by March 5 if not our san francisco boys will lay you out. This is no joke."[9] The signature was a card depicting the Ace of Hearts.

Later, at her Tramonto Drive home, she placed the extortion letter on a desk and wondered what to do. She had worried about slipping into mother roles, but now she faced something more: she feared for her life. The letter was read by studio executives, the publicity department, and Hal Roach himself. Yet, before a course of action was decided, a second letter arrived, scribbled in pencil, in ungrammatical English: "This is the last warning. $10,000 Abe Lyman march 4 new York As nutting he left of your Santa Monica dump." It was signed "Ace." A single letter could have been a prank, but the second was alarming, not only to Thelma, but to Hal Roach and his staff. They decided to publicize the threat. They hoped that public awareness would scare the extortionist.

The letter was given to the *Los Angeles Times*. On March 6, the newspaper published the extortion threat. The article informed readers that Thelma was in seclusion. Rudolph Schafer told reporters that Thelma was worried over the letter and was awaiting action by government authorities. The following day, after the threat was publicized, Thelma recalled a mysterious stranger who had come to the restaurant and wanted her home address for a delivery. Thelma's address was not given, and the man disappeared. In New York, Abe Lyman shrugged off the threat as a practical joke. He said that when he and Thelma broke off their engagement in 1931, they were the victims of pranks.

A reporter gave the extortion letters to Joseph Dunn, an FBI agent. Dunn was skeptical and issued a warning: "I want it distinctly understood that our office will not tolerate nor be used in any cheap Hollywood publicity stunt."[10] Dunn had agents fingerprint Thelma, Lyman, and Mae Whitehead to eliminate a hoax. A third note came: "Remember to pay $10,000 to Abe Lyman in New York or our local boys will wreck your Santa Monica Café. Ace." Federal agents decided the threats were real. The postmarks on the letters indicated they originated in Long Island and New York. Investigators studied the ungrammatical messages and the handwriting for clues. During the last week of March another letter arrived at the Roach lot: "You have failed the Ace," it read.[11] "We shall bide our time. Regards to R.W. Schafer. he remembers me well." Thelma's backround was scrutinized by the FBI, even to the point of noting she had a strawberry birthmark on her right shoulder "about the size of a quarter." Thelma feared a plot by gangsters to extort money from her. She hired three bodyguards and gave Rudolph Schafer a handgun to carry. Santa Monica police kept watch over her home. Federal agents followed her brown Lincoln Phaeton when she drove to the Roach lot. The FBI set out to catch the extortionist. Thelma was photographed with a gun and Roland's white bull terrier. Thelma mailed personal letters from 7274½ Fountain Avenue, the residence of Catherine Hunter, where she occasionally stayed overnight. "She told my mother she was scared all the time," says Bill Todd.[12]

Abe Lyman received a letter in May; it arrived at the Capitol Theatre, where his band performed. It was from Ace: "Dear Sir: Knowing that Thelma Todd is a friend of yours you may be interested in helping her save her life. Wire her requesting her to send you $10,000. When you received same over your next broadcast. The signal shall be all is well. We do not wish to cause you any undue trouble, and request that you regard as a purely business transaction. Respectfully yours, Ace."[13]

On May 10, at 9:30 P.M., Lyman gave the signal "all is well" on his NBC radio show, but Ace never appeared. Instead, Lyman received a postcard: "Well Lyman you failed us but we shall not fail you. My boys on the coast will nab Miss Todd and it take more to free her. Ace."[14] On May 15, another postcard came to the Capitol Theatre: "This is the last warning."[15] But the threatening letters continued: "That Commissioner Davis of Los Angeles gives me a laugh. He thinks this is a joke. Well we mean business. You can write us at Mike Dorgan at 31-18 Newton, Astoria, L.I. Ace."[16] An FBI agent dressed as a deliveryman went to the apartment house, only to discover that "Mike Dorgan" didn't exist. Another threat soon followed: "Pay $10,000 to Abe Lyman in New York and live or our San Francisco boys will get busy. Police Chief Davis of Los Angeles is just a sap."[17]

Thelma suffered a shock on June 27. She returned to her home on Tramonto Drive to find that the residence had been burglarized. Thieves had cut the glass from the front door, gained entry, and stolen clothes and expensive perfume valued at $3,000. Every room in the house had been ransacked. She was photographed with investigators, in the residence in a bathrobe clutching a single key.

A news story reported the incident and gave her address on Tramonto Drive. Thelma believed she was being stalked by a gang, just as the letters threatened. At the Sidewalk Café, telephone messages to Thelma were usually directed to Rudolph Schafer. Thelma kept her whereabouts secret. Only her mother, a handful of trusted friends, and Roach executives knew how to find her. Few were aware she had an apartment above the café. Despite the nationwide publicity, the threats continued: "We are giving you until July to turn over $15,000 or it will be tough on you just address it to the *Los Angeles Times* and we do the rest. Don't fail as we know every move you make. fail us and we wreck this place."[18] Accompanying the message was an arrow that pointed to a clipped newspaper advertisement for La Golondrina, a Los Angeles restaurant.

Although Thelma lived in constant fear, she kept busy. In July, she completed *Twin Triplets* and *Hot Money*, and was paid $5,400 for two weeks of filming. Unknown to Thelma, the FBI was on the verge of an arrest. Agents had studied postmarks of fan letters from the East Coast. They located a fan letter sent to Thelma from "Richard Harding" who requested a photograph. The letter had been mailed from an address on Newton Avenue. The FBI was certain the extortionist lived in the building. Agents examined the handwriting of tenants. Finally, J. Edgar Hoover authorized action. On the evening of August 18, agents arrested Harry Schimanski, a roofer and superintendent of the apartment building. The thin, nervous man had been trailed for days. He was from an indigent family, one of 18 children. Arraigned before a U.S. Commissioner, flanked by federal agents, as well as his weeping wife and children, the frightened man pleaded that he was innocent. Thelma told reporters that she was relieved by the arrest. She had endured months of terror that destroyed her peace of mind. She was also grateful to be cleared of the suspicion that the extortion letters were part of a publicity stunt. "So far as I'm concerned," she said, "there doesn't have to be a prosecution, but I'm ready to follow any advice investigators may give. It would be extremely difficult for me to go to New York to attend a trial."[19] She said the arrest made it possible for her to again go out in public without elaborate police precautions to protect her. But unknown to Thelma, the entire case was unraveling. Doubt suddenly arose when radio station WMCA brought forward a postcard, with a familiar scrawl: "That man had nothing to do with those Thelma Todd notes."[20] The Roach office in New York received a similar postcard. Both were written in the extortionist's familiar handwriting. Abe Lyman came forward with more information: "I have received several phone calls from a man who insisted that the wrong man is being held," Lyman told reporters.[21] "He wrote me two letters, one from Long Island and another from New York, in the same handwriting as the earlier messages." A

Western Union telegram arrived at the Sidewalk Café on October 7 with an ominous warning: "It is with deep regrets that we are again forced to make demands on previous letters which have been disregarded. We think it is advisable for you to take action at once. Ace."[22] The telegram had been sent collect from New York. Two weeks later, a caller claiming to be "Richard Harding" telephoned the Sidewalk Café from New York and asked to speak with Thelma. The café refused to accept the collect call. Federal agents wondered if they had made a mistake. Despite the unresolved case, Thelma stayed busy.

The Hoffman-Schlager Agency on Sunset Boulevard now represented her and sought major roles for their famous client. Pat De Cicco worked as a theatrical agent for the Small-Landau Company, then joined the prestigious Frank Joyce-Myron Selznick firm: "More than an agency ... a powerful organization ... dominating ... but never domineering." Pat was spotted at nightclubs with his friend Howard Hughes and dated a parade of screen beauties; he was linked romantically with Helen Vinson, Sally Blane, and Irene Ware.

Thelma went before the camera in October, cast in *Bohemian Girl,* a Laurel and Hardy comic opera. Thelma was the Gypsy Queen who sang of love and life. Thelma worked on *All-American Toothache* in November, her final production of the year. The handwriting experts felt confident that Schimanski was the author of the notes. His trial was set for November. However, a week before the trial started, the case against Schimanski fell apart. Andrew Viglietta, a reporter for Long Island's *Daily Star,* spoke with a man who identified himself as "Richard Harding." The reporter had followed the story closely and believed Schimanski was innocent. The mysterious "Richard Harding" had telephoned the *Daily Star*: "Please put a piece in your paper that Schimanski is innocent. He had nothing to do with the case. I did it to give Thelma Todd publicity."[23]

When Harding called, Andrew Viglietta kept the confessed extortionist on the line and stalled for time; the switchboard operator transferred the conversation to federal agents. Harding explained his motive: "I mailed those letters to Thelma Todd. Honest. I'm in love with the girl. I tell you I'm in love with her and I had to do something to let her know that I'm her admirer. Why I spent my last ten bucks to wire her orchids for her birthday." Viglietta gained Harding's confidence and arranged a meeting. On November 5, in Times Square, the reporter stood in front of a newsstand as a tall, thin stranger with a pockmarked face approached. The newsman gave the stranger a copy of the *Daily Star.* "I am Dick Harding," whispered the pimply-faced man. The journalist raised his hat and a swarm of federal agents encircled the man with machine guns. "I'll get you for this!" he screamed at Viglietta as he was taken away in handcuffs. Newspapers revealed the arrest of Edward Schiffert, 26, a drugstore handyman who lived in the same building as Schimanski. Schiffert made a full confession to federal agents. Schimanski was released. Edward Schiffert, "the Ace of Hearts," was declared insane and committed to a mental institution.

Thelma felt relief and looked forward to the holidays. On November 28, she wrote a letter to Georges Jomier, an instructor in French, to cancel scheduled lessons. She sent a gracious apology in her even, distinctive script: "My dear Georges, I certainly did think you had forgotten me, not intentionally however. What with the whirl and bustle of the holidays, one must more or less expect it. Indeed I do wish to take French lessons, but I fear it will be somewhat impossible at present. I will be working for at least another week, and then I must do my Xmas shopping and also prepare for our gala opening here New Years Eve. May I beg your indulgence and take the liberty of calling you after the New Year?

That is a promise and not a threat. I do hope it will be agreeable to you, so until — Expectantly and anxiously, Thelma Todd."[24]

On December 12, the *Hollywood Reporter* reviewed *The Bohemian Girl*, complementing Thelma as "the beautiful queen of the gypsies and she looks it and is it." Thelma concentrated on preparations for the opening of the re-modeled Joyas Room, promoted as a new supper club on the second level of the restaurant. She made an exclusive guest list for the event. The public would be allowed to enjoy the elegant restaurant later. Advertisements stated that diners could sit in comfortable booths that overlooked the ocean and enjoy peach, grenadine, or champagne cocktails at $5.00 a glass; afterward, a charbroiled steak was available for $7.50.

At the end of her long day, Thelma retired to an apartment above the restaurant where she and Roland occupied adjoining rooms separated by a locked door that could slide open. Thelma's apartment was reached by an interior stairway or by an exterior staircase on the side of the building. Both doors opened to a living room. Behind the café, close to the exterior entrance, was Castellammare Drive, a narrow street that led to the Wests' residence. Behind the café, steep steps also led to Posetano Drive, a higher street that also led to the Wests' home. Parking spaces at the café were limited, so Thelma usually kept the Lincoln Phaeton in the Wests' garage, parked next to their Hupmobile.

Thelma had a full social schedule arranged for the month of December. One night she attended a party and met Lina Basquette and Lyle Talbot. "Lyle was very charming when he didn't drink, but he had a drinking problem. Thelma was there at a table of several fellows. I remember Pat De Cicco was one, Cesar Romero was another. Thelma was very drunk. On the dance floor she jostled Lyle and me. She said, 'Lina, I've got to see you. I need you, I need you,' in a very loud, drunken way. Lyle pulled me off the dance floor. He said, 'What do want to do with that drunken so and so?' And I said, 'Look, Thelma has a problem, just like you have a problem, and I really should talk to her.' He said, 'Oh, she'll only embarrass you.' So somehow or other I got talked out of it, so I never saw her again."[25]

On Tuesday, December 10, Thelma arranged for a limousine to drive her from the Knickerbocker Hotel to downtown Los Angeles for a shopping trip. The next day, Thelma lunched with ZaSu Pitts and her husband at Perinos on Wilshire Boulevard. She later shopped in downtown Los Angeles. Thelma sent holiday cards to friends: "Christmas Greetings — Fine New Year For You — Thelma Todd." Many cards had a hand-written invitation to the grand opening of the Joyas Room. While having lunch on Friday, at the fashionable Vendome, Thelma glanced up to see Pat De Cicco. Thelma harbored no deep bitterness. In fact, she expected to see him at the Café Trocadero on Saturday night, where she would be the guest of honor at a party hosted by Stanley Lupino. The day before, Thelma had received a telephone call from Ida Lupino. Pat learned of the party and wanted to attend, explained Ida. Pat had met Ida at the Café Trocadero the previous day, a Thursday afternoon, and demanded an invitation. "I hear you're giving a party. Why am I not coming?" asked De Cicco.[26]

Ida explained that his ex-wife would be there and it might be embarrassing.

"On the contrary, it would be swell," he responded. He assured seventeen-year-old Ida that he and Thelma were friendly. So Ida telephoned Thelma and asked for her view. Thelma said that Pat was welcome at the party. Fine, said Ida.

The Lupino family adored Thelma. Ida had come to America in 1933, accompanied by her mother, Connie, to sign a contract with Paramount Pictures. There were press reports that Ida would star in *Alice in Wonderland*. "I'm no Alice," she protested to her parents, who readily agreed. Ida, quite precocious, was already a star in England and was too sophisticated to play naive Alice. After their arrival in Los Angeles, Thelma had been very kind to Ida and Connie. She introduced them to friends and made certain they were invited to chic parties.

Stanley Lupino arrived in Los Angeles in December. He wanted Ida for a British film he planned to produce; the film would be an attempt to boost Ida's career. Paramount agreed to loan Ida, for a price. However, Stanley, Britain's top screen comedian, balked at the steep fee, but he suggested that his visit end on a high note. Why not arrange a party in honor of Thelma, his co-star from *You Made Me Love You?*

Café Trocadero, owned by Billy Wilkerson, was one of filmdom's hot spots.[27] The supper club had opened the previous year. Ida had been a guest at the gala debut, an event hosted by agent Myron Selznick. Also in attendance at the opening were Jean Harlow, William Powell, and dozens of other stars who danced, drank, and guaranteed that "the Troc" was a fabulous success. Located at 8610 Sunset Boulevard, Café Trocadero became one of the most famous nightspots in the world. Guests enjoyed cocktails on a lower level and dined and danced in the upper level. The Trocadero's menu offered such exquisite fare as soft-shelled *crab meuniere*, $1.40; veal chops sautéed a la Viennoise, $1.45; and chateaubriand for two, $4.00. Only the elite were expected to frolic at the Café Trocadero. For the Saturday night party, Ida had prepared a guest list comprised of Thelma's friends and her own circle. The guests were Menlo Polimar, literary agent; Arthur Prince, dance instructor; Al Kaufman, theatrical agent; and Harvey Priester, Thelma's insurance agent and admirer. Also invited were members of Ida's set of young screen performers: Patricia Ellis, sisters Grace and Gertrude Durkin, Tom Brown, and Fred Keating, along with Kelly Anthony, son of Earle Anthony, a wealthy auto dealer. Thelma asked Roland to attend the party, but he declined. He was needed at the restaurant, he said, since Saturday evening would be busy. Thelma loved parties, and she liked the Lupinos. Moreover, she and Stanley both had ideas for another film.

On Saturday morning, December 14, Mae Whitehead picked up Alice Todd at her apartment on Fountain Avenue and drove to the Sidewalk Café. She parked her car on Castellammare Drive, the street behind the café, near the entrance to Thelma's apartment. Alice entered and Mae walked to the garage where the Lincoln Phaeton was parked. She slid the garage door open and drove the Lincoln to the front of the café. At 2:00 P.M., Thelma and Alice drove off. Thelma had an appointment with her dentist, Dr. Ralph J. Arnold, whose office was at 7046 Hollywood Boulevard. Over several months, Thelma had undergone extensive dental work. Dr. Cyril J. Gail had treated Thelma for pyorrhea, an advanced stage of periodontal disease. Dr. Arnold had extracted an incisor and made bridgework. On Saturday, Thelma met Dr. Arnold in his office, room 410, and he prepared a tooth and inserted a temporary crown. After the fitting, Thelma wrote a check to Dr. Arnold for $100, a sum that included past appointments. Afterward, Thelma and Alice went shopping in downtown Los Angeles. At Barker Brothers, a popular department store, Thelma bought a damask set, book ends, a cigarette case, a relish tray, and a clock. Thelma and Alice returned to the Sidewalk Café at 6:00 P.M. Thelma parked the Lincoln Phaeton in front.

By twilight, Thelma Todd's Sidewalk Café was bathed in a reddish glow as the sun faded into the Pacific Ocean. As the December dusk fell, lights twinkled along the coast, and a chill wind blew over the steep palisades. Alice watched as her daughter prepared for the night's fun. Mae Whitehead brought her a metallic gown of shimmering blue. Thelma Todd dressed for her last party.

SIX

Into the Darkness

Thelma descended the staircase radiantly beautiful. The famous blonde curls were adorned with twin-jeweled clasps. A brooch was pinned to her dress. She wore a dark mink caped coat over her blue metallic evening gown. Her fingers glittered with rings, including a huge diamond solitaire. On her dainty feet were blue sandaled heels. Thelma was in high spirits. Alice escorted her downstairs to the café lobby, where Roland joined them. Outside, darkness had fallen, but Thelma's name, spelled with neon tubes on the building, brightened the night. Chauffeur Ernest O. Peters, the hired limousine driver, opened the door. In a joking manner, Roland told her that she must be home from the party by 2:00 A.M.

"2:05," laughed Thelma.[1]

Roland leaned on the limousine door and they bantered back and forth, joking about the time. Alice spoke up. She agreed with Roland and offered her comment that "four hours is enough time at any party."[2] West suggested that any time she stayed out later than 2:00 A.M., to go to her mother's house, so she could get proper rest, rather than driving to the café.

Thelma was ready for a night of fun.

"Don't drink too much," cautioned Roland.[3]

En route to Café Trocadero, Thelma told the chauffeur to stop at a flower shop. She gave Peters a dollar to buy a pink camellia. Thelma pinned the flower to her dress. She wondered aloud if she should accompany her mother home or go directly to the nightclub. At the Trocadero, the doorman said the Lupino party had already started. Thelma bade goodnight to her mother. The chauffeur drove Alice to a market, then took her home. The driver returned to the Trocadero and parked the limousine.

Thelma, the guest of honor, entered the nightspot alone. She was warmly greeted by the Lupinos. She sat with Stanley and Ida in the downstairs cocktail lounge. The guests later went upstairs and enjoyed a dinner of turtle soup, salad, and filet mignon. A chair was placed beside Thelma for Pat De Cicco, but he never came. Word circulated that he was whirling on the dance floor with actress Margaret Lindsay. Ida was stunned, angry that Pat had smooth-talked his way into the party, then ignored Thelma. He didn't even have the courtesy to say hello, a snub that bothered Ida, a teen with a hot temper. After dinner, Thelma danced with Stanley. She observed her ex-mate and Margaret Lindsay sitting together. She introduced Stanley and said, "I think you should apologize to Ida."[4] Pat protested that he had merely been joking when he got himself invited to the party. He had telephoned that afternoon and informed the Lupinos he couldn't attend. "I didn't think you'd break an engagement that way," responded Thelma.[5]

Thelma continued to dance with her host. Afterward, they sat together and discussed Stanley's idea for a film. Thelma also had an idea. Stanley listened to her plan to make another picture in England. She owned the rights to a good story. They sat and discussed the project and agreed to finalize the deal at a meeting. Thelma danced a tango with Arthur Prince. She spotted impresario Sid Grauman and sat with his party, a group that included Richard Roland and the Skouras brothers, wealthy studio executives. Thelma spoke with Roland about her time in New York. Thelma and the Skouras brothers made a $100 bet concerning if they would dine at the Sidewalk Café the next day. Around 1:50 A.M., she asked Sid Grauman to telephone the restaurant, to tell Roland that she was leaving immediately. West was closing the café when the cashier called him to the telephone. Grauman relayed Thelma's message, and West invited him to visit the Sidewalk Café sometime.

The Trocadero usually closed at 2:00 A.M., but Stanley and Thelma again became immersed in the film idea, and they sat talking. Thelma said she felt tired and wanted to leave. Thelma invited the Lupinos to dine at the café. At 3:15 A.M., Arthur Prince escorted Thelma to the waiting limousine. "We'll go home," Thelma told the chauffeur.[6] She leaned from the window and shouted to friends, "Goodbye all of you." Ida Lupino waved goodbye to Thelma.[7] Stanley remarked to his wife: "Oh, my God, Connie, she knows she's booked. I don't think we are going to see her today." On the way home, Ida told her parents what Thelma had disclosed to her, that she wasn't going to live to see another birthday. Her father agreed. "No, darling, I don't think she is; it's her heart."

The chauffeur sped down Sunset Boulevard, reaching speeds of 65 and 70 miles per hour. Thelma was quiet. Peters came to a stop before the café, now dark. She told the driver to send her the bill. He offered to accompany her to the apartment door in the rear, reached by the exterior stairs. "Never mind, not tonight," said Thelma.[8]

As the driver turned his auto around on the coast highway, he saw Thelma approach the outside stairs that led to her apartment, then Ernie Peters drove away.

On Monday, December 16, the city editor of the *Los Angeles Examiner* addressed a group of reporters. Harry Morgan usually passed out routine assignments around noon for the day staff of the newspaper. The telephone at Morgan's elbow suddenly rang. The air grew heavy with excitement as the reporters saw surprise register on the editor's face. Morgan listened in astonishment as George Geiger, the newspaper's West Los Angeles correspondent, informed the editor that Thelma Todd had just been found dead. Morgan jotted notes that would soon be in print. What had happened?

Mae Whitehead had arrived for work around 10:30 A.M. She planned to park in the garage space at 17531 Posetano Road, where Thelma usually kept her expensive Lincoln. The garage belonged to the Wests, as part of the Castillo del Mar residence. Since the café had limited parking spaces, a routine system had been arranged: Whitehead would park her auto in the garage and drive Thelma's Lincoln Phaeton down the hill to the café. Whitehead slid back the wooden garage door as usual, but she was startled by what she saw. Thelma was slumped on the front seat of the Phaeton. She wore the same clothes as the night of the party and her mink coat. The rings sparkled on her fingers. A faded camellia was pinned to her blue evening gown. For a moment, Whitehead believed Thelma was sleeping, but a closer look startled her. Thelma's normally translucent skin was a strange reddish hue. Whitehead tried to rouse her but failed.

Whitehead drove to the café where she broke the news to seventy-year-old Charles Smith, the café treasurer. Roland West was awakened by the ringing of his telephone. Smith relayed the information. Roland hurriedly dressed and called Rudolph Schafer, who lived with his wife in the Castillo del Mar. Whitehead drove Roland to the garage, but she was so upset that coming up the hill she missed the correct street. Inside the garage Roland saw Thelma. Schafer handed Roland a handkerchief. West wiped traces of blood from her lips. Schafer felt Thelma's neck for a pulse, but it was cold. Wishing to avoid publicity, until they could determine what had taken place, Schafer hesitated to telephone from the café. Instead, he drove to a printing

The Wests' garage, 1991 (author's collection).

shop in Santa Monica and called the West Los Angeles police. Captain Bruce Clark soon arrived. Clark and his assistants examined the area closely. They saw no sign of a struggle nor was there a suicide note. A thin layer of dust was on the car. Clark examined the contents of a small, white beaded purse on the seat beside Thelma. The purse contained a house key, cigarettes, lipstick, and four handkerchiefs.

Mae Whitehead called Alice Todd with the terrible news. Soon after, Harvey Priester arrived at the garage with Alice, as detectives swarmed the premises. "She has been murdered!" Alice shouted, emotionally overwhelmed.[9] Later, she spoke with reporters. "It's that heart of hers. Thelma loved life so well," she cried.[10] "She had everything to live for." Harvey Priester was asked to officially identify the body but he was so shocked that he was unable to do so. Alice was placed in the care of a physician. The police surmised that Thelma had walked from the café to the garage. Priester told investigators it was possible her heart gave

December 16, 1935, the nation is shocked by Thelma's death (by permission of Hearst Communications, Inc., Hearst Newspaper Division).

out. Priester explained that Thelma's heart condition had resulted in the denial of an insurance policy. The last time he saw her, she was in good spirits: "She was if anything, gayer than usual Saturday night. I can't conceive of her wishing to kill herself."[11]

In Thelma's apartment the police found over a hundred Christmas presents, ready for mailing. Detectives learned that the previous Friday Thelma had called Harry Dean Carsey, a photographer who had taken her first publicity pictures. Thelma wanted him to send her 45 prints of an early "gag picture," taken the first year she was in Hollywood, a photograph that showed Thelma dressed in children's clothing, decorating a Christmas tree for Santa. The investigators questioned Whitehead. She told officers she had worked for Thelma for four years. Whitehead said she had placed a single key in Thelma's purse to enter the apartment. Roland West informed police that Thelma needed a second key to enter, since an inside door had been bolted. A photographer caught West sitting on the Phaeton's running board, looking forlorn.

Pat De Cicco appeared at the garage. "It's awful, just awful," were the only words he could say.[12] De Cicco tried to enter the garage but was stopped by a policeman. He slipped in though a second garage door, where Roland parked his car, and quickly glimpsed Thelma's body. He then left, overcome by emotion. The investigators doubted that Thelma had taken her own life. They agreed that an accident was most likely. The police theorized that Thelma died from the odorless carbon monoxide fumes from the Lincoln Phaeton. Police believed the death was easily explained. Captain Bert Wallis found only two and a half gallons of gasoline in the 20 gallon tank. The ignition was on and the battery was dead. "There is absolutely no evidence of foul play," said Wallis, "and furthermore there is no motive for any."[13]

Thelma's body was removed from the car, covered with a white sheet, and taken to the Todd and Leslie Mortuary in Santa Monica. Representatives of the coroner's office made a cursory examination. It was discovered that a temporary front crown from the Saturday dental appointment was loose. Coroner Frank Nance ordered an official autopsy to be performed at the County Morgue. Nance said he would call an inquest because of the "unusual circumstances" surrounding Thelma's last months.[14] The extortion letters that had plagued Thelma raised suspicions of foul play. The threat from Ace seemed ominously prophetic, even though Ace had been apprehended. The Coroner's Register listed the personal items found with her: three rings, one wristwatch, three pieces of costume jewelry, one coat, one dress, two stockings, one pair of shorts, one white purse, one cigarette case, one lipstick, one key.

Reporters questioned those close to Thelma. Jewel Carmen, like Roland West and Harvey Priester, told journalists she believed Thelma's heart had failed. Jewel related how Thelma had fainted during *Corsair*. "I recall she was asked why she smoked and sometimes drank if her heart was in that condition, and she replied that physicians told her that she only had five or six years to live anyway and that she might as well have what fun she could."[15]

After the autopsy, county surgeon A.F. Wagner reported that her death was due to carbon monoxide. Rumors circulated that Thelma had spoken with Mrs. Martha Ford on Sunday afternoon, so reporters pressed Dr. Wagner to pinpoint the exact time of death. He said death could have occurred 12 to 30 hours before the body was found, but "it is quite possible that Miss Todd may have come to her death after 4:00 P.M. Sunday. In this cold weather it is difficult to determine how long in the matter of hours a person has been dead." Dr. Wagner found Thelma's heart "organically normal." Dr. Edwin Larson, her personal physician, told reporters he had examined Thelma ten days earlier and found no evidence of heart disease.[16] The coroner explained that tests conducted on Thelma's blood revealed 75 percent saturation by carbon monoxide, with "alcohol thirteen percent." Dr. Wagner said a dental crown had become dislodged when Thelma slumped forward and struck the steering wheel. Dr. Wagner concluded there had been sufficient alcohol in her body to influence her actions; she may have had more drinks than could be determined, since the alcohol had metabolized in her system. The scientific evidence seemed clear, believed detectives. As for her mood, friends at the Trocadero had seen her cheerful. "She was the life of the party, distinctly sparkling," said Stanley Lupino. "We discussed a new film I had planned to make in England, starring her. She told me she cared little, anymore, for the gay whirl of society. Other interests, including her Sidewalk Café, required much of her time, she said. There was nothing strange in her behavior at the dinner. She was escorted to her waiting automobile by Arthur Prince and that was the last we saw of her."[17]

Ernie Peters, the chauffeur, told reporters that Thelma was strangely quiet on the drive home: "On the other evenings she liked to run back the window between us, and we'd chat on the way up the coast. But she didn't say anything much this time. I wouldn't call her glum, but I'd say she had something on her mind."[18]

Pat De Cicco gave a statement to the press: "Until last Friday, I hadn't seen Thelma for a year ... I saw Thelma at the Vendome. We spoke for a moment, quite briefly, and that was the last I saw of her. On Monday morning I was at the Paramount Studio when I heard the report she was dead. I hurried immediately to the scene. I wanted to know definitely. It seemed so unreal that Thelma's life had been so suddenly ended. I wanted to see the proof with my own eyes."[19] Reports surfaced that De Cicco had seen his ex-wife after the meeting at the Vendome restaurant on Friday. In fact, he had been at the Trocadero the night of the party. De Cicco suddenly left town on an evening flight. He said he knew nothing about Thelma's personal life. Hairstylist Frank Chester, Pat's close friend, explained that De Cicco had already made plans to spend the holidays with his mother in Long Island. There were tears in Pat's eyes when he boarded the flight, said Chester. Once in New York, De Cicco blasted the investigation as nothing more than politicians trying to make headlines: "Hollywood has enough headaches without trying to make a scandal out of an accidental death." As for the divorce: "That was gallantry on my part. She put her career before marriage and I allowed her to get the divorce so that she wouldn't injure her career. She was pleasure loving and tempermental ... not the domestic type at all. She had jealous admirers, of course, but no enemies."[20]

Thelma's charity work for the needy was disclosed by the Reverend Harold I. Proppe of the Hollywood First Baptist Church, where Thelma attended services for nine years. The Reverend Proppe praised her: "At Thanksgiving time this year, Thelma delivered thirty baskets herself among poor people. She was always charitable but was never one to let people know what she did. The previous Easter, she had purchased choir robes."[21]

Wanda Gruidl, a former actress, employed in an Oakland drugstore, told reporters of her friendship with Thelma. Known professionally as "Dixie Rogers," she had been an extra, until Thelma spotted her. Amazed by their strong resemblance, Thelma hired her as a stand-in for *Made in Hollywood* and *Redheads on Parade*. "She gave me my chance in films," said Gruidl, "and I have always regarded her as one of the finest women in Hollywood, a jolly sort and delightful to work with."[22] Gruidl had retired to marry. As for suicide? "She would never do that," she said emphatically.

Fred Keating, actor and magician, discounted news stories that Thelma seemed depressed at the party. Keating had not seen her for several years but was struck with her wit and charm: "She seemed to be more vivacious than when I knew her before."[23]

Thelma's death was of nationwide interest. Newspapers in Los Angeles competed for coverage. The *Venice Evening Vanguard* was forced to issue a statement: "For the first time this newspaper today publishes the picture of a corpse.... This newspaper, in order to keep up with its news coverage, is practically forced by metropolitan papers policies to publish these pictures of a dead body, in spite of the reluctance of its management to do so."[24] The city of Lawrence was in a state of mourning. Citizens took great pride in the local girl who became famous the world over. The Todd family was shattered. Thelma had remained close to her relatives. She had written a letter to Uncle Adam and Aunt Gertrude the Wednesday before her death. Wrote Thelma: "Thought I'd be handing out packages to you this holiday, instead of mailing them, but things didn't work quite as I expected them."[25] With the note was a beautiful gift to their little daughter, named after Thelma. Relatives said she had just signed a new contract to make feature comedies. Four days after her death, a large Christmas package arrived for relatives on Bowdoin Street; the package was postmarked December 13.

James Ford expressed his personal grief: "Lawrence and its people found and had a warm spot in Thelma Todd's heart. We often lunched at the First National Studio restaurant and discussed our hometown ... the devotion of Thelma to her mother is well known in Hollywood. Who back home will forget Thelma as a kid, with the long curls, laughing and happily telling you, 'Mother fixed them.' And how we cheered for her when she would take all the beauty prizes. How happy and proud we were. Today here in Hollywood there is a very sad and lonely mother, but all Hollywood is mourning with her."[26]

Hal Roach issued a statement: "She was a favorite with everyone on the lot, from the lowliest employee to the highest. She apparently was joyous and happy and seemed to enjoy her work."[27] Sam W.B. Cohn, director of publicity, sent his colleague Joe Rivkin the following private message: "I know you must have been shocked to hear the tragic news about Thelma Todd. It was a terrible blow to everyone here and we are as much in the dark about the whole matter as are the authorities."[28] Cohn told reporters that Thelma was popular on the Roach lot. She called everyone by their first names, remembering to bring an apple for the gateman each day and was the first to help whenever anybody at the studio faced financial problems. Thelma's closest friends at the studio were Dorothy Callahan, director of wardrobe, and hairdresser Peggy Zardo. Said Patsy Kelly: "Thelma's just kidding us ... I can't believe it. She was so much alive, had so much to live for. Thelma was so happy about her success with the café."[29]

Though investigators were convinced the death was an accident, journalists probed deeper. Reporters asked Roland West why Thelma had gone to the garage. His answer: "As it was necessary for me to stay up late and open the door for her, I told her, when she started for the Trocadero that she should be home at 2:00 in the morning. She replied that she would be home at five minutes after 2:00. At 2:00 I locked the door. I stayed awake until 2:30, then retired. At about 3:30 I was awakened by the whining of my bulldog. I know it must have been Miss Todd at my door because had it been anyone else, the dog would have growled. But she didn't make any noise or attempt to awaken me. Instead, she must have walked up the hill to the garage in which she kept her car and becoming cold, started the motor. Thelma was very considerate," he explained. "I have since learned that she only carried the key to that particular door, but at the time I thought she had the keys to the front door also."[30]

On Sunday morning, West had entered Thelma's apartment and observed an impression on a divan. He assumed she had slept there and gone out. Around noon, H.H. Cooper, an auto salesman, came to the café, to discuss a new car for Jewel Carmen. West's mother visited him at 4:00 P.M. He told her that Thelma was with Alice. At 6:00 P.M. a telephone call from the Skouras brothers said they were coming to dinner with a large party. West responded that Thelma was out "but would be back in a few minutes and for them to come over."[31] At 6:30 P.M. George Baker, a film editor at the Roach Studios, asked to speak with Thelma. Roland said she wasn't in but was expected. He went downstairs, had a drink at the bar, and waited for Thelma. The Skouras brothers arrived. The previous night they had wagered $100 with Thelma, a bet over whether or not they would come to dinner. Late Sunday evening, West was concerned about Thelma's absence; he was rather nervous, and didn't fall asleep until 4:00 A.M.

In memory of Thelma, Roland closed the bar and café, and a wreath was placed on the entrance. Alice remained in seclusion in her daughter's café apartment, attended by a doctor. She saw only three of Thelma's closest friends: Sally Eilers, ZaSu Pitts, and Catherine Hunter.

Though police insisted the tragic death was an accident, the press fueled the flames with unanswered questions. Roland's revelation that he and Thelma shared adjoining apartments, and that he had entered her private room on Sunday morning, made it obvious that they were more than business partners. They were lovers. Thelma's mother, close friends, and industry insiders knew of the romance but not the public, even though the affair had been alluded to in print. Reporters wanted more information from West. The police believed her death was an accident, but curious aspects surfaced. The most puzzling claim was that of Martha Ford, wife of actor Wallace Ford, who informed detectives that she had spoken with Thelma on Sunday afternoon. Mrs. Ford's comments raised suspicions; she spoke of the party at her home at 3528 Laurel Canyon Road: "I know her voice. I couldn't be mistaken. I had invited her to a cocktail party," said Mrs. Ford. "She called herself Thelma, 'your Hot Toddy,' a nickname she always liked us to call her[32] ... last Saturday[33] noon she made the first call to my house. In my absence, my maid, Lucy Polk, answered the telephone. All Thelma wanted was a little general information about the party.... Nothing in the world could ever convince me that it was not Thelma Todd whom I talked to on the telephone between 4:00 and 5:00 Sunday afternoon ... I understood Thelma to say she was Zelma. Since I was expecting a guest by that name, I was rather confused for a moment. Then, Thelma said, 'No Martha, it is Toddy — Hot Toddy.' She then started kidding me about the party and told me that she would be at my home within half an hour."[34] Thelma said she would bring a surprise guest and asked about a shortcut across Ventura Boulevard. Later, when Thelma failed to appear at the party, George Baker telephoned. After six rings at the café, a man's voice answered that Miss Todd wasn't in.

The detectives were skeptical about Martha Ford's alleged conversation. They were sure that Thelma was dead by 4:00 P.M. Sunday. The investigators believed that Thelma, discovering she lacked a key to her apartment, simply decided to pass a few hours waiting in the garage, then died in an accident. How could she have socialized all day Sunday, without contacting her mother and friends? Moreover, why go to West's garage Sunday afternoon, wearing the same party clothes? Martha Ford's statement seemed highly improbable. Roland West agreed: "I am sure she never telephoned anyone on Sunday night and that she was not seen on that day. If she did not communicate with her mother, she wouldn't have communicated with anyone else.... It is regrettable that so many extraneous considerations have entered into the whole affair, but that is to be expected with Hollywood in the spotlight as it is."[35]

Extensive tests were conducted on the Lincoln Phaeton. Douglas Howatt, police fingerprint expert, found a single handprint on the backside of the front seat where Thelma's body was found. He believed it to be Thelma's handprint. Wind had blown dust beneath the thin cracks around the garage doors and left a fine layer on everything. The only area without dust was where Thelma's body was located.

Investigator Frank Cavett examined the position of the body. He theorized that she had started the motor but was overcome by the fumes. She fell forward and struck her face on the steering wheel. As the carbon monoxide filled the garage, she tried to open the door but slid sideways. Cavett found blood on the seat, beneath the steering wheel, eight inches inside the front door; another crimson spot, three inches in diameter, was on the auto running board. Tests would determine if the blood samples contained carbon monoxide. However, newspapers accounts speculated that perhaps Thelma had been knocked unconscious and placed in the garage, to die of deadly fumes.

There were odd developments. Alex Hounie, maitre d' hotel at Café Trocadero, came to police headquarters and asked for protection. He had received a postcard advising him not to testify. On his way home, a large sedan had forced his auto to the curb, with one of two occupants jumping out. They said he had gotten his warning. Reports surfaced that gamblers had wanted to use the Sidewalk Café, but Thelma opposed the idea. Press speculation was intense, until the story was sensationalized to the point that perhaps "Miss Todd was the victim of a powerful underworld clique."[36]

The police revealed that a female officer "about the size of Thelma"[37] dressed herself in furs, evening gown, and slippers. She then climbed the 271 steps directly behind the garage which led to Posetano Road. According to press reports, "The slippers in the test were more scuffed than those of the actress." Then came a report that Roland West had entered Thelma's apartment the afternoon of the party and found Thelma and her mother reclining on a couch "holding hands and crying."[38] Most startling, the owner of a Christmas tree lot claimed he had seen Thelma and a companion at 3:30 A.M. Monday morning. Thelma had asked the man to paint a tree with silver paint but never returned to pick it up. A story in the *Evening Herald and Express* said that a psychic told police the killer of Thelma could be seen in a published photograph of Captain Bert Wallis.

District Attorney Buron Fitts said his office was being deluged with crank letters offering solutions to the death of Thelma. Newspaper articles were filled with dire theories and speculation. To bring all the facts to the public, a Coroner's Inquest would examine the death of Thelma Todd, said authorities.

SEVEN

We the Jurors

On Wednesday, December 18, at 9:30 A.M., the Coroner's Inquest began. Six men of the coroner's jury assembled in the Hall of Justice, Room 102, to sift the evidence in the death of Thelma Todd. The first witness was Harvey Priester who took an oath to tell the truth. Coroner Frank Nance began the questioning.

Q: Please state your name.[1]

A: Harvey William Priester.

Q: Where do you reside?

A: 6853 Camrose Drive.

Q: City of Los Angeles.

A: Yes, sir.

Q: What is your business, profession or occupation?

A: Insurance business.

Q: Mr. Priester, were you acquainted with one Thelma Todd, the deceased?

A: I was.

Q: How long have you known her?

A: Approximately seven years.

Q: Did you see her body here?

A: I did.

Q: When did you see it?

A: Yesterday afternoon, approximately four o'clock.

Q: You recognized her as the Thelma Todd you have known?

A: I did.

Q: What was her correct full name?

A: Thelma Alice Todd.

Q: Where was she born?

A: In Lawrence, Massachusetts.

Q: What was her age?

A: Twenty-nine.

Q: Was she married, widowed, or divorced?

A: She was divorced.

Q: What was her name when she was married?

A: Her name then was Thelma Di [De] Cicco.

Q: Her maiden name was Thelma Alice Todd?

A: That is correct.

Q: She resumed her maiden name after her divorce?

A: She did.

Q: By order of court?

A: No, that was her professional name.

Q: So that her real name by record is Thelma Alice Todd Di Cicco, is it not?

A: I think that is correct.

Q: It is proper for the record that we have the correct name. You don't know whether there has ever been an order of court restoring her maiden name?

A: No.

Q: Will you contact her mother and see with regard to that?

A: Yes, sir, I will.

Q: What was her age?

A: Twenty-nine.

Q: Do you remember the date of birth?

A: July 29.

Q: What year?

A: 1906.

Q: What was her business or profession?

A: Motion picture actress.

Q: Had she any other business or profession?

A: Had a restaurant on Roosevelt Highway.

Q: What was the number of that or location of it?

A: 17576 Roosevelt Highway.

Q: What was the name of that place of business?

A: Sidewalk Café.

Q: What was the date of death, if you know?

A: The date I heard about it first was on December 16, Monday.

Q: Last Monday?

A: Yes, sir.

Q: And at what time did you hear about it?

A: Approximately eleven thirty.

Q: Where were you at the time?

A: I was in the California Bank at the corner of Hollywood Boulevard and Vine Street.

Q: When was the last time you saw her alive?

A: On Saturday night.

Q: Where?

A: At the Trocadero.

Q: What were the circumstances of your meeting her there or seeing her there?

A: There was a party given by Mr. and Mrs. Lupino on Saturday night at the Trocadero at which I was a guest on the same party she was.

Q: Did you go there with her?

A: No, I did not.

Q: You happened to meet her there?

A: She happened to be on the same party. I accompanied another lady.

Q: When did you next see her after that party?

A: Yesterday afternoon down there.

Q: You did not see her before she was brought to this place?

A: I did not, no sir.

Q: Do you know where she died?

A: Well, the place I went to was the garage at 17531 Posetano Road.

Q: Was her body there when you went there?

A: I didn't see it, but they said it was there.

Q: You didn't see it?

A: No, I did not.

Q: When was that that you went there?

A: That was on Monday, December 16.

Q: About what time?

A: I should judge that was approximately two or two thirty, must have been, when I went up there.

Q: You did not look at the body?

A: No, I did not.

Q: What was this place? A house or garage?

A: There was a garage.

Q: Was there an automobile in the garage?

A: There was an automobile in the garage, I saw that, yes sir.

Q: Did you recognize the automobile?

A: I did.

Q: Whose automobile was it?

A: Miss Todd's.

Q: What kind of automobile was it?

A: Lincoln Phaeton.

Q: How long have you known that automobile?

A: Ever since she originally purchased the car.

Q: How long ago was that?

A: That was about two or two-and-a-half years ago.

Q: You know it was her car?

A: Yes, sir.

Q: And although you didn't see her, if she was in that car, that was her own car?

A: That is correct.

Q: Why didn't you look at her?

A: I didn't wish to.

Q: Because of old time friendship?

A: That is correct.

Q: A matter of sentiment. Now, at the Trocadero you saw her and other guests at this party?

A: I did.

Q: What kind of party was it?

A: Well, a party as any party given at the Trocadero, a group of people, approximately twenty, were there as guests of Mr. and Mrs. Lupino and everybody met at the lounging room previous to going to dinner, and then I imagine we went upstairs around ten fifteen to ten thirty.

Q: You mean the dining room is upstairs?

A: No, this is in sort of a cocktail room downstairs.

Q: All right, what happened up there?

A: Then we all gathered as guests do in waiting until that amount of people come and when everybody arrived we went upstairs and had dinner and danced and talked and so forth, like that, and left at — different people left at different times.

Q: About what time did the dinner start?

A: I would say about ten thirty.

Q: About what time did it finish?

A: Well, some people kept on eating, they would dance, finish dinners at different times, I say some were still eating at twelve o'clock.

Q: There was dancing between?

A: Yes, sir.

Q: What time did you leave there?

A: I left there, I would say, approximately two thirty to three o'clock.

Q: Sunday morning?

A: Yes, sir.

Q: Was Thelma Todd there when you left?

A: She was.

Q: You saw her just before you left?

A: Yes, sir, I did.

Q: How was she dressed that evening?

A: She had on a blue gown with sort of glittering material and bright blue shoes, sort of like sandal type, a couple of clasps in either side of her hair and had a ring, a diamond engagement ring on, and she had a little flower like a camellia on.

Q: Where was that?

A: That was on her shoulder.

Q: How was it held?

A: By a brooch.

Q: And did she have any other rings?

A: She had a blue ring on, a cabishon ring, a wedding ring, and the engagement ring.

Q: You talked to her?

A: I did.

Q: Did you dance with her?

A: I did.

Q: Have you since seen that clothing?

A: I have.

Q: Where did you see it last?

A: I got it here yesterday.

Q: You saw all those items that you just mentioned?

A: I did.

Q: The same clothing you saw her wear that night, Saturday night, at the Trocadero?

A: Yes, sir.

Q: And you took them from this office on the order of her mother?

A: That is correct.

Q: I delivered them to you myself on her order?

A: Yes, sir.

Q: And you have inventoried them and checked them and identified them as the same clothing you saw her wear at the party Saturday night?

A: Yes, sir.

Q: Was she still there when you left?

A: Yes, sir.

Q: And that was about what time?

A: I would say anywhere from two thirty to three o'clock.

Q: At any time that night did she say that she intended to go home or how she intended to go home?

A: Yes, sir, she had a chauffeur that she has had on numerous occasions and has had him for several years, the same man.

Q: Do you know his name?

A: Peters, and I asked her how she was going to get home and she said she had this man waiting for her or coming back for her around one thirty o'clock in the morning.

Q: Do you know what she was doing when you left?

A: Yes, sir, she was talking to Mr. Sid Grauman and Mr. Dick Roland.

Q: Was she seated at a table with them?

A: Yes, sir, she was.

Q: Did she appear to be in good spirits at that time?

A: She appeared to be in good spirits all evening long.

Q: Did there seem to be anything in her demeanor that indicated she was unhappy about anything?

A: Nothing at all, and in fact, she was very full of life and full of laughter.

Q: Do you know of any particular thing that might indicate whether or not she was looking to the future and cared to live?

A: Oh, yes, she certainly was, because she had bought her Christmas tree and Christmas packages and Christmas gifts and always enjoyed Christmas and liked that best of all.

Q: She had made preparations for this Christmas?

A: Yes, she had.

Q: Would you know of any reason at all for her taking her own life?

A: None whatever.

Q: Do you know of any enemies she had?

A: None, except the notes I have read about in the paper.

Q: You have known her family and her for several years?

A: Yes, sir.

Q: Do you know of any reason why anyone would want to do her any harm?

A: None at all.

Q: Can you from what you know and all these circumstances account in any way for her death?

A: No, I can't.

Mr. Johnson took over the questioning.

Q: Mr. Priester, were you sufficiently familiar with her affairs to know about her plans as to her marriage or relations with her former husband?

A: Her plans for marriage?

Q: Yes.

A: At the time she was married.

Q: You spoke of her having an engagement ring on this last night.

A: Yes, sir, when I say this engagement ring, it was a large diamond which I imagine is an engagement ring, which she wore on that finger.

Q: Do you know anything of her plans respecting marriage?

A: No, I do not.

Q: Was that a ring that she customarily wore?

A: Yes, sir, it was.

Q: Her husband's name, how do you pronounce that? Di Cicco?

A: Di Cicco.

Q: Was he present at the party last Saturday night?

A: He was at the Trocadero but was not on the same party.

Q: Was he in her company?

A: No, he was not.

Q: Did you see them together at all during that period?

A: No, I did not.

Coroner Frank Nance displays Thelma's purse, sandals, and blue metallic dress (by permission of Hearst Communications, Inc., Hearst Newspaper Division. Hearst Newspaper Collection, Special Collections, University of Southern California Library. Courtesy of University of Southern California, on behalf of the USC Special Collections).

Q: You last saw her, as I understand now, early Saturday morning of December 15?

A: Yes, sir.

Q: And she was still there when you left?

A: Yes, sir.

Q: Was Mr. Di Cicco there?

A: No, he was not.

Q: He had left before that?

A: Yes, sir.

Q: Had there been any discussion or argument of any kind in which Mr. Di Cicco was concerned that you know of?

A: No, sir, none at all.

Q: Were you a friend of Mr. Di Cicco?

A: I was an acquaintance.

Q: Not such as you would call a friend?

A: No, sir.

Q: And you, then, had never discussed the matter of his marriage with Miss Todd?

A: No, I have not.

Q: You spoke of her also having on a wedding ring on the night of the party.

A: Yes, sir.

Q: Was that a ring that she generally wore?

A: Yes, sir.

Q: And do you happen to know where she had acquired either the engagement or the wedding ring?

A: No, I don't, I don't know where she acquired either one of them.

Q: When you were called down to the place where her car was seen by you on Monday, that was Monday afternoon, I believe you stated?

A: At eleven thirty, I went down immediately with her mother, I took her down.

Q: You were notified at eleven thirty?

A: Yes, sir.

Q: And went immediately.

A: I went and took her mother down.

Q: Somewhere around noon?

A: Yes, sir.

Q: And the car was in its customary place in the garage?

A: That I don't know, that is the first time I have ever seen the garage, but the car was in the garage.

Q: You were not familiar with the garage or the premises?

A: No, not at all.

Q: Were you acquainted with the people at the place where this car was in the garage?

A: The place where the car — I didn't even know —

Q: Where you saw the car, did you know who lived there?

A: No, I did not.

Q: And that was not at the premises of Miss Todd, as I understand?

A: No, it was not.

Q: Are you acquainted with Mr. Roland West?

A: I met Mr. West on Monday.

Q: That was the day you went down there?

A: That is correct.

Q: That was the first time you ever met him?

A: Yes, sir.

Q: Did you learn that it was this place where the car was?

A: I knew there was some connection, either his place or his wife's place, but I didn't know which one, but there was some connection, as far as the premises had a connection with Mr. West.

Q: When you last saw Miss Todd, she was talking to friends who were not of your particular party at the Trocadero?

A: That is correct.

Q: And was Miss Todd intoxicated when you last saw her?

A: She was not.

Q: How soon or how near to the time when you left the party had you talked to her?

A: Why, I talked to her, as a matter of fact, I went over to the table with her when she went over to Mr. Grauman's table and she introduced me to Mr. Roland and Mr. Grauman and there was one other gentleman seated at the table with them and then I sat and talked a while and then I went over to my own table and she stayed there the rest of the time. I went over there once more and talked with her and then came back to my table and that is the last time I talked to her.

Q: You think that was about what time?

A: I left somewhere between two and three.

Q: And it was shortly before that?

A: Yes, sir, it was.

Q: Do you know whether there was any reason, apparent to you or known to you, that Miss Todd was avoiding her husband, Mr. Di Cicco, that night?

A: No, there was no reason.

Q: They just didn't get in the same company?

A: Yes, they had nothing in common.

Q: As I understand, you told Mr. Nance they were divorced?

A: Yes, sir.

Q: But you don't know as to her having resumed her maiden name?

A: That is correct. It became final, I think, the first or second of March, 1934.

Q: Do you know of Miss Todd having kept company with Mr. Di Cicco lately?

A: No.

Q: You don't know whether she has or not?

A: She has not.

Q: Have you ever conversed with her, discussed the matter of her former husband with her?

A: Never, except sometimes occasionally, something may have been brought up, nothing as far as anything specific has been brought up, just a general conversation.

Q: In other words, did you have any intimation or otherwise that she might have considered remarrying Mr. Di Cicco?

A: No, she didn't.

Q: Did she mention that she was not considering it?

A: Well, she told me she was through with him absolutely, that is the reason I am basing my statement on that.

Q: How recent did she make that remark?

A: That has been some time back.

Mr. Emerson: You say, Mr. Priester, that Miss Todd told you she had the chauffeur, Peters, coming for her about one thirty?

A: Yes, sir.

Q: She told you that prior to one thirty in the morning, did she?

A: Yes, sir, she did?

Q: Nothing more was said about Mr. Peters?

A: Nothing more, except I went over one time and told her the car was going to be there about one thirty and it was after one thirty and she continued talking and I left and the guests left at the same time.

Q: Do you know whether Mr. Peters was waiting for her at the time you left?

A: I do not, no, sir.

Q: Do you know what drinks Miss Todd had that evening, during the course of the party?

A: No, I couldn't say that; she didn't have so very many, though.

Q: Do you know whether she had any cocktails before dinner or not?

A: I think one. I couldn't say definitely because I wasn't watching all the time.

Q: Do you know whether she had anything to drink during the meal?

A: She had a drink during the meal, yes, sir.

Q: What were they drinking?

A: Drinking champagne.

Q: Do you know of any other drinks that Miss Todd had that evening?

A: No, I do not.

Q: I think that is all.

Frank Nance: Gentlemen of the jury, have you any questions?

Juror: Were the relations between Miss Todd and Mr. Di Cicco friendly up to the time of her death?

A: Yes, they talked.

Q: At the time of her divorce was there anything unusual in the circumstances of her divorce?

A: Well, in any divorce there are certain things brought out.

Q: Any bitterness or enmity between them?

A: Well, there was a slight amount but nothing unusual from the usual divorce procedure.

Q: Nothing to make her resentful of the time they were living together?

A: Well, not except, she held no ill feeling, except she was just through, that is all.

Mr. Johnson: You happen to know whether Miss Todd came to the Trocadero party alone or was she accompanied by anyone?

A: Only that I have been told that her mother accompanied her to the Trocadero.

Q: She had no escort as far as you know?

A: No, she had no escort. I know that definitely.

Coroner Nance: That is all.

Mae Whitehead came to the stand.

Coroner Nance: Your name is Mae Whitehead?

A: Yes.

Q: Miss?

A: Mrs.

Q: Where do you live, Miss Whitehead?

A: 1642 West 36th Place.

Q: That is in the city of Los Angeles?

A: Yes, sir.

Q: What is your personal business or occupation?

A: Personal maid.

Q: By whom are you employed?

A: Thelma Todd.

Q: Have long have you worked for Thelma Todd?

A: Four years in all.

Q: When did you last see her alive?

A: Saturday night between eight and eight thirty.

Q: Where?

A: At her apartment.

Q: Where was this apartment?

A: Above the Sidewalk Café.

Q: Above the Sidewalk Café, on the roof of the building above the café. Well, just what happened there, tell us what you were doing for Miss Todd then and about the circumstances of your being together that night, what you did for her, and what her plans were that evening, if you knew?

A: Well, she was going to the Trocadero, therefore I dressed her that evening about eight o'clock.

Q: All right, and how was she going?

A: In a chauffeur driven car.

Q: Do you know who the chauffeur was to be?

A: Ernie Peters.

Q: Was he going to take her in his car or her car?

A: In his car.

Q: Did you see her depart?

A: No, I did not.

Q: Had she employed him before to take her various places she wanted to go?

A: Yes.

Q: What time did he call for her?

A: Five minutes of eight.

Q: Did she go alone with him or anyone else?

A: Her mother.

Q: Her mother was in the apartment with her and they both left together?

A: Yes.

Q: Did you understand the plan was to take Miss Todd to the Trocadero and her mother to some other place?

A: Yes, she was to be taken shopping and then home.

Q: Where is the mother's home?

A: On Fountain Avenue.

Q: How was Miss Todd dressed that night?

A: She wore a blue evening gown with two clasps in her hair and a mink coat.

Q: Did the coat have a cape?

A: Yes.

Q: A long coat?

A: Yes.

Q: And quite a heavy coat?

A: Yes.

Q: And what ornaments did she wear besides the hair ornaments you mentioned?

A: A diamond pin.

Q: And brooch?

A: And brooch on the left side.

Q: Can you describe the brooch?

A: It is a round pin in rather a bow knot.

Q: Where was the knot, at the top?

A: A knot on the side.

Q: And it was inset with some stones?

A: Yes, diamonds.

Q: Were they all diamonds?

A: No, they were — I don't know.

Q: Two blue stones.

A: More than two.

Q: Some blue stones?

A: Yes.

Q: Where were they?

A: In the top of the knot.

Q: Above the knot?

A: Yes.

Q: Did she wear any flowers?

A: Not when she left.

Q: Did she say anything about getting flowers?

A: No.

Q: Do you know whether she afterwards got a flower?

A: Yes.

Q: What was it?

A: Only that I have heard, it was a camellia, I believe.

Q: After she left to go to this party, where did you go?

A: I went home.

Q: Did you plan to see her the next day?

A: No, I never work on Sundays.

Q: When did you plan to see her the next time?

A: Monday morning.

Q: What time?

A: Ten thirty.

Q: Were you there at that time?

A: Ten thirty o'clock.

Q: Didn't find her there?

A: I didn't go to the apartment.

Q: Where did you go?

A: Went direct to the garage, as I always do, to get the car.

Q: That is your habit, to get the car and bring it to the café for her to use?

A: Yes.

Q: What did you find when you got to the garage?

A: I found her body in the car.

Q: Was the garage open?

A: No.

Q: Both doors closed?

A: Yes.

Q: Were they locked?

A: No.

Q: Tell us what happened?

A: I drove to the garage and parked my car, intending to back hers out as I do, and finding the body there, of course — I — I thought she was asleep.

Q: Where was the body?

A: Slumped in the front seat of her car.

Q: What position was she lying?

A: Just bent over.

Q: Left or right side of the seat?

A: Her head was to the left.

Q: Was it touching the door?

A: No.

Q: Was it on the door?

A: No.

Q: Was it near the door?

A: No, because the door was open.

Q: Well, was it under the steering wheel of the car or was she lying partly under the steering wheel of the car?

A: Partly.

Q: Was she dressed then the same way as she was dressed when you prepared her to go to the party the night before?

A: She was.

Q: Did you notice any evidence of injury?

A: None whatsoever.

Q: What did you do when you discovered her?

A: I first approached the left side because I had bundles in my arms. Then after seeing her there I went around to the right — left side of the car, driver's side, and I thought I could awaken her, that she was asleep, and after finding she was really dead I left immediately.

Q: Where did you go?

A: I went to the café.

Q: Did you notify somebody there about her discovery?

A: I did.

Q: Who?

A: Mr. Smith.

Q: Who is Mr. Smith, I mean what is his capacity there?

A: Business manager.

Q: Business manager at the café, and then what did you do?

A: I asked him to telephone Mr. West.

Q: Did you go back to the garage again?

A: Yes.

Q: Were you there when others came, the investigating officers?

A: Yes.

Q: Now, can you account in any way for her being in her car in that garage instead of being in her own apartment?

A: No, I have no idea.

Q: Is there any reason why she could not have gotten into her apartment if she wanted to that night?

A: Not that I know of.

Q: To get into the apartment, how would she get there?

A: I gave her the key to the side door.

Q: What kind of key is that?

A: Well, ordinary key, door key.

Q: Do you know what a Yale key is as compared with the old fashioned key?

A: It was a Yale key.

Q: Where did she carry that key?

A: In the evening purse, in the coin purse.

Q: And the evening purse was what kind of a purse?

A: It was a small white bag, ordinary size for an evening purse.

Q: Lined with white inside?

A: Yes.

Q: And the coin purse was also white inside?

A: Yes.

Q: And she needed only that one key to get into her apartment?

A: Yes.

Q: Have you heard since that after being let out at the café she walked up the hill to the garage?

A: I don't know that, I understand that.

Q: You have heard that?

A: Yes.

Q: Have you any idea why she did that?

A: No.

Q: Do you know of any trouble she had with anybody?

A: No.

Q: Do you know of any reason why she would not want to live?

A: None whatsoever.

Q: Did she have plans for the future?

A: For Christmas and had done the shopping.

Q: Was she moody or morose or happy and cheerful?

A: Happy and cheerful.

Q: Agreeable person to get along with?

A: Very agreeable.

Q: Have you any way to account for the manner in which she died?

A: I have not.

Mr. Johnson: Had you been employed by Miss Todd for some time?

A: Yes.

Q: Approximately how long?

A: Four years and more.

Q: And you went down there then customarily about ten in the morning every day except Sunday?

A: Not every day. I had my calls every night when I would leave, as to the time I should come.

Q: And you then had no time to come other than the time she gave you when you left the day before?

A: Yes.

Q: And when you left Saturday night a little after eight did she tell you when to come back?

A: Yes.

Q: She told you to come back about ten Monday?

A: Ten thirty.

Q: And you drove your own car back and forth?

A: I did.

Q: What time had you come there on that Saturday, that would be December 14, last Saturday?

A: Last Saturday, five or ten minutes after eleven.

Q: In the morning?

A: Yes.

Q: And you saw Miss Todd that day?

A: Certainly.

Q: Was she there during the entire day after you got there?

A: No.

Q: Did you see her when you got there about eleven?

A: Yes.

Q: And how long was she before she went away?

A: She left about two o'clock.

Q: And was there until about two, did she drive away?

A: She did.

Q: And when did she come back?

A: Around six o'clock.

Q: Did you go away with her?

A: No, I didn't.

Q: Who went with her?

A: Her mother.

Q: Anyone else?

A: No.

Q: In other words, she drove her own car.

A: Yes.

Q: Did you talk to her on the morning of the 14th before two o'clock that day?

A: Yes.

Q: She was apparently in good health?

A: Very good health.

Q: And cheerful?

A: Yes.

Q: When did she come back?

A: At six.

Q: Did she also come back with her mother?

A: She did.

Q: And anyone else?

A: No.

Q: And in that same car that you later saw up at the garage?

A: Yes.

Q: Do you happen to know where she went or where she intended to go when she left about two?

A: To the dentist's office.

Q: Where? In the city?

A: In Hollywood.

Q: Did she discuss that when she got back?

A: Yes.

Q: And stated that she had been to the dentist?

A: Yes.

Q: And did you have any other conversation with her when she came back as to what she had done or who she had seen or anything of that kind?

A: Not particularly.

Q: Do you recall any?

A: Other than speaking of her shoes, she had had a pair of shoes dyed for wearing that evening.

Q: And you remained in her apartment then all that day last Saturday after you got there?

A: Yes.

Q: Do you recall whether or not there were any telephone calls coming into the place?

A: Yes, there were telephone calls from the studio.

Q: Calls to Miss Todd?

A: Yes.

Q: And calls that she answered?

A: I generally answer them.

Q: You answered the phone?

A: Yes.

Q: And then did you call Miss Todd?

A: Yes.

Q: In other words, did she talk over the telephone on that Saturday?

A: Yes, she talked to someone at the studio.

Q: Do you recall whether or not there was more than one telephone call coming in there for Miss Todd on Saturday?

A: On Saturday?

Q: Yes, that particular day.

A: No, other than the studio, not on Saturday, no.

Q: You don't recall that she talked over the phone but one time. Did you have any phone messages that you took for Miss Todd when she didn't talk over the phone?

A: On Saturday?

Q: That same day.

A: On Saturday I didn't receive any calls, any message calls particularly on Saturday.

Q: Then is it your recollection that it was only once that the telephone rang last Saturday at the apartment there?

A: On Saturday, yes.

Q: I mean, from the time you got there about eleven until you left.

A: I had no other phone calls on Saturday.

Q: Now, Mrs. Whitehead, do you recall whether or not Miss Todd phoned out to anyone on that day?

A: Not that I know of.

Q: Whether you know who it was or not, do you recall that she did any telephoning?

A: No, she rarely did, she didn't like telephoning.

Q: Do you recall whether you telephoned out for any purpose at her direction during the day?

A: Yes.

Q: To whom did you telephone?

A: Mrs. Ford.

Q: Did you yourself know Mrs. Ford?

A: No, I didn't.

Q: What message did Miss Todd give you or orders about telephoning Mrs. Ford?

A: That I should call her and accept the invitation on Sunday.

Q: Did you do so?

A: I did.

Q: Had you ever conversed with a woman you understand was Mrs. Ford on the telephone before?

A: Yes.

Q: And you felt that you identified that as the same voice that you understood to be Mrs. Ford?

A: Well, I believe so.

Q: What did you tell Mrs. Ford?

A: That Miss Todd would be very happy to come on Sunday but that she was bringing a guest.

Q: And you understood, of course, that that was some function arranged at Mrs. Ford's home or some place that Miss Todd was going to?

A: Yes.

Q: When you conversed with Mrs. Ford, did you not converse as though you yourself was Miss Todd?

A: No.

Q: You didn't say, "This is Miss Todd," and you would accept her invitation or anything like that?

A: No.

Q: Did you telephone to Mrs. Ford more than once that day?

A: No.

Q: About what time, if you remember, was that telephone call by you?

A: Around three o'clock, as near as I can remember.

Q: Do you recall that it was after Miss Todd and her mother had gone away in the afternoon?

A: Yes.

Q: You know it was while she was away?

A: Yes.

Q: When you drive your car down there in the mornings, when you went down there for your work, where did you ordinarily leave it?

A: I parked it in her stall and took her car down.

Q: Is that the same place where you found it on Monday?

A: Yes.

Q: That was what you recognized as the stall that Miss Todd had in that garage?

A: She was using, yes.

Q: It was a garage with how many stalls or places for automobiles?

A: Two.

Q: And how far from the café was that garage?

A: I should say approximately three blocks.

Q: And was it somewhere up the hill?

A: Yes.

Q: And Miss Todd, as I understood, had an apartment over the café there?

A: Yes.

Q: Right on the boulevard?

A: Yes.

Q: And did you stop at the café ordinarily when you went down, before you drove up to the garage?

A: No.

Q: Did you on Monday?

A: No.

Q: You just drove down and right on up to the garage?

A: Yes.

Q: And left your car outside?

A: Yes.

Q: And opened the garage?

A: Yes.

Q: Did you see any other person around the garage at all last Monday morning?

A: No.

Q: Had you spoken to anyone down there in the vicinity before you saw the body?

A: No.

Q: Had you on any other occasion in your experience there found Miss Todd asleep in her car?

A: No.

Q: That was the first time you ever saw her apparently asleep in the car?

A: Yes.

Q: Did the doors on that particular stall, do they swing out?

A: No, they are sliding doors.

Q: Sliding up or sideways?

A: Sideways.

Q: And the first thing you did was to open those doors?

A: Yes.

Q: And was there any other doorway or entrance way into that stall that you remember, any other way to get into that particular apartment where the car was?

A: No.

Q: Except by opening the two front doors?

A: Yes.

Q: Was there any window in that place?

A: No.

Q: Mrs. Whitehead, I show you here a photograph and ask you if you recognize what that is?

A: Yes.

Q: What is it? The general photograph, what is that of?

A: The garage where I found the car.

Q: Does that show the front of the garage and the doors as you approach the garage?

A: Yes.

Q: And leaving out, of course, this man and all in it, that is a pretty good picture of the place, is it?

A: Yes, it is.

Q: And which one of those doors, as you look at it, was the one in which Miss Todd had her car?

A: The right one, the right hand side.

Coroner Nance: As you look at the picture, it is to the right?

A: Yes.

Mr. Johnson: To get that in another way, did you observe the number, 17531, over this door?

A: Yes.

Q: Was her car in the stall next to that number or the second one?

A: The one on the right close to the number.

Q: It was the one nearest the number which might be called the center of the garage, is that correct?

A: Yes.

Q: That is the door that you have spoken about that you opened?

A: Yes.

Coroner Nance: May I ask the witness if the garage is placed under a hill so there is no possible opening at all, is it cut under a hill or walled up outside entirely?

A: It seems to be set under a hill.

Q: The only openings you know are the doors?

A: As far as I know, yes.

Juror: Is there a wall between the two stalls?

A: No.

Coroner Nance: Is it a two car garage, in other words?

A: Yes.

Coroner Nance: Will you mark that Exhibit A?

Mr. Johnson: Mrs. Whitehead, the stall that Miss Todd kept her car in might be called the center of the garage, is that correct?

A: It might be, yes.

Q: There is one garage stall on the left hand side of that one and a doorway or some other section over on the other side?

A: There was no other door in the garage.

Q: It goes somewhere else but is apparently a door going through there?

A: Yes.

Q: Was that the same stall you found her car in on other occasions?

A: Yes.

Q: She always used that same stall?

A: Yes.

Q: Do you happen to know who used the other stall?

A: Yes.

Q: Who?

A: Mr. West.

Q: Mr. Roland West?

A: Yes.

Q: Do you know upon whose premises this garage was where the car was kept?

A: I understand it belongs to Mr. West or his wife.

Q: He has a house or residence there?

A: Yes.

Q: And was there any garage or place where her car had been kept down nearer the café?

A: No.

Q: How much of the apartment did Miss Todd have where she lived?

A: Two rooms.

Q: And that consisted of her sleeping room and living room, or what were they?

A: Yes.

Q: And a bathroom, I suppose?

A: Yes.

Q: And did anyone live in the apartment with her?

A: Not that I know of.

Q: Did she have any guest occupying the apartment at any time recently that you know of?

A: No.

Q: Now, when you opened the garage door on this last Monday, I believe that you stated that there is no window or other doorway into the garage, except the doors that you used to drive into?

A: Yes.

Q: When you opened the door first last Monday did you observe anything that attracted your attention before you saw her?

A: Nothing whatsoever.

Q: No odor of any kind?

A: No.

Q: Not noticeably warm in there?

A: No.

Q: And was the car motor running?

A: No.

Q: Was your attention drawn to anything else that seemed to be unusual before you saw her in the car?

A: Nothing.

Q: And she had her clothing about as you had last seen her on Saturday evening, is that correct?

A: Yes, sir.

Q: Was there anything different about her clothing or dress that you observed?

A: Nothing at all.

Q: Did you get any notice of this camellia being on her dress?

A: I didn't notice.

Q: Did you observe whether or not her jewelry was on her?

A: I did not.

Q: Did you observe whether she had that white evening bag or purse that you had seen?

A: Yes.

Q: Where was that?

A: Lying on the seat.

Q: Next to her?

A: Yes.

Q: And that was the purse in which you had seen her put the key to her apartment?

A: I put the key in there.

Q: You put the key in there for her?

A: Yes.

Q: Did you tell her?

A: Yes.

Q: When you did that, you told her you were putting the key in the purse to the apartment?

A: Yes.

Q: Did you find it there when you found the car?

A: I didn't touch the purse.

Q: Is there any way of going from her garage down to the apartment without going down around the road?

A: No.

Q: There is no stairway or pathway?

A: Further down, but you have to go down the road first, there is a stairway.

Q: It is a shorter cut than going down the road?

A: It is about the same.

Q: When you put the key in the purse on Saturday evening, did you observe whether there was any money in there?

A: Yes.

Q: Was there any?

A: I put thirty-five cents in there.

Q: Put thirty-five cents?

A: Yes.

Q: Was that all that was in the purse?

A: That is all.

Q: Did she say anything at that time, that is, when you last saw her, about stopping to buy a camellia?

A: No.

Q: You didn't know she had such intention at all?

A: I didn't know that.

Q: Are you familiar with the doors to her apartment to which you gave her the key, do you know how that door works?

A: In what respect?

Q: How it opens and how it is locked?

A: It is locked with a key from the outside.

Q: Is there a spring lock or Yale lock, that they commonly call a Yale lock? Do you know what a Yale lock is?

A: Yes.

Q: One something on that fashion. Maybe not as big?

A: Yes.

Q: That was the kind of key you gave her?

A: Something on that order, yes.

Q: And you recognized it as the key to that door leading to her apartment?

A: Yes.

Q: Was that the door down on the ground or top of the stairway?

A: Top of the stairway.

Q: How do you approach the place to go up that stairway?

A: You can come up from the highway by the stairway or come up the back way.

Q: In other words, do you have to get in the café building and then go upstairs?

A: No.

Q: You can go up outside?

A: Yes.

Q: There is no door or key or obstacle, you walk right up the stairway to her door, is that correct?

A: Yes, sir.

Q: Now, is there any way of getting into her apartment, I mean legitimately or properly, without going through that door?

A: Without going through the café?

Q: No, I mean any other way to get into that apartment except going through that door that you gave her the key to. If you don't understand just say so.

A: No, I don't.

Q: You gave her a key to the apartment?

A: Yes.

Q: Is there any other way to get into the apartment?

A: Not unless you come through the café.

Q: If you come through the café, where do you land up into her apartment?

A: Well, it is the side door.

Q: This key that you gave her is to what door, where does it lead to? Into her apartment?

A: Into her living room.

Q: The other door that you speak of coming from the café, where do you go into the apartment there?

A: Living room.

Q: Same room but different part?

A: Yes.

Q: Is there any manner of locking those doors from the inside?

A: They can be.

Q: I mean, is there a bolt on the inside of that particular door?

A: One for the key and one lock that can be locked inside.

Q: In other words, in addition to that key and the lock that it is for, would you say just one other bolt?

A: Yes.

Q: And that is a bolt that can be used on the inside?

A: Yes.

Q: Mrs. Whitehead, did you leave before or after Miss Todd on Saturday evening?

A: Left after.

Q: Left after she did?

A: As far as I know. She went downstairs before I did and I didn't see her leave.

Q: She went out of the apartment before you did?

A: Yes.

Q: And her mother also?

A: Yes.

Q: She went out the side door?

A: She went out the other door.

Q: And when you left, which door did you leave?

A: The side door.

Q: So when you left, the door that she had the key to was not bolted on the inside?

A: Could not have been. I could not bolt it on the outside.

Q: And do you know whether the other door that leads up from the café was bolted on the inside when you left?

A: Yes, I bolted that door from the inside.

Q: You are sure of that?

A: Yes.

Q: Do you remember doing that?

A: The bolt with a key, I bolted that.

Q: I see, the bolt with the key.

A: Well, I bolted the door from the inside and went out the side door.

Q: In other words, the door from the inside was locked from the inside and no one could get in from there?

A: It could have been opened with the key.

Q: I am distinguishing the lock from the bolt. When you locked the door from the café, did you switch the lock on or the bolt?

A: Just the lock.

Q: So anyone could have come in there if they had had a key?

A: Yes.

Q: Yes.

Coroner Nance: Did you open these garage doors regularly yourself?

A: When I go for the car.

Q: Were they hard to open?

A: No.

Q: Do you think it would be difficult for Thelma Todd to open those doors herself?

A: No.

Q: She operated them?

A: Yes.

Q: Did she often go up and open the doors and get the car herself?

A: No.

Q: You spoke of a telephone message that you placed to Mrs. Ford for Thelma Todd saying she would accept an invitation and would have a guest?

A: Yes.

Q: Do you know who that guest was?

A: No, I don't.

Q: Don't you know who that would be?

A: No.

Juror: The other phone message, how did you know it was from the studio?

A: They always say it is the studio.

Q: And you never put the car back in the garage?

A: No.

Q: You always take it out in the morning?

A: Yes.

Q: And you took it out Sunday morning?

A: Saturday morning.

Q: She always drove her own car?

A: Yes.

Q: Never had anybody drive it for her?

A: Very seldom.

Q: And she drove it in when she got through in the daytime?

A: No, I was not there, I don't know.

Q: Usually how did she put it back there?

A: I think she had one of the boys put it up.

Q: Was there any living quarters or anything above this garage, was there any rooms or anything above the garage where the car was kept?

A: I understand there are. I don't know.

Q: You don't know whether anyone is living there in those apartments?

A: No.

Q: Was it customary to have the door on the garage unlocked?

A: It has never been locked, as far as I know.

Q: She would drive the car in and leave the doors unlocked?

A: As far as I know. I always found them unlocked.

Q: You found them closed?

A: Yes.

Q: But not locked?

A: No.

Mr. Johnson: I just wanted to ask Mrs. Whitehead a little more about those keys. Do you know now whether the same key to that so-called side door would open the lock on the other door?

A: No, it wouldn't.

Q: It is a different key?

A: Yes.

Q: And the same type lock, Yale lock?

A: Yes, it is the same type lock.

Q: Do you have any key that you keep in your possession to the apartment?

A: Only the one key to the side door.

Q: That is the same one that you gave Miss Todd?

A: Yes.

Q: And do you know whether she had any other key or not?

A: Not that evening, no.

Q: Well, did she lose her key or wasn't there another key to that door?

A: Yes, she has keys to that door but she didn't want to carry them all.

Q: Didn't want to take it off her bunch of keys, so you gave her your key?

A: No, I didn't give her my key; off her key ring.

Q: Did you have a key that you carry to that apartment?

A: Yes.

Q: And you still had that after you gave her a key Saturday night?

A: Yes.

Q: Do you know of anyone else that has a key or keys to that apartment?

A: I don't know.

Q: Do you know of any other person in any apartment whom Miss Todd has told you has a key to the place?

A: No, she has not told me of anyone having the key.

Q: You don't know of anyone else having a key to the door leading from the café?

A: No.

Mr. Emerson: Mrs. Whitehead, on Saturday, when you took your car and went home, you had it parked in the garage in the usual place where you kept it?

A: No, Saturday I didn't have my car up there. I walked Saturday morning and got her car.

Q: You didn't have your car there at all?

A: Not in the garage, no. I drove to the apartment, because I had her mother, I brought her mother.

Q: Out from Los Angeles?

A: Yes.

Q: And did you come in a car?

A: In my own car.

Q: In your own car?

A: Yes.

Q: Saturday?

A: Yes.

Q: And where did you park your car?

A: At the rear of the café, in the back of the café.

Q: You didn't take it up and put it in the garage?

A: No.

Q: When you left Saturday night, did you know where Miss Todd's car was?

A: No, I had no occasion to go to the front.

Q: You had no occasion to go to the garage?

A: Only when I went up to get her car Saturday morning.

Q: When you went up and brought it down, was there any car parked in the garage beside hers?

A: I don't remember. I didn't notice particularly.

Q: Do you remember ordinarily whether there was another car parked there?

A: Generally, yes.

Q: Mr. West was ordinarily using the other half of that garage and you would see his car in there?

A: Yes.

Q: When you came Monday morning to get Miss Todd's car, was there any car parked in the garage?

A: Yes.

Q: Mr. West's car?

A: Yes.

Q: Did you notice his car?

A: Yes.

Q: When you found Miss Todd there, Mr. West's car was also parked in the garage?

A: Yes.

Q: And I understand there is no division between the two cars, they were in there parked side by side?

A: Yes.

Mr. Johnson: Did you find anything in the garage or about the car in the way of a note or any letter or anything?

A: Not a thing.

Q: Nothing at all?

A: I didn't notice anything.

Q: You didn't notice any note around the switch to the car?

A: No, I didn't notice a thing.

Q: Was Miss Todd in a position there right back of the steering wheel when you saw her first?

A: Yes.

Q: And did you observe whether her feet were down on the pedals or where they were?

A: They were not on the pedals.

Q: Which side of the compartment were they?

A: There were on the driver's side but were not on the pedals.

Q: Just down on the floor board?

A: Yes.

Q: And the steering wheel and the driver's seat is on the left hand side of that car, is it?

A: Yes.

Q: And her head was slumped a little over towards the left when you first saw her?

A: Yes.

Q: As far as you know, no one had been in there or had seen her body before you did?

A: No.

Q: I show you this photograph, Mrs. Whitehead, and ask you if you could recognize what that is?

A: She wasn't lying down that way when I saw her.

Coroner Nance: Describe the difference between the picture and the way you saw her.

A: She was more upright, just with her head down.

Q: Mr. Johnson: You think she was seated more upright than she is there?

A: Yes.

Q: This picture indicates that she was slumped over toward the left.

A: She was slumped over toward the left but not that far.

Coroner Nance: You don't know whether she had been moved after you first saw her?

A: I don't know.

Q: You were not there all the time.

A: No.

Q: But the impression you got, she was sitting back of this wheel in the normal position of a person who was about to start the car or drive?

A: Yes.

Q: This photograph will be marked Exhibit Two.

Mr. Johnson: Mrs. Whitehead, did you observe any blood from her face or mouth?

A: Yes.

Q: What was it.

A: Around her nose.

Q: And was her head against any part of the car?

A: No.

Q: Or her face?

A: No, it was not.

Q: And where was her head or face resting?

A: On her chest, slumped down.

Q: Slumped over forward?

A: Yes.

Q: You saw how her arms were?

A: Her arms were in her lap.

Q: Both of them?

A: Yes.

Q: She was dressed and all as she appears in this picture?

A: Yes.

Coroner Nance: Was her head below the steering wheel when you first saw her?

A: No, not below, wasn't that far down.

Q: Was it as low as the lower edge of the steering wheel?

A: Well, practically.

Q: Gentlemen of the jury, any questions?

Juror: Do you know whether she had been accustomed to fainting spells?

A: No.

Q: Never complained of any dizzy spells of any kind?

A: No.

Q: Who did she rent the garage from?

A: I don't know how that was arranged.

Q: Were there other living quarters above the café on the same level with Miss Todd's apartment?

A: I don't know anything about it. I had nothing to do with the café whatsoever; I don't know.

Q: You were never upstairs in this house?

A: No.

Q: That is all. You are excused.

After a five minute recess, the proceedings recommenced. Ernest O. Peters was sworn in.

Coroner Nance: State your full name.

A: Ernest O. Peters.

Q: Where do you live?

A: 348 1/2 North Gardner.

Q: City of Los Angeles?

A: Yes, sir.

Q: What is your business, profession, or occupation?

A: U-Drive automobile proprietor.

Q: Proprietor of the business?

A: Yes.

Q: Did you often drive for Thelma Todd, the deceased?

A: Yes, on various occasions.

Q: How long have you known her?

A: The last three years.

Q: When did you last drive for her?

A: Saturday night.

Q: Where did you pick her up and where did you take her, just tell us what happened?

A: I picked her up at the Sidewalk Café at eight o'clock and drove from there to a florist's on Wilshire Boulevard.

Q: Do you know what she did at that florist's?

A: I went in and I bought a camellia for her.

Q: Do you know whether she put it on her dress?

A: Yes.

Q: Where did she put it on?

A: On the left side.

Q: How did she put it on?

A: I gave her a pin.

Q: At that time what was she wearing?

A: A mink coat and blue dress.

Q: Where did you go?

A: West to the Trocadero café.

Q: Who else was with her, if anybody?

A: Her mother, Mrs. Todd.

Q: And you first took Thelma Todd to the Trocadero café?

A: Yes.

Q: What time did you arrive there?

A: Twenty-five minutes after eight.

Q: Did you have instructions to call for her?

A: Yes, I did, after I took Mrs. Todd home.

Q: What time did you return?

A: I took Mrs. Todd out shopping and then took her home and then I started back to the Trocadero.

Q: What time did you arrive at the Trocadero the second time?

A: Approximately five minutes to nine.

Q: Did you remain there until the party was over?

A: I did.

Q: Did you take Thelma Todd somewhere from the Trocadero?

A: I took Miss Todd from the Trocadero to the Sidewalk Café.

Q: What time was that?

A: That was approximately three fifteen.

Q: Three fifteen Sunday morning?

A: Yes.

Q: Last Sunday morning. State what happened when you got to the Sidewalk Café at three fifteen Sunday morning.

A: Well, I pulled up to the corner, as usual, because she goes up a side entrance to her door, and I stopped the car right parallel with the door, with the door parallel to the curb, and I got out and I went around and opened the door and she said she didn't think she had left anything.

Q: That is the door on the car?

A: The door on the car, yes, and she said she didn't think she left anything and I looked and I said no, and she said, "Send me the bill, I believe I owe you some money," and I said, "That is all right, don't worry about it," and I then closed the door, as my usual custom and started to accompany her and she said, "No, never mind, not tonight."

Q: Are the steps level with the sidewalk?

A: Yes, on a level with the sidewalk.

Q: All right, go ahead.

A: That was all.

Q: Did you drive away?

A: I turned the car around and drove out onto Roosevelt Highway and stopped, which placed me on the right side of the highway nearest to her walking up the driveway. I stopped and saw her walking off and the last I saw was her turning to go into the apartment.

Q: Do you know whether she attempted to get into her apartment?

A: When she turned the corner I was approximately three hundred feet from her.

Q: When you let her out did you see her attempt to get into the doorway, into the apartment?

A: That is one hundred feet away from the car when I let her out and then one hundred feet back and she has to walk up and back and so I could not see her.

Q: You saw her walking away from her apartment after you got some distance away from her?

A: No, walking towards the apartment, the only way for her to proceed, towards the apartment.

Q: Did you have any intimation that she had any intention of going anywhere except into the apartment?

A: Not a bit.

Q: Did you see her at all after you left?

A: No, sir.

Q: What was her physical condition as to sobriety at the time you left her out?

A: She was quite sober.

Q: Was she talkative?

A: Not a bit.

Q: Was she good natured or talk to you at all?

A: Never spoke to me from the time she got in the car when she said, "We will go home," until she got out.

Q: Was she unsteady at all?

A: Not a bit.

Q: Did she make any other engagement except ask you to send your bill?

A: Not at all.

Q: Was there anyone else around there at the time?

A: Not a soul; had there been, I would have proceeded to the door with her.

Q: The weather was good and the night was clear?

A: Very good; the wind was blowing.

Q: Rather cold?

A: Cold.

Q: Are you able in any way to account for her being found dead in her automobile some distance away?

A: Absolutely none.

Q: From your association with her, have you known her to be morose or when she was inclined to not care to live?

A: No, never. She has always been very genial with me, always talking.

Q: Did she seem hopeful of the future?

A: Very.

Q: Do you know of any enemies she had?

A: I know none, sir.

Q: Or any difficulties she was in at all?

A: Not a bit, none whatsoever.

Q: When you went in to get this camellia for Miss Todd did you pay for that with your own money or did she furnish the money?

A: Miss Todd gave me a dollar bill.

Q: You say you came back to the Trocadero about nine o'clock?

A: About five minutes to nine.

Q: Did you see or hear anything from Miss Todd until she came out ready to go home?

A: No, sir, I did not.

Q: That was when?

A: That was approximately three fifteen.

Q: When she came out to go home, did anyone come out with her?

A: Yes, a gentleman escorted her to the car.

Q: Did you know him?

A: I didn't know him but I can recognize him.

Q: You don't know his name?

A: I don't know his name. I have seen him before.

Q: About what time was it when you arrived at the Sidewalk Café?

A: Well, we drove directly from the Trocadero and at that time in the morning there wasn't much traffic and we drove fairly fast all the way home, which was her custom.

Q: It was her custom to drive fast?

A: We always drive very fast.

Q: Did you have any reason to go fast or like to go fast?

A: She liked to go fast and wanted everybody else to go fast.

Q: What time was it, then, when she got out at the Sidewalk Café?

A: I should say a quarter to four; would not take me over half an hour, possibly, from the Trocadero at that time in the morning.

Q: The last you saw of her she was walking towards her apartment?

A: That is right.

Q: And from where you stopped the car to where she entered the building, about how far was that?

A: There is an incline that goes up to the right opposite my car where I let her out and then she had to turn around and revert right back on an incline and when I left her she had just turned the corner and her back was towards me and I was just moving at the time and looking at her and then I drove away.

Q: Was it your custom to take her where she entered the building or clear up to the apartment?

A: I usually took her clear to the door.

Q: And you suggested doing it that night?

A: I did, yes, sir.

Q: And she said she didn't care for it?

A: Didn't care for it that night.

Mr. Johnson: Did you observe whether she had the key ready to open the door to her apartment?

A: I did not, no.

Q: As I understand you now, when you parked in front of the café down there at her place, were you on the side of the building nearer Santa Monica or away from Santa Monica?

A: Nearest Santa Monica. The entrance is just this side of the cocktail room where she walks through the arch and up the walkway.

Q: You mean the arch at her café?

A: Yes.

Q: Not the big arch across the street?

A: No, not the big arch but there is a small arch where she had to walk through to get over the sidewalk and when I come around the corner and see no one else at the café I usually stop there because I know she goes that way.

Q: When you last saw her with her back towards you, was she on her way to the apartment?

A: Yes, sir.

Q: Was that the door that would be called the side door?

A: That I don't know.

Q: Did you know of a passageway leading up from the café to her apartment?

A: I do not. I am not acquainted with the café.

Q: The door she was headed for was the only door you knew of?

A: Yes, sir.

Q: The door you have taken her to before?

A: Yes, sir.

Q: Did she ever tell you before she didn't want you to escort her to the door?

A: No, never.

Q: In fact, she has always asked you to?

A: Yes, sir.

Q: That was the one occasion she didn't want you to?

A: Yes, sir.

Q: How many times have you taken her home?

A: I should say five times in the last year.

Q: Any times before that?

A: Yes.

Q: Over a period of what time?

A: Over a period of a year or a year and a half. I have it all on record on my books.

Q: You have a record showing what time you got back to your market or drive-in place?

A: Yes.

Q: Is that punched in on a card or something?

A. No, just written down.

Q: You write it in yourself?

A: Yes.

Q: What time did you get back there?

A: Four twenty.

Q: Stop at any place going back?

A: Yes.

Q: Where did you stop?

A: At Armstrong and Schroeder.

Q: Have anything to eat then?

A: Yes, had a bowl of milk.

Q: And back to your place when?

A: Four twenty when I opened the office door.

Q: Did you take anyone else away from the Trocadero at the same time you took Miss Todd?

A: No.

Q: Did you see her with anyone else there when you took her?

A: Only the man that escorted her to the car.

Q: Who was that?

A: That I don't know his name.

Q: That is all I have.

Mr. Emerson: You say there were no lights in the café when you drove up?

A: No, the café was closed.

Q: Could you see the windows of the apartment?

A: No, I could not, not from where I stopped the car. There were no lights in the building on any way.

Q: If there were lights in the apartment you were where you could have seen them?

A: I hardly think so because I am off on the side and the top of the car would obscure my view.

Juror: Mr. Peters, when Miss Todd gave you that dollar bill did you see any other money?

Q: Did you see her take that dollar bill out of her purse?

A: I did not. I went to inquire if they had any camellias in the shop and when I came back I said yes, they have them, and she gave me this dollar.

Q: Have you a picture of that café and the entrance to the apartment?

Mr. Whitehead: None available.

Juror: You say there was someone escorted her to the car?

A: That is right.

Q: You don't know who he was but you could recognize him?

A: Yes.

Q: Is he in this room now?

A: I haven't looked. I haven't seen him.

Coroner Nance: He didn't accompany you further than the car and didn't follow you and wasn't in the neighborhood of her café when you let her out there?

A: No, there wasn't anybody there at all.

Juror: Mr. Peters, on these five occasions that you drove Miss Todd home in the evening, did she always enter her apartment in the same manner?

A: Yes.

Q: Never through the café?

A: Never through the café. When I let her out at the café there was no reason for me staying any longer.

Coroner Nance: I think that is all.

Roland West takes the stand.

Q: State your full name, Mr. West.

A: Roland Van West.

Q: Where do you live, Mr. West?

A: I live at 17520 Robelo Drive and at the Sidewalk Café.

[17520 Revello; a different entrance to the home].

Q: What is your business, profession or occupation, Mr. West?

A: Well, at the present — I was a producer and director.

Q: Of pictures?

A: Of pictures, and now I am a landlord.

Q: Are you also in the café business?

A: No, I am not in the café business, but I will be.

Q: You were acquainted with Thelma Todd, the deceased?

A: Yes, she was one of my best friends, if not my best friend.

Q: You have been associated with her for how long?

A: I have known her for four years. I have been associated with her in business about two years.

Q: Are you interested with her in this café business?

A: Only that I am financially back of the café.

Q: Now, you say that you live at the café?

A: I live at the café.

Q: Now, what are the apartments at the café, the living apartments, how are they arranged?

A: Well, there is one main room and the outside one is always Miss Todd's and that is as large as this court room and it is divided off with pillars and whenever I sleep at the café I went into the back room and there are folding doors which are locked between and outside the lobby is all private and couches out there and places to sleep.

Q: How many entrances to those apartments?

A: The main entrance is through a room which has never been opened and occupied as a ladies' boudoir and going from there is the main room to the main apartment.

Q: One entrance that went though the café?

A: Not through the café, the café is on the left.

Q: Is there any entrance though the café?

A: There is no such entrance through the café.

Q: Were you there last Saturday evening in that apartment?

A: I was there and escorted Miss Todd and her mother to the car.

Q: Did you have any conversation with her before that about what she was intending to do that evening?

A: I knew what she was intending to do and had been invited by her to go along.

Q: Will you please relate in your own way what that conversation was and what happened?

A: Well, she said, "Can you go tonight?" and I said, "Not Saturday night, because we are very busy," and she said she had been very busy buying Christmas presents and was rather tired and I said in a joking manner in front of her mother and everyone else up there and the chauffeur, I said, "Be home by two o'clock," and she said, "I will be there at two five," and every time I said that she would open the door and laugh and I said two o'clock and she said two five.

Q: Was it all in fun or in good spirits?

A: Well, I think you can ask the chauffeur or mother.

Q: But as far as you are concerned?

A: As far as I was concerned, it was laughing, and I said, "Be home at two o'clock," and she said, "Two five," and it was joking, as everyone would notice.

Q: Did you say, "If you are not home at two o'clock I will lock you out?"

A: No, I said, "After two o'clock the outside door is locked."

Q: What did you mean by that?

A: Well, we have heard people around there and I had bars put up on the window.

Q: Prowlers?

A: Prowlers, the manager told me that, and I had bars put on the window especially after she got those messages and she never would go to that door on Saturday night, and she had three keys, one for the main door, one for the main entrance door, the back apartment, and the outside door was a separate key, and she never used that door on Saturday night except once and it was locked and she wanted to get in and she said she rapped and rapped on my window and she was down there and could not get any answer and I had been very tired that night and I thought I dreamed that the pane was broken and looked up and the curtain was moving and she said, "The door is locked," and I said, "Why haven't you got the other keys?" and I got up and got in a bathrobe and let her in a and went back to my place. That was an experience to let her know she could get in that door.

Q: Mr. Peters had stated he left her there at the doorway where he was accustomed to leaving her and the maid said she had a key, described as a Yale key, was that key sufficient to let her into that apartment?

A: That particular key, it wouldn't; I put the lock on that door myself that Saturday night. It is put on every night either by myself or the manager.

Q: How did you expect her to get in under those circumstances?

A: I didn't know until Monday morning that she didn't have her keys. The maid told me she had only one key to the outside door.

Q: She didn't have the other keys. Let's see what they look like.

A: There is the pass key that Miss Todd had to the main door. This is the key to the outside. I thought she had these keys. She had more keys, like to the ladies' boudoir, that I haven't got, and if I had known she didn't have that one key, I would have stayed up and waited for her.

Q: Where did you go?

A: I didn't go anywhere, I was at the café until closing time, which I imagine was about two o'clock, when I received a message from Mr. Grauman.

Q: Where were you when you received the message?

A: I was in the cocktail lounge.

Q: At the café?

A: And one of the cashiers called me and I went into the main dining room and talked to Mr. Grauman.

Q: What was the message?

A: That Miss Todd was talking to the Skouras boys and said she was leaving immediately.

Q: What time was that?

A: That was about five minutes to two, and I talked to Sid and I said, "When are you coming down" and so forth and said nothing else, said bring your mother down and that was about the amount of the message.

Q: Did you remain there at the café then?

A: After I got the message I went upstairs and got the dog and through the side door and took him for his walk and then brought him back and locked that door, bolted it, the other door was not bolted, the main door, the way we always use, and went into my room, closed the apartment, locked it and took the dog in with me and covered him up.

Q: Now, did you hear any sound after that?

A: I fell asleep. I would not know; I imagine about two thirty. I was awakened about three thirty by the dog whining and he never whines — he has a habit of whining when he gets uncovered, and I looked over to see, to cover him up and he was all covered, and I looked at the clock and it was exactly three thirty. Whether that clock was right or not I don't know, it was a table clock, and I called out to see if Miss Todd was home and received no answer, but I heard the water running in the building and figured that there was nobody up, figured she had come in from the outside the regular way and gone to bed, and the dog was quiet, and I went to sleep.

Q: How long did the dog whine?

A: As soon as I waked up he whined.

Q: Didn't bark?

A: No, no bark.

Q: And you didn't get up?

A: No, but when he whines I knew he would know her.

Q: Did it to occur to you there was a double lock on that door?

A: I didn't know she didn't have a key to the main door. I didn't know what keys she had, I never knew that until Monday morning.

Q: When you retired you assumed she had key to get into the apartment?

A: Yes.

Q: How far is this garage from the café, Mr. West?

A: There are two ways to get to the garage, one steps and one a walkway. Miss Todd used to take the steps, she never wanted to walk, but if we ever come home and knew there was no one to take the car up, sometimes she would take the steps and I would take the walk down. The garage was as far as that building [indicating building].

Q: The Federal building?

A: Back of the Old Gold sign.

Q: Would there be any way to get assistance on finding herself locked out, any one around there where she could get assistance that time of the morning?

A: Miss Todd is very considerate and she knew she could arouse me and if she got in at three thirty or four o'clock and knew she didn't have her keys, knowing that she didn't have her key she might have walked up there because I made that remark to her and said "If you don't come home you can always go to your mother's," but she never did, and she could always rouse me very easily.

Q: Had she ever gone to the garage that way?

A: Never.

Q: Ever been locked out that way before?

A: Yes, when she broke the pane of glass to wake me up.

Q: She could have done the same thing that night is she wanted to?

A: You could not keep Miss Todd out of any place if she wanted to get in.

Q: Do you know why she went to the garage?

A: I don't know whether she ever came to the apartment because when you come up these stairs, as the chauffeur will tell you, you walk this far and continue twenty-five feet and go up on the stairs and go on around to the garage or continue on around to this door.

Q: On that particular occasion, or any time recently, had you noticed she was at all moody about anything?

A: Miss Todd was never unhappy; she had everything to be happy about, everything.

Q: Was she making immediate plans for things that were pleasant?

A: Yes, she was finishing a Roach contract and Mr. Schenck told her in front of me that as soon as she was finished he was ready to sign her up; she has her mother she was taking care of, and has her café, and has everything in fact.

Q: Did she appear to be in good health?

A: Fine.

Q: Never complained of any —

A: Yes, she used to have fainting spells.

Q: Fainting?

A: Yes.

Q: She wasn't accustomed to vigorous exercise?

A: She never walked; you could never get her to walk.

Q: It is quite a climb up to that garage for a person who is not accustomed to exercise?

A: It is a climb for anyone.

Q: The mink coat that she was wearing, you knew that?

A: Very well.

Q: It is very heavy?

A: Yes, very heavy.

Q: And if one has been at a dancing party and exercising that way, several hours in the evening and has to climb a hill that would be rather fatiguing for one not used to exercising?

A: The chauffeur told me she was very tired when she got out of the car, he had never seen her that way so she must have been tired before she even started to climb.

Q: Do you know of any reason in the world why this death occurred and the way it did, can you give us any help as to what occurred?

A: Well, the only help, perhaps she had tried that door, didn't want to waken anybody, may have thought she would go to the car, stay there and wait until the porters come in the morning, which is six o'clock, and say she went there at three thirty or four, she may have got chilled, and started the car and may have thought she would drive down to her mother's, started the car and warmed it up and then open the doors — she would never think of little details —

Q: Did you ever discuss the effect of carbon monoxide gas with her?

A: Oh, no.

Q: She knew nothing about it?

A: No, no, knew nothing about it.

Q: You know the car very well, do you?

A: Yes.

Q: Consumed a lot of gas?

A: Yes, you can go from one gas station to the other. It is always empty, always just about that much in it.

Q: If the motor is turned on with the door closed, how long do you suppose it would take to fill that garage with smoke or fumes from the exhaust pipe?

A: Well, I don't know. I tell you, here is a thing that has never been brought out: The treasurer lives above that garage and he closed up that night and he said, "I went home at two thirty and read until three thirty before I went to bed," and then you know the plaster in that garage has been taken off—

Q: What is his name?

A: Mr. Smith. The plaster in that garage has been taken off and you could hear any sound.

Q: Did he tell you he slept there that night?

A: He lives there above the garage and went there about two thirty and said he didn't go to bed until three thirty.

Q: Is Mr. Smith here?

A: No.

Q: He wasn't subpoenaed?

A: No.

Q: Can you get him here this afternoon?

A: You will have to ask Mr. Schafer whether he has anything to do.

Voice: I doubt it very much. I think he went to see his daughter at Santa Ana.

A: I asked him what time he goes up that night, he said, "I went home about two thirty and then read the paper until about three thirty." He said maybe fifteen minutes later, might have been a quarter to four, and all those windows are open and his wife happens to be in Detroit and then he said, "I went to bed," and he said, "I never heard a sound."

Q: Is he deaf?

A: No.

Q: Does he have normal hearing?

A: Yes, he is about seventy years old.

Q: Do you recall that the night was rather windy?

A: Very windy.

Q: Was the wind making a lot of noise that night?

A: Yes, there is a lot of trees around there.

Q: Would that confusion of sound be so that you might not hear a motor?

A: I think you could hear a motor because I think a motor right under you and the fumes would go through there.

Q: Was that a quiet engine?

A: Oh, no, when you start that thing you could hear it all over, twelve cylinders, very loud.

Q: You feel if you were upstairs over that garage in Mr. Smith's apartment, you would hear the car running downstairs?

A: I believe when that car started it would waken anyone because that car when it started would make more noise than breaking a pane of glass.

Coroner Nance: Any questions?

Mr. Johnson: You had a car in the compartment on the other side?

A: On the other side.

Q: What kind of car did you have?

A: Hupmobile coupe.

Q: Eight?

A: Eight cylinders.

Q: Do you own the premises there where that garage is?

A: Yes, I own it — they are in Mrs. West's name.

Q: There is a house in connection with the place there?

A: There is a house in connection with the garages and there is a house above, very big house, tremendous house.

Q: You mean in addition to the apartment over the garage?

A: In addition.

Q: Is that the address you first gave on Robelo Street?

A: Robelo Street, that is the main house.

Q: Is that all a big estate?

A: Yes, all one.

Q: Do you have quarters there in the house, too?

A: In the main room, yes. I used to go in at 17520 Robelo Drive and there was also a garage up there which I could use when I got up there.

Q: Another garage?

A: Another double garage. We would bring our cars to the upper entrance and would go down to the lower entrance and have the chauffeur take the cars down below.

Q: That is the garage where Miss Todd kept her car?

A: That is the garage I used when I was down to the café.

Q: Two different garages?

A: Two different garages, two below and two above.

A: But two garages.

Q: Did anyone occupy the big residence on Robelo?

A: Yes, my brother-in-law and his wife down below; you see this house, the main part is on one level and below that it is, hillside, is where the manager, my brother-in-law, he lived, and down below that, still down, is this garage with another apartment over.

Q: You mean he is the manager of the estate?

A: He is the manager of the café for Miss Todd.

Q: What is his name?

A: Schafer.

Q: That is Mr. Schafer?

A: Yes.

Q: Mr. Schafer, then, takes the pathway to the big house where he lives?

A: He goes around to Robelo Drive.

Q: Does he go the same road that Miss Todd takes to the garage?

A: He can go by that way, I don't know just which way he goes.

Coroner Nance: We will take an adjournment at this time until one thirty. All witnesses will be back at one thirty.

At 1:30 P.M. Harvey Priester was recalled.

Coroner Nance: Mr. Priester, did you get the information as to the correct name?

A: I did.

Q: What is the correct name?

A: Mrs. Thelma Di Cicco.

Q: How do you spell the last name?

A: Capital D, i, capital, C, i, c, c, o. And also there was an error that I made in the final decree of divorce, that was March 2nd, 1935, instead of 1934.

Coroner: All right, thank you.

Roland Van West is recalled.

Mr. Johnson: Mr. West, did you ever know of Miss Todd walking from the café up to the garage?

A: No, I don't remember of her ever walking up there.

Q: That was a distance of three or four hundred feet?

A: Would that building over, that red building, if that is three or four hundred feet, it would probably be that distance.

Coroner Nance: Between three and four hundred feet.

Mr. Johnson: And that was up hill all the way from the café?

A: Yes.

Q: And she was not one addicted to walking?

A: Never.

Q: Didn't care about walking. Your last conversation with Miss Todd was regarding her getting home about two o'clock?

A: That is correct.

Q: And just about two o'clock did you have a telephone message from Mr. Grauman?

A: Just about two o'clock.

Q: Did you know Mr. Grauman, were you acquainted with him?

A: Very well.

Q: Just what was the conversation?

A: He says, "How are you, Roland?" he said, "Thelma wanted me to call you up and tell you she was leaving. We are with the Skouras brothers," and I said, "That is fine" and he said, "She is on her way," and I said, "When are you coming down to see us and bring your mother?" and he said, "I was down one day and you were not around," and he said, "I was down about a week ago and you were not around," and he said he would be down in a few days.

Q: You assumed from his conversation she was about to be on her way back to the café?

A: Yes.

Q: And then you remained until about two thirty or three?

A: No, I went upstairs then and took the dog out, because they were closing up, and I took the dog for a walk.

Q: You say you let the dog out or took him out?

A: I took him out for a walk.

Q: What time did you finally retire?

A: Well, about 2:15 or 2:30.

Q: And did you say then that you went to sleep?

A: I went to sleep, I don't know, in a very short while.

Q: About what time would you say that you probably went to sleep?

A: Well, I would not want to specify a time because I have been specifying times on Saturday and Sunday night and I could not remember just what time it was.

Q: Well, some time probably before three?

A: I know it was before three.

Q: Miss Todd didn't appear and you had heard nothing since Mr. Grauman telephoned?

A: I heard nothing since Mr. Grauman telephoned until I heard the dog whine.

Q: Did you know when you went to bed that the bolt on the door she would enter the place was locked on the inside?

A: I didn't know the door that she would enter the place was locked, I locked the inside door, she had keys to the main door.

Q: She had the keys to that door, didn't she?

A: She had the keys to two doors.

Q: Wasn't that the key to the side door?

A: No.

Q: Wasn't that the customary way for her to come in?

A: No, it was not the customary way for her to come in. She come in the other doors as much as the side door. She never come in that door on Saturday nights, because it was always bolted when the maid left on Saturday night. It might sometimes be bolted at eight o'clock at night, and if the dog was taken out he was taken out of that door, because that is a dead entrance and if the dog was taken out at two o'clock in the morning they would take him out by that door and bolt it again.

Q: When did you bolt that door on Saturday night?

A: I bolted the door when I brought the dog in.

Q: Did you also bolt the other door?

A: No, I didn't bolt the other door.

Q: The side door was not bolted before you bolted it that night?

A: Not that night, to my knowledge; I don't remember it being bolted, it was just a catch you open. You turn it twice, it is a double lock.

Q: Cannot be unlocked from the outside?

A: No, cannot be unlocked from the outside.

Q: What time did you wake up Sunday?

A: I waked up, I heard the dog whining at 3:30, that was what the clock said on the table.

Q: You mean you were awakened and then went to sleep again?

A: I went to sleep—first, I got up and examined the dog to see if he was uncovered, he always whines when he is uncovered, and I covered him up and lay there a few minutes and heard the water running in the other lady's boudoir and figured it was Miss Todd.

Q: What is there in the way of partitions or doorways, if anything, between the bedroom you were occupying and the apartment of Miss Todd?

A: There is double doors with locks on both sides.

Q: Sliding doors?

A: Sliding doors, solid wooden doors.

Q: Were those doors locked that night?

A: These doors were locked.

Q: From your side?

A: From my side.

Q: And is there any way of communicating, that is, talking from the quarters that you are occupying with Miss Todd over in her quarters except by opening those doors?

A: No, only by talking loudly you could hear through those doors if you pull the drapes back.

Q: And when you ascertained it was three thirty in the morning you didn't make any particular inquiry to see if Miss Todd was in yet?

A: No.

Q: Did you have any information or knowledge as to how Miss Todd was going to come back from that party?

A: I knew she had Ernie to drive her.

Q: You expected she would come back the same way she went?

A: That is it.

Q: And what time, then, did you get up, that is, for the day, on Sunday?

A: I think I got up between nine and eleven; I think that was Sunday, nine and eleven.

Q: And you hadn't been awake or up or disturbed for any purpose since 3:30 that morning, is that correct?

A: That is correct.

Q: Then when you got up Sunday morning and dressed, did you find anything there regarding Miss Todd?

A: I went out to see, opened the doors, rapped, went out—

Q: You mean went out where?

A: Out into the big room, like this court room, and saw she wasn't there, and then I went into the lady's boudoir, opened with my pass key and examined the huge couch in there because she had slept on that couch and there was what I considered an impression on that couch, thought she had slept there because nobody else could have done that. Then I figured she had got up and went to her mother's.

Q: Got up and gone to her mother's?

A: Gone to her mother's.

Q: Did you make any investigation as to her clothing or what clothing she had left or taken?

A: No, because she had so many clothes that I could not tell, I don't think anyone could tell.

Q: Didn't keep a check on that?

A: No.

Q: When did you go through the double doors into her particular quarters after you got up that morning? When you got up or later?

A: No, I went right on through. I rapped and then went through.

Q: In other words, you didn't wait until you got your breakfast or anything of that kind, but you started to making some inquiry?

A: That is right, not to making any inquiry then.

Q: I mean some investigation.

A: Yes, I went on through and went into the lady's boudoir and looked in there; picked up the newspaper, got the newspaper out in the lobby and came back and read it.

Q: Upstairs all the time?

A: Oh, yes; I just had a bathrobe on and partially dressed.

Q: Then did you stay upstairs there all day?

A: No, I finished my paper, my newspaper, and then I rung for breakfast because when I didn't have the servants at the house, that is why I always lived down there, we have servants, have everything there, and I had my breakfast after I read the newspaper.

Q: And then you remained up there the rest of the day?

A: No, I remained there between twelve to one o'clock, at the latest, I don't know exactly what time, and then I went downstairs.

Q: All the time up until you went downstairs, about one, you heard nothing whatsoever regarding Miss Todd?

A: No, I thought she had gone to her mother's.

Q: And you didn't make any inquiry about her?

A: Not until I got downstairs.

Q: And then what happened?

A: Well, I asked the boy that takes care of Miss Todd's car which car she had used.

Q: You say you did ask the boy?

A: Yes.

Q: What is his name?

A: Bob.

Q: Is he employed there at the café?

A: Yes, he is employed there at the café. He is one of the bartenders, but he handles Miss Todd's car, which she pays him for herself, keeps it clean and takes care of it. He does not take care of my car.

Q: Where was this boy Bob when you talked to him?

A: Back of the bar.

Q: What did he tell you about the car?

A: Well, he said, "Mr. West," he said, "we are so busy I haven't had time to go up there today."

Q: That was the first time you did speak to him that day about the matter?

A: About the matter or anything else.

Q: You did order your breakfast?

A: Yes, but I didn't speak about Miss Todd.

Q: Is that all you said to him, just asked which car she had taken?

A: Which car she had used.

Q: You meant between what cars?

A: Between the Hupmobile or the Lincoln.

Q: Between whether she had taken her Lincoln or your Hupmobile?

A: That is right.

Q: Then he said he didn't have time to go up, then what happened?

A: Well, I stayed down there for a few moments and I met a Mr. Cooper, and he was getting a car from my wife and I told him to go up to Mr. Smith and get a check, she was to get it on the 3rd day or for Christmas and to get the check from my treasurer.

Q: All right.

A: And then Mr. Cooper stayed around and talked to me an hour or two hours maybe, or an hour and a half, and he said, "You never let me buy you a drink," and I said, "I don't drink much," and he said, "I don't drink much, but let me buy just one." And so he bought me a cocktail and as Mr. Cooper left my mother came, and she is a very old lady, and wanted to go upstairs, always come up to see me and always have to lift her and always stay every Sunday until Sunday night, and she asked for Miss Todd and I told her Miss Todd had gone to her mother's.

Q: Did you get any telephone calls on Sunday?

A: After my mother left I went into my place, I was very tired, nervous for some reason. I don't know why, and I lay there, and about six o'clock the telephone rang and they said Los Angeles is calling and wanted Miss Todd, and I said, "Miss Todd isn't here," and they said, "Who is talking?" and on that phone I always give the same answer, Mr. Schafer, Miss Todd's manager, and they said, "Do you want to talk to the party on the phone? Miss Todd isn't there." They repeated the message, and this man said yes, and he talked to me and told me he was Mr. Skouras, and he said he had made a bet with Thelma to come to dinner and bring the family, eleven of them, and I said, "Miss Todd isn't here, but we are expecting her any minute." And he said, "Just wait a minute, I will call you back." And in about fifteen or twenty minutes later he called again and said that we are all coming, there will be eleven will be there, between seven and seven thirty. I went to the house phone and called Mr. Schafer and told him that Miss Todd had a party, they told me they had met her at the Trocadero, and a party of eleven for dinner, and to see them get the best service for they were Miss Todd's friends and told him they would be there any moment, and the reason I said that "any moment" I knew she went out with an evening dress, I couldn't see any other way she could have any clothes if she went to her mother's, and I think it was about six thirty. A little later, maybe five minutes or ten minutes, there was another call came in and asked who it was, and the information I gave was the usual answer, said it was Mr. Schafer, and he said it was a Mr. Baker, Mr. George Baker and I said, "Miss Todd will be here in a little while," and he said, "Will you deliver a message to call up North Hollywood?" and I said, "What is the message?" and he said, "I am calling for Martha Ford, and Miss Ford wants to have her call her up," and I said, "I will tell her," and then I looked at the time and it was seven o'clock and I thought I would go down on account of the Skouras coming, and because I had met Mr. Skouras through Mr. Schenck and I sat in the cocktail lounge and they came in and one of the Skouras boys introduced me to the other Mr. Skouras and the other people told me about this bet that Miss Todd made and asked me why she is not here, and I said she would be here and wanted to make them know she was interested in their business, which she was, Saturday night, and they said, "Yes, we met her last night," and when they went in to dinner I went in to dinner and they were in another place and came back to my place and talked to me and could not get over Miss Todd not being there. Well, neither could I.

Q: Did you expect Miss Todd was going to be there at this time?

A: Well, I knew the only engagement she had was this cocktail between three and seven, and I knew from the dinner they ordered they could not get out of there before eleven and knew she would positively be there before they left.

Q: Did you communicate with the Hollywood telephone number, did you endeavor to make contact with that telephone number at North Hollywood?

A: No, no.

Q: Did you make any inquiry anywhere regarding the whereabouts of Miss Todd?

A: No, I never did that.

Q: Did you leave the café, I mean, the building there itself, that day at all, Sunday?

A: Never left the building.

Q: Make any further inquiry, of Bob or anyone else, as to the cars in the garage?

A: Not me.

Q: You didn't make any inquiry of anybody?

A: I would not.

Q: Well, you didn't?

A: I didn't.

Q: And you kept your car in there without locking the garage?

A: Kept both cars in there without locking the garage, and the keys in the car.

Q: Then you did remain there at the café Sunday evening, too?

A: Sunday evening, I stayed there until twelve o'clock, Sunday night, and then went to bed, took the dog for a walk and was in bed by twelve o'clock.

Q: And you had heard nothing from Miss Todd, of course?

A: Not a word.

Q: And the guests had come and gone downstairs?

A: Well, those guests left about eleven, I imagine, eleven or twelve o'clock.

Q: Then you slept as usual there Sunday evening after you went to bed, about midnight?

A: No, I didn't sleep.

Q: What did you do?

A: Just lay awake until about five o'clock.

Q: You mean you could not sleep?

A: Could not sleep.

Q: And when you got up, that is, for the day, on Monday, when did you get up?

A: Well, I think I fell asleep around five or six o'clock and I was awakened by the house phone, buzzing very heavily — when I say "heavy," it has never buzzed that way before.

Q: Air of business?

A: Ringing once, twice, three or four, five or six times.

Q: Then what was that?

A: That was from Mr. Smith, he told me the maid had come from the garage and told him there was something terribly wrong with Miss Todd and she says she thinks she is dead.

Q: And did you go up to the garage then?

A: I put on a pair of trousers and shirt and coat and the maid took me up to the garage and when she took me up she missed the road and she was excited, and one of the employees down from the house and he said he thought she was taking me to the doctor because I was white as a sheet; that is what he told me later. Do you want me to go on?

Q: Yes.

A: I came to the garage and rushed in the door and there was Miss Todd lying there. I put my hand onto her face and there was blood and I wiped it off on my handkerchief, drops, and I then sent May to go up, she could not go through the garage, and I said, "Stay in the car and go around and get Mr. Schafer and his wife as quick as you can." And she sent them down and they came down and opened the door from the inside and then I then I told Schafer, I said, "You go get the police and get a doctor." And he jumped in the car and I said, "May, you go down and get the mother." I went in the car — I think the door, I don't know how I got this thought, that the door had been closed, but I found out now, I think the mother told me later, the door was opened in the car and I looked over there and I saw the switch and Mrs. Schafer was over there, and I walked up and down the place and went on the other side and looked to see how much gas was in the tank and it was almost empty, and I know from the position that she was trying to get out of that car, I know that, because otherwise she would not have been turned in the way she did, and the door would not have been open. She was trying to get out of that car.

Q: The door of the car was partly open?

A: It was wide open, not partly open.

Q: Did you talk to Mrs. Whitehead of that?

A: No, I didn't speak to her because I didn't have a chance from that time on. The first opportunity I had about speaking about the door was with her mother that night, and the mother told me, she said, "May said she opened the door," but the mother must have misunderstood her, May must have said she opened the garage door, because I heard her say on the stand this morning that door was open and that is the first time I heard her say the door was open, and I know how positive she was trying to get out of the door.

Q: What condition did you find the ignition?

A: The ignition was on.

Q: Anything else about the car?

A: The only thing, there was a little dust this side of the seat and I looked over and looked down at the gas and there was just about that much gas in the car, I imagine about three or four gallons.

Q: You looked at the gauge on the dash?

A: Looked at the gauge on the dash and I lit a match to see that.

Q: Were there any lights on in the garage?

A: None. The door had been left open, the garage door was open.

Q: I mean as to the lights of the car or in the garage.

A: I could not see that, because the car was turned around and was facing out, because if Miss Todd ever took a car in she never backed a car in.

Q: The car was backed into the garage?

A: Backed in the garage, which she or I never did, because it was quite a trick to back the car into the garage.

Q: Do you know when the car was taken out of there the last time, when it was backed in, I mean, if it was before that Saturday night?

A: That car was taken up there at two o'clock, when we closed, or thereabouts, and backed in by the boy that handled it. He was the only one that would back the car in; I don't know exactly what time, but I imagine about two or two twenty.

Q: Which car are you speaking about?

A: The Lincoln.

Q: You say Bob did that?

A: Yes, my car was facing in.

Q: Are you stating of your own knowledge that Bob did that?

A: I am stating of my own knowledge that Miss Todd never backed the car into the garage.

Q: You haven't talked to Bob, that he backed the car in?

A: No, but I have been told that he did that.

Q: What is his other name?

A: I think it is Bob Anderson.

Q: Is he here today?

A: Yes.

Q: You saw nothing else about the car that attracted your attention?

A: Yes, I opened the back to see if there was a robe in it, because I figured Miss Todd had come up there, she was very considerate, could not open that door and would go up to the car and sit in there, and that was the only cold night we have ever had down at the beach and I was trying to figure out what happened, and I looked for the robe and there was no robe.

Q: Was there a robe that had been carried in the car?

A: There was a very valuable robe, but I found it afterwards; it was in the apartment.

Q: That was approximately what time Monday when you went up to the car?

A: Well, I should say between ten and ten fifteen.

Q: Mr. West, were you engaged to marry Miss Todd?

A: No.

Q: Were you acquainted with her former husband, Mr. Di Cicco?

A: No, I never met him.

Q: Had you ever discussed with her, her relations or her feelings toward him?

A: Well, I have known Miss Todd a good many years; I knew her before she married Mr. Di Cicco; she was a great friend of mine.

Q: My question is, had you ever discussed with her or had she discussed with you her situation with Mr. Di Cicco?

A: No.

Q: Never at all?

A: No, only that she got a divorce from him.

Q: Well, you knew he was around here?

A: Around where?

Q: Living in this vicinity.

A: Oh, yes, I knew about it, but I had never met him.

Q: You didn't know anything about him from her?

A: I knew all about her friends, and I never met Mr. Priester until Monday; he was a very good friend of hers, but I never met him. I knew all about him.

Q: Then you had discussed with her this Mr. Di Cicco?

A: Oh, I talked to her about him, yes; I knew her before she married him, and afterwards.

Q: Do you know of any intention or contemplation she had of remarrying him again?

A: Oh, no.

Q: Did you ever know of anything of that kind?

A: I knew that could not be.

Q: Why couldn't it be?

A: Because I am talking to you the same way.

Q: Well, she and he were friendly, were they not?

A: She was friendly with everyone; she loved everyone; she liked everyone.

Q: Your relations with Miss Todd were more or less intimate, were they not?

A: She was my best friend, one of my best friends, I should say.

Q: Did you have any suggestion from her or otherwise that she might contemplate leaving you and resuming marriage relations or otherwise with her former husband?

A: Leaving me?

Q: Yes.

A: I could not have any such thought.

Q: Nothing like that had ever been suggested?

A: I could not have such thoughts or she would not have such thought; there could not be anything like that. She was my partner, also.

Q: You feel that the car was driven into the garage at some time after you went to bed?

A: The car was taken up — you mean on Saturday night, yes, it was taken up after I went to bed.

Q: Her car?

A: I heard it start.

Q: In other words, before you went to bed, the time Miss Todd left that evening, around eight o'clock, where was her car?

A: In front of the café where she usually left it.

Q: You mean some time after that?

A: No, after I went to bed the car was taken up to the garage.

Q: From in front of the café?

A: Yes. You want to know how I know it was taken up afterwards?

Q: I presume Mr. Anderson told you?

A: No, he didn't tell me at all. You see, around 2:15 all guests had gone and there were only two cars left, one for Mr. Smith's, a little small four cylinder car, and Miss Todd's car, and Bob is a young fellow and he likes to make noise and when he starts that car he makes a noise with it and you can hear all over the place. He told me, "You can start that car without making a sound," he explains it to me, he told me at lunch, "You don't turn the ignition, but start the starter and give it two or three rounds and then turn the switch and it will start up very quietly." He is very young and he likes life, and I heard the car start after I was in bed.

Q. Then the car was in that position in the garage when you saw it up there Monday?

A: When I saw the car in that position it was facing out.

Q: Was that the customary way to put it in there?

A: I often seen it that way, I don't know whether it was customary, and I have seen it put in that way when it was taken down to the Standard station by the boys down there to recheck the battery, because the battery has been run down several times.

Q: Did you find your car, the Hupmobile, in the garage Monday morning?

A: Yes, my car was in there, and facing straight in, the opposite way, and Mr. Schafer took my car to go after the police.

Mr. Johnson: That is all.

Coroner Nance: Any questions, gentlemen of the jury?

Juror: Has Mrs. Todd's mother got a telephone?

A: Yes, she has, but I have never called up Miss Todd's mother in my life.

Q: Were you friendly with Miss Todd's mother?

A: Very, but I have never called up.

Q: What time were you informed of Miss Todd's death?

A: Mr. Smith informed me.

Q: About what time?

A: Well, if I got up there at ten, he notified me at five minutes before ten; if I got up there at 10:15 they notified me at ten minutes past. I put on trousers and shoes and no tie.

Q: It was before half past ten Monday morning?

A: By the clock that was on the dresser it was before half past ten.

Q: Do you know anything about the condition or status of her financial affairs?

A: Yes, I do.

Q: Were they good or bad?

A: Very good.

Q: There wasn't anything bad?

A: No, nothing; and everything is left to her mother.

Q: Mr. West, you made a statement to the effect that you asked this man Bob whose car —

A: Which car?

Q: Which car she took?

A: No, which car Miss Todd used that afternoon.

Q: Which car Miss Todd used that afternoon?

A: That is correct.

Q: And he said the Lincoln.

A: No, he said, "I don't know, I haven't had time to go up."

Q: That is correct. Then it is presumed that your car, the Hupmobile, and the Lincoln were both standing outside?

A: No, both in the garage.

Q: Well, but if you asked the question, "Which car was used —"

A: Yes, sir.

Q: Wouldn't you naturally assume there was one or the other cars to use outside there?

A: She could use both; they were both in the garage. She could use either one she wanted to. I wanted to know which car she used.

Q: I get the point. You presumed she went to her mother's?

A: I presume she went to her mother's.

Coroner Nance: Just one question about that hearing the water in the boudoir some time after you retired.

A: Yes, sir.

Q: About what time was it?

A: That was after the dog whined, and after the dog whined, at three o'clock or three thirty, it was within five minutes after that.

Q: Did it continue to run?

A: No, it shut off. And I asked Mr. Schafer about that when this thing broke out, and he told me it could have been the carbonator that pumps water through the fountain.

Q: There were no leaks that you saw the next day, nothing of that sort?

A: No.

Q: There is a mechanical device that pumps water?

A: By electricity.

Q: And it could have been that?

A: That is what he told me.

Q: And you thought it was the water in Miss Todd's room?

A: Yes.

Juror: You said when you looked in the lady's boudoir there is a sofa in there that had an impression that you assumed had been left by Miss Todd?

A: Yes.

Q: If that is the case, why would you assume she had gone into the garage to sleep there?

A: I didn't assume that at that time. I assumed she went to the garage after I found out what had happened. I assumed this when I formed the impression she had slept there until daylight and then gone to her mother's.

Q: Afterwards, when you found her dead, you assumed she had slept in the car?

A: Then I found out. May told me when she was found dead that she only had the one key. That is the first time I knew she had only the one key, and I said, "Why did you give her the one key?" And she said she had so much in her purse.

Q: What is your opinion about who left the impression on the couch?

A: I thought it was May or Miss Todd at some other time, because no one else ever goes in there except Miss Todd or May.

Q: Then the impression may have been there before?

A: It may have been there before.

Q: Does that combination lock have to have two keys to open it?

A: No, coming in the front you have to have a pass key for the front door, which has the bolt.

Q: There is a flight of stairs on the outside up to that door?

A: No, those stairs are heavily carpeted, and no one ever goes up there except the help to clean up.

Q: They are on the outside?

A: No, they are on the inside.

Q: No outside stairs?

A: Yes, the steps that she comes in. The other is not the same. This is the only entrance that the building owns to the upstairs. The chauffeur brought her up to the main stairs, but she turned and went back from where he was and went around and come up this other stairs because she had only this one key.

Q: There are more than two rooms over the café?

A: Oh, yes, there are twenty rooms over the café, roughly.

Q: Are those sleeping quarters?

A: No, there are only two sleeping quarters — three sleeping quarters.

Q: Was it customary to leave these cars with the ignition keys in them and the doors unlocked?

A: We did, always left them.

Q: The cars might have been taken off by anyone that come along?

A: Anybody could have taken them.

Mr. Johnson: Mr. West, had you ever had any dispute with Miss Todd about her returning late from some function?

A: Well, it is a matter whether you could call it a dispute if I said to her to be home at two o'clock because your asset is your beauty, and her mother said, "Yes, four hours and a half is long enough," and Miss Todd said, "I will be home at 2:05," and she laughs and I laugh back, and say, "Two," and I told her, "Any time you have to stay out later than two go to your mother's, that will save you that half hour of sleep, you must have your rest because your work depends on you," and she was the most beautiful woman in the world, and that was my advice.

Q: Did you ever have any argument with her at any time about her staying out late?

A: I never had an argument with Miss Todd at any time in my life.

Q: Did you at any time reprimand her because she had stayed out later than certain hours that you thought was proper?

A: Not reprimand; I would talk to her. You could not reprimand Miss Todd. Miss Todd had everything a man has, she had money and had plenty of everything; you could not reprimand Miss Todd; she was an individual with the strength of any man in this room.

Q: She wasn't entirely financially independent of your cooperation?

A: Yes, she was entirely independent of me financially in every way.

Q: I understood you to say you were backing her financially.

A: Maybe I said it wrong. I put up the building, I own the building, I put the equipment in that building, and the reason I put the equipment in, it cost so much I would not ask anybody to put equipment in to carry out my ideas, but Miss Todd carried out my ideas and run the place according to my ideas, but she had the finest and best equipment of any place in this city.

Q: Your answer, I take it then, is there never was any real disagreement or dispute between you as to her hours?

A: Never between Miss Todd and I.

Q: Had you ever told her if she didn't get home before two o'clock you would lock her out?

A: Yes. I didn't say I would lock her out, I said I would lock the doors, always the outside doors. And I told you the door was locked one Saturday night and she wanted to get in and she got in from that outside door.

Q: That is when she broke the window pane?

A: That is it. She could get in better than you and I if she wanted to get in, and nobody could make her do anything she didn't want to do. You could advise her and talk to her and she would judge what is right.

Q: Did you have the Hupmobile car out of there at all on Sunday?

A: No.

Q: When did you have it out of there before Sunday?

A: Did I use it myself or Miss Todd use it?

Q: When was your Hupmobile out of the garage before Sunday that you know of?

A: I couldn't tell you. The only time I had used the Hupmobile or any car, I don't think I have used the car any time for a month, I very seldom drive, I don't go to the city or go to town or don't go anywhere.

Q: Do you know of your Hupmobile being out of there Saturday?

A: No, it could not have been used there Sunday, because no one can use the Hupmobile except Miss Todd, and she used the Lincoln to go down town to have the tooth put in.

Q: You don't know how many days before it had been the Hupmobile had been taken out?

A: Miss Todd may have used it a week before.

Q: But you didn't have it out Saturday or Sunday or Monday?

A: No, no.

Q: And no one else that you know of?

A: No, no one else has any right to.

Coroner Nance: That is all.

Robert John Anderson was the next to be queried by Coroner Nance.

Q: State your full name, please.

A: Robert John Anderson.

Q: Where do you live?

A: 1217 Sixth Street, Santa Monica.

Q: What is your business, profession or occupation?

A: I am a bartender at the Sidewalk Café.

Q: Employed by Thelma Todd?

A: Yes.

Q: Now, it has been stated that you took care of her car?

A: That is true.

Q: Did you place the car in the garage for the last time Saturday night?

A: I placed the car in the garage for the last time Saturday night.

Q: At what time?

A: At approximately two twenty.

Q: That was Sunday morning?

A: Sunday morning.

Q: Where was Miss Todd at that time?

A: I don't know — yes, I do — she had gone with Ernie Peters in his car.

Q: You don't know where she went?

A: No.

Q. You put the car in the garage. How did you put it in? Head it in or back it in?

A: Always, always back in so it will be easy for her to take the car out in the morning.

Q: What was her habit?

A: Drive the car directly in, headed in.

Q: Do you know anything about the circumstances of her death? Were you there to see her in the car?

A: No.

Q: Where were you at the time her body was discovered in the car?

A: Home, asleep.

Q: Did you have any intimation she might meet with that sort of accident?

A: I haven't the slightest idea. It was as great a shock to me as anyone else.

Q: Had you ever talked to her about gas fumes from an automobile?

A: No, I never had occasion to discuss it with her at all.

Q: Did you know about carbon monoxide at all?

A: Only what the police told me when they were out there.

Q: Did you know anything about it before?

A: Oh, yes.

Q: Ever discuss with her how dangerous it is to run a motor in a closed garage?

A: No, never mentioned it.

Q: How much carbon monoxide gas do you suppose would be expelled by that car?

A: I was told by one of the detectives that one half of one percent of carbon monoxide gas would kill and the amount there was accumulated would depend on the ventilation.

Q: There would not be any ventilation if the doors were closed?

A: Well, there was some space around the doors.

Q: That car was a great gas burner?

A: Yes.

Q: Does it have a large exhaust pipe?

A: Yes.

Q: Can you give us any clue at all, do you know anything about it other that what you have told us?

A: None whatsoever.

Mr. Johnson: Mr. Anderson, when you put the car in the garage that early Sunday morning, were the doors then shut, the doors of the garage?

A: My procedure was to pick the car up in front of the café, drive it to the garage, back it in, push the ignition button off, and lock the ignition and leave the key in there and then get out and close the doors and the reason I turn the lock in the ignition was to be absolutely certain the ignition would not be on and run the battery down. One time someone else took the car up and the ignition was left on and could not start the car the next day and after that I took the key off, to be positive.

Q: Did you do that this Sunday morning?

A: Always did.

Q: Did you shut the doors of the garage?

A: Yes.

Q: Were they locked?

A: No, never locked.

Q: What ventilation other than the space around the doors is there when the doors are closed?

A: Facing the garage from the outside, on the left door, there would be a space of perhaps an inch at the top and perhaps as much at the bottom. Other than that there would be very little.

Q: No other windows or ventilating spaces?

A: No, there is a pane there but not open; nothing that I know of.

Juror: Are the walls of this garage painted with whitewash?

A: Just the natural cement.

Q: When you backed the car in how close was the exhaust pipe from the wall?

A: It is a matter of probably a foot and a half because it backed directly up against some old tires and I believe a suitcase.

Q: There was something in between the car and the wall?

A: Yes.

Q: However, with your knowledge of that particular automobile, if it had been running any length of time, the exhaust would make a black mark on anything it would hit in the rear?

A: That would all probably depend on the speed that the motor was operating.

Mr. Johnson: Mr. Anderson, did you ever see Miss Todd start that car?

A: Yes, I have seen her start the car many times in the morning.

Q: Did she have any difficulty in getting it started?

A: No, she was an expert driver.

Q: She was a good driver. Did the car make quite a considerable racket when it was being started?

A: Well, of course, I have heard what was said in the courtroom but I was under the impression there wasn't a great deal of noise connected with it. It was a large motor and operated quietly when it was idling. The only time it would make a loud noise would be if you opened the motor wide when you started. It was very easy to start the car without any noise, starts very quietly, start it up and idle it, start it right away.

Coroner Nance: I understand it was quite windy that night?

A: Yes, sir.

Q: Do you believe if Mr. Smith was living overhead he would be able to sleep and the motor going downstairs and not hear the motor?

A: Well, under the circumstances, Miss Todd might have come in and was extra careful to start the car and not waken him and with the wind blowing around and trees around there, it is possible he would not have heard it. He is an elderly man and tired after a day's work and probably slept very sound.

Coroner Nance: I think that is all.

Robert Cooper comes forward.

Coroner Nance: State your full name.

A: Robert H. Cooper.

Q: Where do you live?

A: 1135 South Cardiff.

Q: And what is your business or occupation?

A: Automobile salesman.

Q: Were you acquainted with Thelma Todd, the deceased?

A: Yes.

Q: Do you have some knowledge —

A: I wanted to explain to you how I happened to be up here. I was doing my duties yesterday morning, trying to sell an automobile to the Homicide Squad, and happened to see a bunch of men over at the desk and I said, "What is going on?" and they said, "There is a bunch of reporters trying to solve the Thelma Todd mystery," and I said, "That is too bad, I happen to know Miss Todd," and I was subpoenaed to appear.

Q: What do you know about this Lincoln car?

A: Well, I know this, that her car had what we call a "blow-by" in the motor, that is an excess amount of oil being used.

Q: Oil or gas?

A: Oil. That means your cylinder walls are out of round.

Q: Would that have a tendency to generate more carbon monoxide?

A: No, it has nothing to do with that.

Q: Was that a condition that obtained if the motor was not going?

A: Well, the fact you drive a motor, the more "blow-by" and that is the more oil you use and of course, the condition with the idling, the "blow-by" would be forced out.

Q: Are you acquainted with the operation of carbon monoxide gas?

A: No, just what I have heard.

Q: Do you know whether this condition that obtained in that automobile might have contributed to her death by carbon monoxide poison?

A: Well, a car of that size, the exhaust pipe on the end is very large and spreads out, if I am not mistaken, a quite large pipe, and the end comes flat and must be at least three or four inches and that car being a twelve cylinder car would throw off very, very much gas.

Q: Did you see anything in that light you have described which would have contributed to her death?

A: No, the oil has nothing to do with the carbon monoxide death.

Q: You know nothing about what she did Saturday night or Sunday morning or what she did or what was found Monday morning?

A: No.

Coroner Nance: I have nothing further.

Mr. Johnson: Mr. Cooper, do you know anything about the mechanics of the thing, as to whether a car of that type with what you call the "blow-by" trouble, would do if the engine was running idly?

A: Yes, the "blow-by" condition in an automobile, it will run smoother than if you are running it otherwise. If you are idling it, that "blow-by" oil is up on the top of the cylinders and as the compression comes down it forces oil wherever it will go, throws it over the breather and sometimes comes through the floor boards of the car and also gets up in the plugs and there is a possibility in a car that has "blow-by" when you idle you will stop because the plugs are being fouled.

Q: In other words, if it is running idle it will stop or the engine die quicker than in another car without the trouble?

A: Oh, yes, because if the "blow-by" is bad enough the oil will get around the plugs, right where the plug fits in.

Q: Coroner Nance: That is all.

Mrs. Wallace Ford then came forward.

Coroner Nance: State your full name, please.

A: Mrs. Wallace Ford.

Q: Where do you reside?

A: 3528 Laurel Canyon Boulevard.

Q: Are you a housewife?

A: Yes.

Q: Mrs. Ford, you are acquainted with Thelma Todd, the deceased?

A: Very well.

Q: When did you last see her alive?

A: About three or four weeks ago, downtown, I think it was near the Broadway, Hollywood.

Q: Have you talked to her since that time?

A: I haven't seen her since that time; I talked to her on Sunday.

Q: This last Sunday?

A: This last Sunday.

Q: About what time did you talk to her?

A: I should judge it was about 4:30; I have been told it was ten minutes after four, just as I came in here.

Q: Will you state the circumstances?

A: Yes. I had told Miss Todd's maid — it might be her mother, or her maid, she didn't say when she talked — about a party, and gave her the address and the time and the phone number, so they would all be set.

Q: You had invited her to a party at your home?

A: I had invited her to a party at my home that was to be at seven on Sunday night.

Q: What did she say in this conversation?

A: Well, the first thing she said was, "Hello, this is Thelma," and I said, "When are you kids coming out," and I thought it was Velma, another girl friend, and she said, "Who do you think this is?" and I said, "Velma," and she said, "No, it is Hot Toddy, Toddy."

Q: Was that a nickname?

A: That was a joke between Thelma and myself.

Q: All right, go ahead.

A: I don't know the exact sequence, whether one thing was first or the other, but the substance of the conversation was, she said, "What are you wearing at the party?" and I said, "I am wearing hostess pajamas," and she said she had on an evening gown and I said, "Whatever you are wearing will be all right," and she said she was bringing someone with her and I asked if it was a girlfriend and she said no, and I asked who it was and she wouldn't tell me, she said, "I want to have the fun of seeing your face when I come through the door." And she mentioned something about going through a short cut or something like that and I said I didn't know much about that part of the country and I said if you know all about it, all right, there is such a place, and she said, "I will take a chance," and she spoke of the address being wrong, and she said, "I will be there in half an hour," and I said, "All the lights will be on and you can't miss the house because there will be plenty of cars there," and she said, "O K."

Q: She didn't arrive?

A: No.

Q: Did you try to reach her?

A: My brother-in-law, George Baker, called her about the party.

Q: About what time did he try to talk to her?

A: I don't know exactly what time he called, I haven't asked him.

Q: Sometime after or during the party?

A: Oh, no, it must have been in the neighborhood of 6:30 or 7:00, because she called me about between 4:15 and 4:30. He began to worry in about forty-five minutes.

Q: Did you receive a message from her on the day before?

A: I wasn't at home. She called the maid.

Q: And accepted your invitation?

A: Yes, her maid was talking to my maid.

Q: You didn't talk to her personally?

A: No, the maid made that mistake.

Q: You were not at the party at the Trocadero?

A: No.

Q: You know what Miss Todd was wearing? Of course, you know about her wardrobe?

A: No, I would not know what she had or what she didn't have.

Q: Do you suppose she would probably wear the same gown to your party Sunday afternoon as she wore Saturday night?

A: Well, it would have depended on the dress; cocktail dresses and dinner dresses are sometimes very much alike.

Q: Did you suppose if she had purchased a camellia on Saturday evening on her way to the Trocadero, she would have that same faded camellia on her dress Sunday afternoon at four o'clock?

A: I should not think so. I think it would be mussed up.

Q: And you think if she was found dead in the same gown with that camellia, you still feel she talked to you Sunday afternoon?

A: I know she talked to me Sunday afternoon.

Q: Do you think you could be mistaken?

A: Oh, no, I could not be.

Q: Well, you believe you could not be?

A: Well, as sure as any human being could be.

Mr. Johnson: I didn't perhaps get it myself, when did you first invite Miss Todd to your party?

A: I can't be sure of that date, whether it was Wednesday or Thursday or Friday.

Q: Of last week?

A: Yes.

Q: And did you invite her over the telephone?

A: Yes, I invited everyone by phone.

Q: You telephoned to her and told her about the party at your place?

A: I didn't speak to Thelma, I spoke to the maid, although I thought it was either the maid or the mother, I didn't make any distinction.

Q: You knew you were not talking to her?

A: I knew I was not talking to Thelma, certainly.

Q: Did you get a reply back to the conversation?

A: No, there was no reply back because the maid said she had gone Christmas shopping, and you know what that is, and she said, "I will put the message where she can't possibly avoid seeing it."

Q: Then what did you do next?

A: The next I heard was about 4:30 or 5:00 on Saturday, and my maid told me Miss Todd had called — and had told her she was bringing a guest, and asked the maid, I guess, what I was wearing, because she said I was wearing hostess pajamas — I think I may be a little confused or mixed up what the maid said.

Q: Then from what you were advised Saturday and Sunday, you would infer Miss Todd had accepted your invitation and would be present?

A: No, the acceptance was given to my maid on Saturday afternoon.

Q: And on Sunday you knew that?

A: Certainly.

Q: And knew it Saturday evening?

A: Certainly, I knew it by 5:00 or 5:30.

Q: Did she call you the next day?

A: She called me.

Q: I see. In other words, you didn't sit down and call the phone number of Miss Todd?

A: No, I called them on whatever day I gave the invitations.

Q: I mean on Sunday.

A: Oh, no.

Q: Your phone rang and someone told you Miss Todd wanted to speak to you?

A: No, my phone rang and I answered it myself.

Q: She said, "This is Miss Todd?"

A: No, she said, "This is Thelma," and I thought she said, "Velma," another girl I knew, and she said, "Who do you think this is?" and she said, "Toddy, Hot Toddy," and then the conversation from there.

Q: That nickname "Toddy" or "Hot Toddy," wasn't anything secret between you and Thelma?

A: Oh, no, I think perhaps I started it.

Q: But her friends in general called her that?

A: I think probably they do.

Q: How many times have you talked to Miss Todd, or whom you understood to be Miss Todd over the phone?

A: I don't know how many times, never kept account, would not have been any reason.

Q: Could you tell how many times in the past month?

A: Not once in the past month until Sunday afternoon.

Q: How many times would you say in the last few months?

A: Perhaps twice or three times.

Q: You have a good many conversations over the phone, I suppose?

A: Not a great many but enough so I could not be mistaken.

Q: You have a pretty complete telephone service in your home?

A: Well, there are three extensions.

Q: Three extensions and the main phone?

A: No, two besides the main phone.

Q: And you sometimes talk over one phone and sometimes another one in your home?

A: It all depends, yes.

Q: Wherever you happen to be?

A: Wherever I happen to be or what the circumstances are.

Q: What time did this conversation occur on Sunday?

A: I should judge between 4:15 and 4:30. I should say closer to 4:30.

Q: And the party began at what time?

A: At three. Thelma mentioned had the party started and I said you bet it had.

Q: Had many guests arrived yet?

A: Not very many, perhaps twelve, divided between the living room and the various places outside.

Q: Twelve or so had arrived?

A: Yes.

Q: And before they were all there there were several hundred?

A: Oh, yes, there was a great many.

Q: How many? Three or four hundred?

A: More than that. I couldn't estimate. The caterers know how many, I don't.

Mr. Johnson: That is all.

Coroner Nance: That is all, thank you.

Abram R. Kallmeyer was summoned next.

Coroner Nance: State your full name, please.

A: A.R. Kallmeyer.

Q: You are a police officer, city of Los Angeles, are you not?

A: I am.

Q: Since the death of Thelma Todd, the subject of this inquiry, have you made some check of the telephone calls from the Todd home to the Ford home?

A: I have.

Q: Will you state the results of your investigation of that matter?

A: The first call that I investigated was a call at eleven twenty-seven, from Miss Todd's apartment to the Ford home, eleven twenty-seven Saturday morning, the fourteenth. There were no calls from either her apartment or the café phoned on Sunday, or previous to the finding of the body, after the call on Saturday morning.

Q: Coroner Nance: Any questions, gentlemen?

Mr. Johnson: In other words, there wasn't a call from Mrs. Ford's telephone to Miss Todd's place, or a phone call from Miss Todd's place to Mrs. Ford's place, on Sunday?

A: I wouldn't know of a call from Mrs. Ford to Miss Todd. My investigation was only from the Santa Monica exchange, which was Miss Todd's phone numbers. The phone numbers coming from North Hollywood to Santa Monica, I have no check.

Q: No phone calls from the Santa Monica phones of Miss Todd's to Mrs. Ford?

A: Only on Saturday, at eleven twenty-seven.

Q: Do you have the phone numbers, or number of Miss Todd?

A: Yes, I have.

Q: What is that?

A: The one in her apartment is Santa Monica 21988. The one in the café is 27302.

Q: Both toll calls from there, are they?

A: The 27302 is a pay phone. The other is a private phone in Miss Todd's apartment.

Q: I say, there is a toll call —

A: Toll call from 21988 on Saturday morning. That is the only call at anytime Saturday; none at all Sunday.

Q: You have the telephone number of Mrs. Ford?

A: North Hollywood 0132.

Mr. Johnson: That is all.

Coroner Nance: That is all.

Rudolph Schafer was the next to testify.

Q: State your full name, Mr. Schafer.

A: Rudolph Henry William Schafer.

Q: Where do you reside?

A: 17520 Ravello [Revello] Drive.

Q: What is your business, profession or occupation?

A: I manage Miss Todd's café.

Q: You have been associated with her for some time?

A: I opened the café for her.

Q: Did you see her last Saturday night?

A: No sir, I didn't. I had been away on my vacation for a week. I came home Saturday night I didn't stop at the café, went right home.

Q: With respect to the café, how far is your home?

A: About six blocks.

Q: When did you last see her alive?

A: About eight days ago, before I went on my vacation.

Q: Then when did you see her next?

A: When I saw her in the car the first thing the next morning.

Q: On what morning?

A: Monday morning.

Q: About what time?

A: It was between ten and fifteen minutes after eleven o'clock, exactly.

Q: How did you happen to see her there?

A: Well, I was in bed, and Miss Whitehead, Miss Todd's maid, came up, and my wife happened to be getting up before I did, and Miss Whitehead told my wife that Miss Todd was in her car dead, so I immediately got up and dressed and went down.

Q: What was the position of her body in the car when you first saw her there; where she was in reference to the steering wheel, for instance?

A: Well, she was sitting on the right hand side of the car, and her body had slumped over to the left of the steering wheel.

Q: I will show you a photograph. Do you recognize this picture?

A: Yes, sir.

Q: Was that the position she was in when you saw her there?

A: Well, I was standing on the other side of the car when I first saw her, but that is the position she was in.

Q: Did you remain there until the officers came?

A: No, I went and called the officers.

Q: You called the officers?

A: Yes, sir.

Q: Where did you have to go to call the officers?

A: I thought I would go into West Los Angeles, in order to eliminate any publicity right away until we found out what it was all about. While I was going in Santa Monica — took Mrs. West's car out of the garage, it was sitting next to Miss Todd's car — I stopped in the printing shop up there, and went into their private office and made the call, called West Los Angeles.

Q: Did you observe her clothing, or anything about her personal appearance, other than the fact that she was slumped over and appeared to be dead?

A: Well, I naturally —

Q: Did you think she was dead; did you examine her to see whether she was or not?

A: I merely just touched her head, and she was cold.

Q: Did you notice some blood?

A: Yes, there was blood over her mouth and run down on the seat right where her head was.

Q: Did you notice any evidence that she had been ill at the stomach?

A: Well, I tell you, at that time it was hard to determine, because the blood was all over her mouth. Any other evidence, there was none.

Q: Did you accompany the police back to the garage?

A: Yes, sir. I waited at the café for them and took them up to the garage.

Q: And you were present there while they made their investigation?

A: Yes.

Q: What was the position of the automobile, with reference to being headed in or out?

A: It was backed in the garage.

Q: It was facing out?

A: Yes, sir.

Q: Do you know anything else that would help us to solve the mystery of how she happened to be found there dead?

A: Nothing.

Q: Do you know of any reason of her taking her own life?

A: I don't think that is possible.

Q: Do you know of any enemies she had?

A: No. She was planning on opening our upstairs part of our business down there, and she was just as occupied in it and making plans for the future, just like the rest of us naturally.

Coroner Nance: All right. Mr. Johnson?

Mr. Johnson: Mr. Schafer, are you related to Mr. West in some way?

A: By marriage.

Q: In what way?

A: My wife and Mr. West's wife are sisters.

Q: You say you were away all week until Saturday evening?

A: Yes, sir.

Q: And did you talk to anybody at the café when you got back Saturday evening?

A: No sir, I didn't stop at the café, because there was a crowd there, and I was unshaven, and I had been away just resting, and I went right on home.

Mr. Johnson: I have no other questions.

Coroner Nance: Gentlemen, have you any questions? That is all.

Bruce F. Clark, being first duly sworn testified as follows:

Coroner Nance: State your full name, please, captain.

A: Bruce F. Clark.

Q: You are a police officer, City of Los Angeles, are you not?

A: Yes, sir.

Q: And you made an investigation of the death of the deceased in this case?

A: I have.

Q: Were you the first detective on this case?

A: I was.

Q: Please state to the jury what you found there; just give them the picture as you got it first hand.

A: I received a call to go to the Sidewalk Café, to meet Mr. Schafer, and I met him there shortly before twelve o'clock, on Monday, the sixteenth, and followed him uphill. It is only a short distance by air line, but the road stretches back and forth about three times, and we both stopped and parked our cars in front of the garage, and entered, and we found the deceased lying in the front seat of the car. She appeared to have been sitting about the middle of the seat, with her head over toward the driver's door, and her feet were on the floor, near the pedals, underneath the pedals, which would indicate that she had been sitting behind the wheel.

Q: I will show you this picture marked Exhibit G. Is that the position in which you found her?

A: Yes, that is. I opened the door, which I found closed, and took this from the right side of the car. It shows her lying with her head against the left door.

Q: Did you also have some photographs made?

A: Yes, I did.

Q: This photograph of the garage, Exhibit A, you had had that made?

A: Yes, that picture shows the two garage doors. I have one more picture here if you would like to see it, showing the car. The front of the car as it is in the garage.

Coroner Nance: Mr. Johnson, did you see this picture?

Mr. Johnson: I think I have seen it, yes, Mr. Nance.

Coroner Nance: Shows the car facing outward?

A: Yes, sir.

Q: And the door was open there? All right, continue, Mr. Clark.

A: I felt of the deceased, and saw that rigor mortis had set in; she was cold, and apparently had been dead sometime. There was a small amount of blood at the nostrils, and at her mouth, and I noticed that she was wearing a wedding ring, square cut diamond ring, and some ring on her right hand, but I didn't notice what it was.

Q: Diamond ring and the wedding ring were on her left hand?

A: Yes.

Q: And the bluish stone ring was on her right hand?

A: Yes. The purse was laying beside her, open, as the photograph shows, and she had some pins in her hair, some kind of brilliants of some kind, and she was wearing a very faded flower. I could not tell what kind it was, but it was on her buttonier, and held with a pin, kind of a round pin, tied like a bow, and the flower was very wilted, looked like it had been dead for at least a couple of days.

Q: What was the color of the dress she had on?

A: It was kind of a dark blue, with a kind of brilliant sheen appearance.

Q: Sort of metal weave over the blue?

A: Yes.

Q: Gave it a sheen appearance?

A: Yes. She was wearing a heavy fur coat, kind of thin hose and sandals.

Q: To match her dress?

A: Yes, bluish sandals. I examined the bottom of her shoes, and they had the appearance, or gave the indication she had walked quite some distance on cement. The bottom of her soles were scuffed up quite a little bit, and there was no blanket in the car. Of course, we notified the Homicide Squad immediately, and were instructed by Captain Wallace, of the Homicide Squad, not to disturb anything until he arrived, and we waited for the other officers to come.

Q: After you received instructions, did you call the funeral director to take charge of the remains?

A: Yes.

Q: At Santa Monica?

A: Yes, and I called the radio car to find the nearest phone to talk to your office, to see if that would be O.K., to have the body removed as soon as possible, to Todd & Leslie, or whatever place you might suggest.

Q: And the body was removed from the car by the funeral director, and taken to Todd & Leslie's in Santa Monica?

A: Yes.

Q: And nothing was touched or disturbed in any respect?

A: Nothing, we left everything as it was. I looked in the purse for a note of any kind, and I found no notes, no writing and no papers. I turned that over to the Homicide Squad.

Q: What did you find in the purse?

A: About four handkerchiefs of hers, and a cigarette case and lipstick, and white coin purse, containing nothing but a key, a Yale key.

Q: Just one key?

A: Just one key.

Q: You took that to your station?

A: I left that in the purse and turned it over to the Homicide Squad when the body was transferred from Todd & Leslie to your office.

Q: The doors of this garage were open when you got there, weren't they?

A: Yes, one door was open, showing the front of the car as the photograph shows.

Q: Did you notice the switchboard in this car?

A: I looked casually; I noticed the ignition was on, and I looked and saw there was gas in the car. The officers drained out a gallon of gas, and there was still enough gas in the car to drive it down to the road and back, so there must have been some gas in the car.

Q: How large an area is that garage?

A: Twenty by twenty-four.

Q: Are there any openings at all except the doors?

A: Just openings around the door, about an inch, at the bottom, and I believe about two inches at the top, of the sliding doors.

Q: Are the sliding doors difficult to operate?

A: Well, just about an average door.

Q: Miss Todd wasn't a very strong appearing woman.

A: A child could open them. She could have done it easily.

Q: Did they make very much noise in operation?

A: No, sir.

Q: One could open those doors and close them without disturbing anybody around?

A: Easily. I opened them and closed them myself and there was very little noise. A child could have done it.

Q: When the doors were closed there was very little opening around the edges for ventilation?

A: That's right.

Q: Did you try that motor yourself to see how much gas it gave off when the motor was running?

A: No, I didn't start the motor. My men drove the motor down the hill and back and it threw off quite a bit of fumes.

Q: At that time and while you have been on this investigation, have you talked with the maid, Miss Whitehead?

A: I did.

Q: And Mr. Peters, the driver?

A: I didn't talk to Mr. Peters.

Q: Did you talk to Mr. West?

A: I did.

Q: And Mr. Schafer?

A: I did.

Q: Did you talk to Mr. Anderson?

A: No.

Q: Well, did Miss Whitehead and Mr. West and Mr. Schafer tell you the same thing when you first talked to them as they told to this jury today?

A: Yes, sir.

Q: Have they altered their story in any way at all?

A: Not in any way. I haven't found any discrepancies.

Q: From your investigation, does it appear that this death could have been caused by some homicidal agency?

A: I have been unable to find anything indicating murder or suicide. I believe it was accidental purely. I haven't been able to find anything that would indicate anything out of line at all.

Mr. Johnson: Captain, did you state about what time you arrived at the car where the body was?

A: I didn't look at my watch when I arrived, but I left the station about twenty minutes to twelve, approximately.

Q: What time would you say you got there?

A: I don't think it took me over ten or fifteen minutes.

Q: Something like just before twelve you got there at the place where the body was found?

A: That's right.

Q: Did you find any indications that she had had a struggle with anybody there at the time she died?

A: No, sir. I examined the body carefully and looked at it and I could see nothing to indicate any type of struggle. For instance, on the back of the seat of the car there was a lot of dust and I touched it with my hand and it left a distinct mark, and if there had been any type of a struggle, I think they would have been compelled to disturb that dust.

Q: You found no weapons of any kind in the car or around there?

A: No.

Q: And her clothing did not indicate that she had been attacked in any way?

A: It did not. There was nothing torn or nothing disturbed.

Q: Nothing to indicate any robbery?

A: No.

Q: Her jewels and all were there?

A: That's right.

Q: That is, there were some there, at least?

A: At least all that she was supposed to have.

Q: And no note?

A: I looked carefully for evidence of any message and I found nothing, and there were absolutely no marks on her body in any way; just a speck of blood on her nose and on her mouth.

Q: Did you see the little purse that she was carrying with her there?

A: I did.

Q: Did you make any examination of it?

A: Yes.

Q: Did you determine what was in it?

A: Well, I just stated the articles that were in there. There was a cigarette case, a small coin purse containing this Yale key, lipstick, and I think about four handkerchiefs.

Q: One Yale key?

A: One key, and there was nothing else in that little coin purse except a single key.

Mr. Johnson: That is all.

Coroner Nance: That is all.

Dr. Wagner took the stand.

Coroner Nance: Your name is A.F. Wagner?

A: Yes sir.

Q: Autopsy surgeon for Los Angeles County. Doctor Wagner, have you made an examination, a post-mortem examination, of the body of Thelma Todd, the subject of this enquiry?

A: I did.

Q: Have you made this report?

A: I did.

Q: Please state to the jury your findings as to the cause of death in this case.

Dr. Wagner read the report: "I performed an autopsy on Thelma Todd December 17, 1935, at the Los Angeles County Coroner's Mortuary and found the exterior of the body presenting a red discoloration and on examination of the blood, I found it to contain seventy-five to eighty percent of carbon monoxide saturation. On opening the head, the brain showed a scarlet red color of the blood and the organs of the body were similarly colored. On opening the body I found all the vital organs normal, that is, free from organic disease. There were no marks of violence anywhere upon or within the body. A superficial contusion on the lower lip did not penetrate beneath the skin. The cause of death was carbon monoxide poisoning."

Coroner Nance: Mr. Johnson, would you like to ask the doctor some questions?

Mr. Johnson: Doctor, would you kindly give some little explanation of the manner in which this poison works upon the human system and how it affects a person?

A: The poison is drawn in, a little bit of it, by each breath, and it accumulates in the body until the blood is practically saturated. In the living body, however, it never becomes saturated, that is, it don't take up as much carbon monoxide gas as it would outside of the body, so that when we have the blood saturated, we call that one hundred percent. When we test the blood for the amount of carbon monoxide it has in it after we do an autopsy, that is expressed in terms of that one hundred percent. If we get above seventy percent, that is fatal. Some can take in more before they die. It goes as high as eighty and ninety percent, but that is about the limit. It is merely, it takes some time, too, out in a garage where the motor would be running and generating some of the carbon monoxide, it would take a few hours before there would be sufficient carbon monoxide accumulate in the blood to cause death.

Q: As I understand it, that sort of poisoning is only effective when it is breathed into the system.

A: Absolutely.

Q: In other words, if your body were exposed and you would have fresh air to breathe, it wouldn't hurt you?

A: Had enough air to breathe —

Q: If your head was outdoors, sticking out of a door, and your body was inside a room, it wouldn't affect you, would it?

A: Your head sticking outdoors, you probably wouldn't get any carbon monoxide, but if you have carbon monoxide outdoors you can get it as quickly as in a room. People have died when the doors of the garage were open. It makes no difference, when the carbon monoxide appears in the air, you have to breathe it in.

Q: You have to breathe it into your system before it injures you?

A: Yes, but the room doesn't have to be closed up.

Q: When your system does become sufficiently saturated, that is, your blood stream does become sufficiently saturated, so that it is affected, how is it demonstrated? What is the affect upon a person?

A: The effect is the same as asphyxiation. It is an internal or blood asphyxiation. Besides keeping the oxygen out, it also keeps the oxygen from the tissues. The carbon monoxide takes the place of the oxygen in the hemoglobin of the blood, so the final result is an asphyxiation. Carbon monoxide [dioxide] retains its hold upon the hemoglobin, which the carbon monoxide does not do. That is given off the minute it comes in contact with water.

Q: And it would be somewhat the same manner as breathing in any kind of obnoxious gases?

A: Yes, it would have that effect.

Q: When it becomes sufficiently strong and the blood stream is sufficiently saturated to be injurious, what is the first organ or organs that would be affected?

A: Well, it is the blood that is affected and of course, not being able to carry oxygen to the brain that is really affected. All the tissues of the body, however, are filled with blood and therefore become red, which it holds against the free agents that we use for the test.

Coroner Nance: Is that why the victims become drowsy first?

A: The victims become drowsy first and yet there is quite a difference in the experience of some people who have had this carbon monoxide. We had one man in my experience here that has had such a large amount of carbon monoxide that he was practically at death's door and a companion of his did die and that man, after he survived, told us there was no premonition or anything occurring; that he felt all right until he finally sank down, so it must act differently on different people. Unfortunately, those who have so much carbon monoxide in their blood usually die and they can't tell us how they felt, but those who survive, of course, have had various percentages. A person can have as high as forty or fifty percent of saturation of blood with carbon monoxide and may not know it and may get rid of it after he gets where there is no carbon monoxide.

Q: Is there any way you can tell us what goes on in the blood stream when the blood stream becomes saturated? Does it just choke off the heart?

A: No, it chokes off the oxygen.

Q: It has its first effect upon the lungs?

A: No, it has an effect upon the brain centers that control the vital processes and they become starved of oxygen and that is the end of it and it is, after all, an internal asphyxiation.

Q: Is there any hemorrhage indicated in this trouble?

A: No, that isn't an essential feature of the poisoning at all, but most cases, especially after they have been dead any length of time, most bodies, for that matter the mucous membrane congests and they bubble up a little swath that is bloodstained, and these cases do the same thing, but when these cases do it, that swath is usually fairly red, inasmuch as that blood has come out before they were fully saturated with the gas. The blood that was seen around this case had no significance other than just the poisoning of the gas. It did not mean that it was due to any bruise or any fall or any violence at all.

Q: You do not refer to that as a hemorrhage, about the nose and mouth?

A: That is the only hemorrhage that I saw.

Mr. Johnson: In other words, you mean there wasn't any indication of any contusion or injury and it might, but would not necessarily follow, from this carbon monoxide poisoning?

A: No. It would occur without carbon monoxide poisoning. The blood coagulates less rapidly in carbon monoxide poisoning than it does in other conditions. Inside the lip and beneath there was no bruise at all. It must have been due to the lip coming in contact with a hard object.

Q: Do you know anything about her organs or about the condition of her body in any way, that would have any bearing upon her death, except carbon monoxide?

A: That is all.

Q: And you can determine that by analyzing the blood, independently of where she was found or what you were told about it?

A: Absolutely. It don't make any difference where they are, if they have it in the blood, that can be shown and be seen.

Mr. Johnson: That is all.

Mr. Emerson: Did you see the body soon enough to form an opinion as to how long [after] the party [she] had been dead?

A: Well, that is a hard question to answer because of the fact so many elements enter into it. When the weather is quite cold, as it was on that night, I remember it was, a body won't show the post-mortem effects you would get in the day time or in the warmer weather. She had been dead some time, some hours. As close as I think anybody can get at it, at least by observation of the body itself, she could have been dead anywhere from twelve to thirty hours. My best judgment was it was about eighteen hours.

Coroner Nance: That is, from the gross appearance of her body?

A: Yes.

Q: Regardless of any history?

A: Yes, independent entirely of a history.

Mr. Emerson: That would be twelve to thirty hours from the time you made your examination?

A: Yes.

Q: And just when was it you made the examination, doctor?

A: That examination was made on the evening, I guess, around, half past four to five o'clock?

Q: Coroner Nance: Last Monday evening?

A: Yes, somewhere around five o'clock, probably a little before. I have that on my sheets.

Q: Doctor, you were present when the body of Thelma Todd first came in the morgue here, were you not?

A: Yes.

Q: You saw her before she was disrobed?

A: Yes, sir.

Q: Saw her when she was first brought in by the representative of the Todd and Leslie Mortuary?

A: Yes.

Q: Had the covering been taken off?

A: Yes.

Q: You saw that she was fully clothed, even to the fur coat?

A: Yes.

Q: Did you observe the clothing she had on?

A: I did not.

Q: There was a bright red discoloration around the skin that was exposed?

A: Yes.

Q: After she was disrobed you made your examination as quickly as possible?

A: I did.

Q: And you made this test for carbon monoxide, you had that made, and made one for yourself independently?

A: I did.

Q: Subsequently you examined the organs and found them to be normal?

A: They were perfectly normal.

Q: You found the characteristic coloring throughout the organs of carbon monoxide, did you not?

A: I did.

Q: There was no degeneration of the organs in any way and you also examined the stomach?

A: I did.

Q: You found a considerable quantity of food in the stomach, did you not?

A: I did.

Q: About how much?

A: About half full.

Q: There is a history. It has been the testimony today she was on a dinner party on Saturday night that lasted until eleven thirty or midnight, before it was finished, and she went to her home. Is it possible anyone could have held that food in that condition or would it have been digested by that time? How long does it take a meal to digest?

A: Normally it takes six to seven hours for a stomach to empty itself. Digestion doesn't all take place in the normal stomach. Under perfectly healthy conditions, it is supposed to empty itself in six hours but most people are not quite normal, and it usually takes a little longer, and also if there are other circumstances, like excitement, ingestion of alcoholic liquors, and previous delayed digestion from some cause, not necessarily any organic cause, but just indigestion, then it takes considerably longer.

Q: On this point as to the probability as to how long she had been dead at the time she was found, taking into consideration the stomach full of food, undigested, is it possible she could have died sometime around five or six o'clock on Sunday morning? Is it likely she might have?

A: It is possible.

Q: In view of the fact that she wore the same clothing as she had worn Saturday night, is it likely she had gone somewhere else after she had taken the meal at the Trocadero and had a full stomach, with a meal she had gotten later? Assuming Mrs. Ford has said she would be at her party and would be there, is it possible she could have been going somewhere and had another meal after that, when all her personal appearance was the same as it had been the night before?

A: Taking all those facts into consideration, with the condition of the body, showing it had been dead, I figure, at least a minimum time of twelve hours, probably a little longer, I think she died some time Sunday morning, anywhere from five to six o'clock on to eight o'clock. In the first place, it was testified here that rigor mortis had set in when she was found. If that is the case, rigor mortis usually, with glaring exceptions, may vary greatly, rigor mortis usually is supposed to set in in six hours; in a case of carbon monoxide that is delayed some, so she must have been dead quite some time for rigor mortis to develop the way it did. My best judgment, from all the facts taken into consideration, she died some time Sunday morning.

Coroner Nance: Gentlemen of the jury, have you any questions to ask the doctor?

Juror: Was there an analysis made of her brain?

A: For alcohol, yes, only.

Q: What did it show?

A: It did contain alcohol, rather a moderate amount of alcohol, not enough to consider it as a cause of death at all, but probably enough to have caused her to be what we call somewhat under the influence of liquor, and yet not greatly. In fact, a person that is accustomed to taking alcohol frequently, every day, would probably hardly be affected by the amount that we found. The amount that we found, however, is not necessarily an amount that might have been used the night before, because alcohol oxidizes very quickly in the system. As long as anybody breathes, they oxidize that alcohol, and there is always a little more than we can find at death.

Q: What percentage did that show?

A: I showed thirteen one hundredths percent. The maximum amount that the brain can take up is six tenths or sixty one hundredths, and this is thirteen one hundredths percent.

Q: What would represent an intoxicated condition?

A: Well, somewhere in between there. Some people could get intoxicated at thirteen one hundredths percent. Those who are unaccustomed to alcoholic liquor, we hardly call them intoxicated until they get up twenty-five one hundredths percent. Then you have to have a normal condition, not regarding exceptional cases, and some people die at thirty-five one hundredths percent. There is another thing that enters there. It depends entirely when the alcohol is taken. Some might have been consumed in the afternoon of that day and some during the evening and some during the meal, during the time passed at the café, and some of the earlier alcohol might all have been gone.

Q: I was interested if there was enough to make her drowsy?

A: It is quite possible, yes, sir.

Coroner Nance: Have you anything further, gentlemen?

Mr. Johnson: Nothing, Mr. Nance, unless it could be established a little farther that she had on the same clothing.

Coroner Nance: We will take care of that by another witness. Dr. Wagner, you did not examine the clothing, I believe?

A: No.

Russel Monroe was called to the stand.

Q: State your full name, please.

A: Russel Monroe.

Q: Where do you live?

A: Los Angeles.

Q: And you are a deputy coroner, Los Angeles County, are you not?

A: Yes, sir.

Q: Mr. Monroe, you assisted in receiving the body of Thelma Todd at the morgue here?

A: Yes.

Q: On Monday afternoon about —

A: Three forty-five.

Q: And you assisted in checking over her personal effects?

A: Yes.

Q: Will you describe the clothing she had on at that time and what the personal effects were?

A: Yes, sir. She had on a fur coat with a cape attached to it, a bluish silver and gold dress, light colored stockings, blue sandals.

Q: What jewelry was she wearing?

A: She had on a white wedding ring set with diamonds, a white wrist watch set with diamonds, an engagement ring, a large white stone, and a blue stone in a white ring.

Q: Did she have a brooch?

A: Yes, there were three pieces of custom jewelry, two attached to the collar and I believe the third attached to the dress, that had a pink gardenia on it.

Q: What was the condition of that flower?

A: It was quite withered as though it had been on, oh, a number of hours, I would not guess how many, I know nothing about the condition of flowers, how quickly they wither.

Q: That was on what part of her dress?

A: I believe it was on the left side of her dress.

Q: Near the shoulder?

A: Yes.

Coroner Nance: All right.

Mr. Johnson: It wasn't a gardenia. It was pink, was it not?

A: It was pink.

Coroner Nance: Of course, it is a well known fact that gardenias are always white. It had a pinkish appearance, as though very faded and aged?

A: Yes.

Q: The sort of flower a woman would wear if she were going to a party? Was it in a condition she would wear to a party, when you saw it?

A: When I saw it, it was much too withered for that.

Coroner Nance: For the purpose of the record may I correct your statement. You said three pieces of custom jewelry. You did not observe that brooch very carefully?

A: It appeared to be custom jewelry to me.

Coroner Nance: Well, I thought so too, when I first saw it, but it was a very handsome brooch but that is immaterial. You turned that property in to the record room there and made an inventory and reported it all?

A: I did.

Coroner Nance: I think that is all, gentlemen.

Mr. Johnson: That is all.

Coroner Nance: Mr. Priester, you need not come to the stand. You have heard this list of property. Did you receive that property for the mother?

Voice: Yes, sir.

Coroner Nance: As stated here, and was it the same property and the same clothing as has been described by Mr. Monroe?

Voice: Yes, sir, it is.

Coroner Nance: All right. Gentlemen, have you any further questions or any witness you would like to call again? All right, that is all the evidence we have for you at this time, gentlemen. Please retire to the jury room with the clerk and deliberate upon the evidence that has been presented to you and determine how, when and where the deceased came to her death and whether her death was homicidal, suicidal, accidental or natural. Now, please retire with the clerk.

The Coroner's Jury rendered the following verdict: "From the evidence submitted to the jury the death of the deceased appears to have been accidental but we recommend further investigation to be made in this case, by the proper authorities."

EIGHT

The Long Goodbye

After the six men of the coroner's jury recommended further investigation, District Attorney Buron Fitts ordered a grand jury probe, declaring, "So far, nothing conclusive has been brought forward to show that this may have been a murder, but it is obvious that the whole picture is far from clear."[1] Newspapers repeated speculation that Thelma may have been poisoned or drugged and then placed in the garage to die by asphyxiation. A chemist was instructed to conduct a complete analysis of Thelma's vital organs, including a search for any traces of poison. "The grand jury will look for murder," said Deputy District Attorney George Johnson: "If murder was not possible, perhaps even probable, the grand jury would not be interested. The question of murder must be answered."[2]

A telegram was sent to Pat De Cicco in Smithtown, Long Island: "Your hasty departure from Los Angeles raises questions in connection with Miss Todd's death which only your presence here can explain."[3] De Cicco received a subpoena requiring him to testify. The press further fueled Thelma's "drive to death" with a theory she had been alive the day after the party.

Reporters stated that a drugstore clerk said she had seen Thelma enter a telephone booth around 4:00 P.M. Sunday afternoon, but a police check of all calls made from the drugstore that day failed to disclose a call made to Martha Ford's residence. More sensational was the story of Patricia D'Este, a numerologist who recalled a party in honor of Jack Warner, an evening when Thelma was a special guest. The party was hosted by A. Ronald Button at his home at 2263 Maravilla Drive. D'Este had been brought to the event by director William Dieterle and his wife. D'Este was sitting on the porch when a smiling Thelma approached. The seer remarked that Thelma had a brilliant future, after hard work to attain her position. D'Este was surprised by Thelma's reply: "I don't want any future. I don't want to live anymore." For a moment, the numerologist thought she was joking, but Thelma didn't smile. D'Este told Thelma her future was bright. But she responded she didn't care, then asked, "Will I marry this year?"

"You will if that is your desire," said the reader.

"Will I be happy if I marry?" asked Thelma.

And who was the man? Thelma declined to give a name. And what about a trip to Europe? D'Este said that she would take a trip, but she did not know the destination, since

R.H.W. Schafer, Roland West, Robert Anderson, and Mae Whitehead at the grand jury investigation (UCLA Charles E. Young Research Library, Department of Special Collections, Los Angeles Times Photographic Archive. Copyright © Regents of the University of California, UCLA Library).

she could only base her readings on the "vibration you happen to be in." After further conversation, the women shook hands, Thelma smiled and said to send her a bill.[4]

Then Jewel Carmen made headlines. She claimed she had seen Thelma alive Sunday evening. When first questioned by police, the day after Thelma's body was found, Carmen said she had not seen Thelma for several weeks. Two days later, she summoned police to her home with a different story. She had seen Thelma in the Lincoln Phaeton on Hollywood Boulevard Sunday evening. Thelma was in the company of a "dark complexioned man, probably a foreigner."[5] Jewel admitted that she had been evasive when first questioned by detectives but declined to explain why.

Jewel now told a different story to investigators. She was questioned in the presence of Mr. and Mrs. Roman Romero and Sonia Ardell, her close friends who worked in the film industry. Police quoted Jewel's new explanation: "I first learned of Miss Todd's death when Mrs. Ardell telephoned me at 3:30 P.M., Monday. I was so dumbfounded, I couldn't speak, but told her it was impossible because I had seen Thelma with a dark complexioned man in her car on Hollywood Boulevard at 11:15 Sunday night."

However, when Jewel was interviewed by Louella Parsons, she made no mention of sighting Thelma and insisted that she and Roland were not estranged. But the columnist knew the truth: "The staunchest friend that Roland West will ever have is his blonde wife, Jewel Carmen, who has been living away from him for nearly a year."[6] Jewel told Parsons she had been in ill health for the last year and lived quietly with friends. "As far as I know, Miss Todd was only associated with Roland in a business way and I think that now she is gone it is wicked for anyone to make any other suggestions.... Naturally, I am upset now over this horrible tragedy, especially since I am sure that Thelma died of a heart attack. You had only to see the puffy shadows under her eyes to know that she suffered from a heart affliction."

Jewel now recounted how she had seen Thelma. Returning from the San Fernando Valley, after a trip with friends to Mount Wilson, she recognized Thelma on Hollywood Boulevard: "I stepped on the gas and drew as close as possible. Sitting next to the driver was Miss Todd. I recognized her from a smart hat I knew she wore and from her golden curls."[7] Added Carmen: "Driving the Phaeton was a foreign-looking man. He wore a salt and pepper hat and overcoat to match. He was of dark complexion, but before I could get a good look at him they turned South on Vine Street." But investigators discounted Jewel's sensational story. When Thelma was found, she wore no hat, and had not worn a hat to the Trocadero party. Most significant, it was unlikely the Lincoln had been driven after Robert Anderson backed it in the garage. Jewel insisted she was not mistaken but was unsure if Thelma wore a hat. Jewel said she occasionally met with Thelma and Roland to discuss business. Jewel said she lived with Mother Grey, her spiritual adviser. Jewel now admitted the estrangement. "I have always been very fond of Miss Todd. I last saw her about two months ago and I never objected to Miss Todd keeping her car in my garage down at the beach. Thelma knew that she was welcome and she also knew that she could have used my house there at any time ... I haven't talked to Mr. West for a long, long time. I entertain only the friendliest feelings for him and I believe he thinks the same of me. I have always known of Mr. West's feelings for Miss Todd. We have discussed the matter many times. Mr. West was a gentleman at all times. We have been separated for more than two years yet there has been no talk of a divorce. I understand Mr. West, and Mr. West understands me."[8]

Jewel gave another interview. She did not believe Thelma could have died from carbon monoxide since "the place is entirely too well ventilated."[9] Jewel's comments created more sensationalism. Just when the Coroner's Inquest brought plausible answers, a firestorm ignited; coupled with Martha Ford's story of a conversation with Thelma on Sunday afternoon, Jewel's curious tale gave the impression that Thelma was alive on Sunday night. Most sensational, Jewel confirmed that Roland and Thelma were more than close friends; it was now evident to all that they had been lovers and shared adjoining apartments above the café. Reporters realized that Roland had not been totally forthcoming concerning his relationship with Thelma.

Reporters located Charles H. Smith, the occupant of the room above the garage. Smith said he had closed the café at 2:00 A.M. He arrived at his apartment just as Bob Anderson was backing the Lincoln in the garage. Smith offered to drive Anderson back to the café, but the bartender said he would walk. Smith was certain he had fallen asleep around 3:30 A.M., after reading in bed: "I know because I have two clocks ... I was awake again three or four hours later, and got a cup of hot water, a regular habit of mine. It soothes my nerves."[10] Smith slept until 11:30 A.M. the next morning. "During all that time in the apartment I heard no unusual sound or anything to make me think anything out of the ordinary had happened. The wind was blowing the trees noisily and the surf was pounding with unusual violence which might possibly have prevented me from hearing anything."

The day after the inquest, Thelma was prepared for the final farewell. Alice decided there would be two services, one for Thelma's fans and the other for close friends. Reporters from the city newspapers arrived in the pre-dawn hours. By 7:30 A.M. thousands stood outside Pierce Brothers Mortuary at 720 W. Washington Boulevard. They waited patiently beneath an overcast sky to pay their last respects. Before dawn, Percy Westmore had gone to the mortuary at the request of Alice Todd. Thelma lay in an orchid casket dressed in blue satin pajamas, a Christmas gift from her friend Dorothy Callahan. Twin lamps cast subdued light on her body. Westmore applied makeup and curled the blonde hair. As a final touch, he placed a necklace and earrings on Thelma.

Patsy Kelly and Dorothy Callahan knelt before the casket and prayed in silence. Before the doors were opened, floral arrangements were brought to the chapel. There were white roses from Alice; a wreath of lilies to *Alison* from Roland West; red roses and gardenias from Harvey Priester. Joe Schenck sent pink roses; Chaplin sent lilies. On a table was a silver-framed portrait of Thelma, selected by Harvey Priester. The doors opened and mourners filed past Thelma. An attendant arranged pink camellias in the casket, fresh flowers sent by Alice. Thelma's loyal fans bade farewell until 1:00 P.M., when the doors were closed; 3,000 visitors had passed through the chapel. The casket was transported to Forest Lawn cemetery in Glendale.

The private service was held in the Wee Kirk o' the Heather at 3:30 P.M. The stone church had been the site of many celebrity funerals, including those of Will Rogers and Marie Dressler. Hundreds of spectators lined the cemetery road. Alice Todd arrived with Roland West and Mae Whitehead. There was no mistaking the message conveyed by Alice. The sinister theories about murder pointed to West, hinted journalists. But Alice chose Roland as her honored escort. Alice knew how much her daughter had loved him. After the shock of Thelma's death, Alice regained her strength and composure. Before the service began, she gave her first formal statement to reporters: "Even as she came first in my life, so I was first in hers, that I know…. People who say they saw her or talked to her must be mistaken. Certainly she would never let a whole day pass without communicating with me." Alice said Thelma's death was an accident: "The circumstances were typical of her. That she turned on the motor of her car in order to keep warm, without thinking of the danger of monoxide fumes, is more than possible. Thelma was impetuous. She was careless in little things. She was not mechanical-minded. Often she would have some little trouble with a car, and not have the least idea of what the difficulty was. Much as she might have heard of carbon monoxide poisoning, I am sure she might have been heedless of the danger on the spur of the moment. It was so characteristic of her to be that way."

Alice clarified stories of heart trouble. Thelma had enjoyed good health in recent years, but "about four years ago, after a tonsil operation, a doctor told us she had a heart murmur, at that time she suffered a few fainting spells, but she had not been troubled in that way for several years. She did not like to walk because she had injured her ankle once while skiing … but she could outwalk most anybody when she wanted to … I know Thelma was considerate. If she returned home at an hour approaching morning, like 4:00 A.M., and found the door locked, she might decide not to rouse anybody. That would be just like her to wait until daylight, knowing that it was only a matter of two of three hours until someone would let her in. She never worried about time anyway, that was also typical of her … the loneliness of the walk would not frighten her because she had no fear, none whatsoever…."[11] News reports gave detailed accounts of the celebrities and friends who came to pay their

***In death she sleeps in serene loveliness**, December 19, 1935 (by permission of Hearst Communications, Inc., Hearst Newspaper Division).*

last respects. The flower-scented chapel was packed with the famous. Dvorak's *New World Symphony* swelled on the organ, played by Irene Robinson, Thelma's friend. Alice Todd sat beside Roland West. Among those in attendance were Stan Laurel, Oliver Hardy, Hal Roach, ZaSu Pitts, Patsy Kelly, Sid Grauman, Joe Schenck, Ivan Lebedeff, George Stone, Lois Wilson, Minna Gombel, Wallace and Martha Ford, Charley Chase, Sally Eilers, the Lupino family, Ray Hays, A. Ronald Button, and Catherine Hunter.

The Reverend Harold L. Proppe eulogized Thelma: "She was one of the most genuine persons alive. To know her was to love her. She was the same woman at all times. She never forgot her acquaintances. I have lost a great personal friend, and the industry a great actress."[12] He paused. "Your years of life were like a lovely song, whose sweet singing we no longer hear. For those who know you there is no dread of age. Death is no conqueror; you merely smiled as you greeted another friend." Tears streamed down the face of Patsy Kelly, noted reporters. The preacher's voice was filled with emotion, and he also wept: "In the church we called her Thelma, she wanted it that way. She was genuine. She was real. She loved little children and of such is the kingdom of heaven. She has departed this life for a newer and more beautiful existence. Her spirit will help guide us through the meandering paths of life that yet remain for those of us here whose hearts are heavy as we look for the last time upon the blessed face of this most gracious of little ladies. Amen!"[13] The music of Handel's *Messiah* broke forth. Alice sobbed when the casket was closed and taken to the crematorium. Alice had personally asked Jack Luden, Thelma's classmate from the Paramount School, to be with her daughter at the very end. After the shiny limousines departed, the body of Thelma Todd was consigned to the flames. Reporters observed the wisps of smoke that curled from the crematorium chimney. The ashes were sealed in a brass urn. While the service had been conducted in Los Angeles, family and friends gathered on Bowdoin Street in Lawrence for an hour of silence and prayer. Although she was physically gone, Thelma remained a subject of interest for reporters and fans throughout the nation. The investigation continued.

On the fifth floor of the Hall of Justice, eighteen grand jurors assembled. The witness testimony was secret, but nothing prevented those summoned from talking to the press. Reporters lined the hallway, shouting questions at witnesses when they entered or exited the chamber. Actress Margaret Lindsay, clutching white gloves, swept through the hall. Lindsay testified for 30 minutes, then disappointed reporters by ignoring their questions. Roland and Jewel sat near the entrance of the courtroom. Jewel wore sunglasses and a dark beret. She was accompanied by a physician who said his patient was on the verge of a nervous collapse. For days Jewel had remained secluded in her apartment at 317 South Ardmore. Jewel asked a friend to make a statement for her. Jewel now admitted her mistake in believing she had seen Thelma and a dark, handsome man: "Miss Carmen thought at the time it was Thelma, but she knows now she was mistaken. The police were wrong in quoting her as having said she followed the car."[14] Jewel's physician asked that she be allowed to testify as soon as possible. Reporters hovered around her, asking questions, but she had few words. "I am not feeling very well," she said.[15]

Foreman George Rochester led the probe into speculation that Thelma had been murdered. Newspaper reports had reached a frenzied peak: Was she the victim of the most fiendishly clever plot ever conceived in a slayer's twisted brain? The sly innuendo reminded the curious that Roland West had directed "mystery films" with diabolical plots and characters. Reporters searched for anything that would incriminate him. The grand jury found a witness who stoked the flames. "Sensational Disclosures At Todd Inquiry" trumpeted the *Los Angeles Examiner*.[16] The witness was seventeen-year-old Ida Lupino. She told reporters about a conversation that had supposedly electrified the jurors: "During my party at the Trocadero the night of December 14, Thelma and I slipped off by ourselves for a moment. She said to me, rather coyly, 'How's your love life?' 'Oh,' I replied, 'I haven't any just now.'" Replied Thelma: "'I'm in the middle of the most marvelous romance I've ever had, with a man from San Francisco who is just too good for words. He's a businessman. You know what gentlemen the San Franciscans are.' 'Is that so? Surely you don't have to go all the way up to San Francisco?' 'Oh, yes I do,' said Thelma."[17]

Ida felt Thelma was happy that night because she was "so terribly in love." Stanley Lupino had overheard his daughter's conversation with Thelma, which took place in the cocktail lounge in the early evening, before dinner. Stanley corroborated the conversation but maintained, "it was said in a hasty joking way."[18] Despite Stanley's clarification, the "mystery man from San Francisco" made news throughout the country, along with more press speculation. Was the businessman the guest Thelma wanted to bring to Martha Ford's party? Did he poison Thelma? Was Roland West jealous? Investigators began questioning Thelma's friends about her personal life. As reporters scrambled to find the alleged lover, police witnesses demolished Martha Ford's story of the Sunday afternoon telephone conversation. Behind barred doors, Ford had repeated her story. She again insisted she spoke to Thelma: "This is Thelma, Toddy, your Hot Toddy."[19] But Mae Whitehead refuted the claim: "I never heard her use such a nick-name, either 'Hot Toddy' or 'Toddy,' but I do know she objected to its use."[20] Other friends also verified Thelma's dis-like of "Hot Toddy."

A trio of investigators conducted tests to determine how fast carbon mon-oxide could have overcome Thelma. Investigator Frank Cavett, detective Joe Whitehead, and police chemist Ray Pinkert recreated the death scene. White-head got behind the steering wheel of the Lincoln and Pinkert shut the garage door. As the motor idled, Joe Whitehead looked at his stopwatch. Only a minute and a half later, coughing, with watery eyes, Whitehead banged on the garage door. The team estimated that Thelma would have been overcome by fumes within two or three minutes. Ray Pinkert went upstairs to Smith's apartment. When the Lincoln ran at idling speed, nothing could be heard. It was deter-mined that the motor, running normally, still could not be heard in the area where Smith had been sleeping. When the motor raced at fifty to sixty miles per hour, only a light sound was heard in the bedroom. Robert Anderson demon-

Jewel Carmen at the Coroner's Inquest (UCLA Charles E. Young Research Library, Department of Special Collections, Los Angeles Times Photographic Archive. Copyright © Regents of the University of California, UCLA Library.)

strated how he had parked the car. Exhaust marks on the rear garage wall were examined by the trio. They concluded the Lincoln had not been moved after Anderson parked it.

The grand jury listened to a parade of witnesses. Sid Grauman complained about being summoned, since he had only stopped at the Trocadero for an omelet. Grauman had tele-phoned Roland as a courtesy. On Christmas Eve, a story claimed that Thelma's body had undisclosed injuries; specifically, that her neck appeared swollen and torn on the inside. Dr. Wagner came forward and emphatically denied to reporters that such swelling was seen in his autopsy. More confusion resulted when Helen Ainsworth spoke with a reporter. She was an employee of Robert Galer's fashionable dress salon in Beverly Hills. Ainsworth had lunched with Thelma on the Tuesday before the Trocadero party. According to press reports Thelma told her: "There is going to be a change in my life this week. I'm pulling out of there, if you know what I mean. I probably will be broke as a result of the change, so I'm paying my dressmaker's bill while I have the money.... But you shouldn't feel that way," responded Ainsworth. "Why not? I don't know why I'm living the way things are. There must be a change." Added Thelma: "You know, Helen, I've been going to a psychoanalyst in Hollywood and he's psychoanalyzed me pretty thoroughly. He looked into my eyes and said that I had been under the stress of weird dreams and mysteries and worries. He told me I hadn't, for the last year or so, made the right use of my brilliant brain and my youth and beauty. And, my dear, he hit the nail precisely on the head."[21] Ainsworth's testimony was interpreted in press accounts as evidence she was "pulling out" of the Sidewalk Café, indicating a split with Roland West.

When Pat De Cicco stepped off the airplane, court officers placed him in "technical custody." De Cicco was furious. "What the hell is the matter with you guys," he fumed.[22] "I wired the district attorney I'd be here, didn't I?" While in New York, De Cicco had railed against the investigation. Grand jury members were also grumbling to reporters about a waste of taxpayers' money; thus far, no evidence of murder had surfaced.

The day after his return, reporters crowded around De Cicco as he strode down the fifth floor corridor. Although speculation of foul play centered on Roland West, Thelma's ex-mate was close behind. Reporters were curious about his odd invitation to the party, social rudeness, and temper. Could he have harmed her? West sat calmly in a dark corner of the witness room, his overcoat in his lap, as the brash De Cicco entered the court chamber. The eyes of the two men met for an instance, noted reporters, but there was no warm recognition. De Cicco shared his testimony with the newshounds. "She had few close friends," De Cicco had told the jurors. "Miss Todd had a lot of acquaintances but not many friends in whom she could confide her troubles, if she had any. I saw her only about five times in the last two years, after we divorced. Roland West was the last man in her life, according to what I heard. I can't imagine her committing suicide. She had plenty of money, probably about $200,000. There was no possibility of reconciliation between us, and I had made no overtures on that line. We were just good friends."[23] De Cicco said that, although he had not seen his ex-wife often, he did represent her during the previous year, negotiating contracts with Hal Roach, RKO, and British producers. His work earned her $90,000. As for his appearance at the Trocadero party, he maintained he was "only kidding" when he accepted Ida Lupino's invitation.[24] "I went to the Trocadero with Margaret Lindsay, and the only time I saw Thelma was when we danced near her. She said, 'I think you ought to apologize to Ida.' And I replied that I hadn't meant Ida to take me seriously about coming. Thelma laughed and that was all there was to it. I took Miss Lindsay home between 12:00 and 1:00 A.M. Saturday night and then went home myself." He denied being "the mystery guest" and said he knew of nothing in Thelma's life that would have led to murder.

ZaSu Pitts was questioned about the holiday lunch with Thelma. Pitts said there was no mystery guest present, only her husband. "I never saw Thelma happier in her life. We went shopping and Thelma bought a lot of Christmas wrappings and seals and I'm sure she meant to be alive and observe Christmas."[25] As for romance: "A couple of years ago Miss Todd confided to me that she was interested in 'someone up north,' but she never told me the name of that man."[26] As Pitts left the throng of reporters, a stranger came forward and placed an invitation in her hand. She was invited to a meeting where a spiritualist could converse with Thelma's spirit.

A. Ronald Button answered questions about illegal gambling. "The only thing that I can recall that might have worried her was in her statement some time ago that a group of gamblers wanted to open up games in her café," said the attorney. "She told me that she was opposed to any gambling.... The last few times she came to my office she seemed to have something on her mind that she wanted to talk about but she never did. It was not like her, for she usually spoke fully and freely of everything she was doing. I do not think Miss Todd committed suicide, nor do I think she climbed those stairs from her café to her garage of her own volition. I believe that someone knows something about this case which should be told."[27] As for her involvement with the Sidewalk Café, the financial end was handled entirely by West. Button acknowledged that Thelma was very fond of Roland. Thelma had not spoken to him about any other man in her life in recent months. Button said he had heard reports that the café was to be opened to gamblers at the first of the year although he couldn't confirm the rumor.

Actor Duke York told reporters that he was the mystery guest Thelma planned to bring to Martha Ford's party, along with British wrestler Lord Lansdowne. York said he had dinner with Thelma the Thursday before her death. Thelma was going to introduce them as the Duke of York and Lord Lansdowne under those titles and pretend they were British aristocrats visiting in Hollywood. Roland scoffed at York's tale, stating he knew who the mystery guest was going to be, since Thelma liked to attend parties with an escort: "Sometimes it would be me. Sometimes it would be her mother. Sometimes it would be someone else."[28] York responded that he had telephoned repeatedly when he didn't hear from Thelma on Sunday but got no answer. West challenged York to disclose the telephone from which the calls were supposedly made, as all Sunday calls to Thelma had been traced back to their source. West said Thelma intended to attend the party alone. Deputy D.A. George Johnson said the ongoing investigation was filled with honest evidence and obvious faking. He regretted that it was becoming a publicity event. Unless tangible evidence was presented after the holidays, the case would be closed.

West was angry the inquiry dragged on, and he was the target. He was scheduled to be the last witness. Although tired of answering questions, he faced the reporters: "It is terrible in one way that all the private moments of her life must be searched out but, on the other hand, it is best that the inquiry be exhaustive and thorough. Ten years from now, someone will not be able to break out with a new solution of the so-called 'Todd Mystery,' if there ever is a mystery, because then the authorities can pin such a party down to these facts."

Thelma's fame brought international interest, West acknowledged, so the public had a right to know all the information about her death. Then he added a bitter note: "I always thought third degrees were conducted in a room. I never knew there was anything like this. It is pounding, pounding, rush and wait." His voice broke, "Thelma Todd's death was the greatest shock of my life." He paused and regained his composure. "For days after her death I could hardly talk. My mouth dried up, my throat burned, yet, police detectives and investigators plied me with questions. They have taken five statements from me so far ... I don't think anyone knew Thelma Todd better than I did. She was a keen, witty, powerful personality. We were partners. If she wanted to buy lunch, she bought it. I bought mine. Would you believe it? I never bought Thelma Todd anything — no jewelry, no clothes, no presents. The only flowers I ever bought Thelma were the flowers they put on her casket." West was distraught but continued. He was not Thelma's business manager; she handled her own contracts. He denied she was leaving the Sidewalk Café. "I know an influential producer who told us that when Thelma finished her contract he wanted her for feature roles. Thelma was ready to start a new phase of her career, and she had everything to live for — money, position, beauty. That was the only thing I ever concerned myself with in

Thelma's life — her work and her beauty. I often told her she should watch her hours. I know she drank very little the last few weeks. Her beauty was her career, and I wanted her to keep her independence because as long as she had beauty she had her film career, and the money gave her independence." Did he ever fight with her? "No one could row with Miss Todd, or strike her, and get away with it. I know I never did. We have argued, but never in anger. Maybe she did what I wanted her to do, maybe she didn't."[29]

West told reporters that in the event of his death, Thelma would have received half interest in the café business and restaurant property, which would have brought her $30,000. West revealed that he and Thelma had executed their wills together. Thelma had been living at the café for over a year, said West. As for the Sidewalk Café, there had never been any profits. He was the sole owner and Thelma had nothing guaranteed, except the will. Roland estimated Thelma's estate to be around $60,000. There was no life insurance policy. West underwent three hours of questioning on December 27. To the query, "Did you ever strike Thelma Todd?" he responded with an indignant denial.

Thelma's party clothes were brought to the jury chamber: the mink coat, the shimmering blue dress, silk stockings, and blue sandals.

Earl Calder, a night watchman, testified that he had passed the garage fifteen times between midnight and dawn on December 15. As he patrolled the area, the wind was strong and the surf crashed on the beach far below, but he had neither seen nor heard anything unusual: "I never saw the garage door open, never saw a light, never heard a sound that attracted my attention."[30]

Catherine Hunter, described as a buxom blonde, came forward and spoke to reporters. She told investigators that she was completely mystified by her close friend's death and could offer no solution. Hunter answered questions at her bungalow apartment on Fountain Avenue, where she had seen Thelma the day before the party. Hunter said she had known Thelma for nine years and was probably her closest female friend. They were so friendly that Thelma often visited Hunter's modest bungalow and sometimes spent the night. She was confident that if Thelma had been alive Sunday, she would have heard from her.

As 1935 passed into 1936, the investigation dropped from the front pages. But the parade of witnesses continued. Robert Galer and Helen Ainsworth, his assistant, returned for more questioning. Both agreed that when Thelma had entered the dress shop with ZaSu Pitts, Thelma wasn't her usually sparkling self. But both rejected the suicide implication, recalling that she had ordered a new hat and set a date for a fitting. They protested that they had been misquoted or misunderstood in statements that Thelma was "pulling out."[31]

"She did not say that," said Ainsworth.[32] "She said, 'Let me see my bill. I'll be broke next week,' an obviously flippant remark which referred to her shopping spree for Christmas gifts." As for the "changes" she was to make, Galer explained she was referring to new arrangements with a film studio. "She seemed decidedly unhappy, and that struck me as a little strange, since she was so glorious a girl but, knowing the artistic type, I put it down to a mood of depression."[33] Before leaving the dress shop, Thelma paid the outstanding bill of $20. Ray Hays, Thelma's former business manager, testified that she had terminated their agreement a year earlier, but she had no financial worries, As for personal problems, "if she had them, she certainly never confided in me to that effect."[34]

Roland West told the police that he feared harm from "threat after threat."[35] Threatening letters were mailed to him. "Each time I venture into the open, I fear an attack from ambush, and I have not allowed myself to be seen around the Sidewalk Café because of the possibility that some deranged person might come here for the express purpose of killing me."

Flash bulbs popped as Ida Lupino approached the grand jury room. She was the star witness. On the stand she made sensational comments. "Thelma often told my father, Stanley Lupino, she wouldn't care if she were run over by an automobile tomorrow because she didn't care about living."[36] Ida spoke of Thelma's "morbid streaks" and bad heart, how she had collapsed on the set in England, warned by physicians that she must give up picture work in order to live. "Thelma told me the night of her last party at the Trocadero restaurant, 'I am in love with a businessman and I did so want to bring him to this party tonight, but he is in San Francisco and won't be back for several days.'" While sitting at the bar, Ida told Thelma: "Gee, I'd like to quit all this and get out of Hollywood, it's too much of a strain." Replied Thelma: "I've been trying to do that all of my life, there is just one way you can pull out. Come on, let's have a drink."

Ida spoke of Thelma's "death complex," how on numerous occasions, she would say, "I would be the happiest girl in the world if some catastrophe would befall me ... life isn't worth the candle, while we're here we should laugh and be gay and have fun."[37] The last time she saw Thelma, the night of the party, she was being escorted to her car by Arthur Prince. "She turned toward the Trocadero as she got into her car, placed her hand on her forehead and made a sweeping gesture, as though saying farewell to all of Hollywood."[38] Ida Lupino was furious that Pat De Cicco had contradicted her. "I called Thelma and told her about inviting De Cicco, and she seemed extremely pleased to hear it. At her suggestion, a place was arranged for him next to her. We regarded him as her escort, although she had pointed out that they didn't wish to come together, since it wouldn't look right. Both Thelma and I were surprised and hurt, therefore, when Mr. De Cicco did not appear at our party. And we were even more hurt and surprised when De Cicco entered the Trocadero with Margaret Lindsay. At her first opportunity, Thelma bawled him out."[39]

Ida Lupino's claims of Thelma's "death complex" provoked puzzlement. Did Thelma commit suicide? However, thus far, there was no indication of murder. Public interest in the case was waning. Some jurors also felt it was time to end the investigation. But George Rochester, the foreman, aggressively pushed the case along. The Foreman issued a warning to the jury panel not to be led astray from their search for murder evidence by testimony of witnesses that Miss Todd welcomed death and sometimes appeared to be despondent.

On Friday, January 4, the 18 members of the grand jury went to the Sidewalk Café. They climbed the 271 steps directly behind the café and later examined the garage. They studied the garage's oak, hand-carved sliding doors and listened to investigator Bruce Clark explain how he had found Thelma slumped behind the wheel of the Lincoln Phaeton, how her pink toenails were visible in the sheer silk stockings. The group returned down the hill. Reporters were barred from entering the Sidewalk Café. Roland West appeared, cocktail in hand. He was stylishly dressed in a blue blazer, white shirt, tie, and gray flannel pants, noted reporters. He guided the jurors to the living quarters and showed them the three doors that opened to the two apartments. The locks were examined. West showed the closets in Thelma's bedroom, with the bed, table, chairs, and chaise lounge. Then he pointed out the ladies' boudoir and the double doors which separated his room from Thelma's. Jurors commented that knocking on one of the doors would have likely roused West.

Downstairs, the panel looked over the stylish chromium cocktail bar. The jurors sat for lunch in the dining room, supervised by Rudolph Schafer. The reporters ate at a nearby hot dog stand on the beach. Beside worry of the threatening letters, Roland was plagued by souvenir hunters who were descending on the restaurant. They stole silverware, napkins, and even wrapped sugar cubes imprinted with Thelma's face. Rudolph Schafer had caught a man trying to chip a brick from the café exterior.

The following day, Catherine Hunter came to the Hall of Justice to formally testify. The reporters rushed toward her, aware that she was Thelma's closet confidante. Hunter told the journalists what she would tell the grand jury: "I definitely know that Thelma never thought of taking her life, had no financial worries, and was loved by all who knew her, which in itself is reason enough to want to live. I know this not only from Thelma, but from her mother, Mrs. Alice Elizabeth Todd, who is, like Thelma, one of my closest friends, and who is certain, with all of a mother's love and instinct, that Thelma did not kill herself."[40] Hunter denied seeing any morbidity in Thelma during their years of friendship. Marion Wilkinson, an elderly resident of the Fountain Avenue bungalows, and a close friend of Thelma and Alice, told the jury panel that she had engaged in a confidential talk with Thelma before her death. Thelma said she was "very happy" in her romantic and professional life.[41]

After her third appearance before the grand jury, Alice Todd, dressed in black, stepped into the hallway. She summoned reporters, quite upset: "This grand jury investigation and the manner in which it is being conducted is the work of cheap politicians looking for jobs at the expense of my daughter's name. She is dead and is not able to defend herself. But I am here and I will defend her good name. I certainly am convinced that Thelma's death was an accident. If I am satisfied, I don't see why anyone else is interested."[42] This was Alice's second interview of the day. She spoke for 25 minutes, filled with anger. Alice scoffed at stories of her daughter's romance with a businessman in San Francisco and denounced reports that she and Thelma wept a short time before they departed for the Trocadero. Of Thelma's relationship with Roland West, she had earlier remarked: "He treated Thelma very nicely, he treated us all very nicely."[43] She said Thelma kept no diary or even a telephone book. "Nothing could convince me that my daughter's death was other than an accident. There was no reason why she should end her life or that anyone should murder her."

After Alice blasted the investigation, Captain Bruce Clark emerged from the jury chamber. "We were convinced at 4:30 P.M., the day of the discovery of the body, that death was entirely accidental."[44] Detective Joe Whitehead presented scientific evidence to the jurors as did chemist Ray Pinkert. Their tests indicated carbon monoxide fumes would have killed Thelma within minutes. In addition, Pinkert said he had made the walk from the café to the garage in a new pair of shoes; they showed less wear than a walk on ordinary pavement.

When told of Alice's bitter attack, Foreman Rochester shrugged his shoulders, smiled, and refused to comment, as did the jurors. But Alice's defiant attitude had sent a shock wave through the crumbling investigation. Two days later, Roland West confronted the grand jury, angry and defiant: "I will not answer any questions that might reflect on the character of Miss Todd. Anyone in my position would do the same thing. I will gladly tell anything they ask about myself." When asked if he would pose for a photograph, West complied and remarked: "A photograph, like a glimpse in a mirror, is just an illusion."[45]

On January 8, Captain Hubert Wallis of the Homicide Bureau, said the case was officially closed. As he explained: "The death has been listed as accidental with possible suicidal tendencies."[46] However, Captain Wallis had told the grand jury there was no motive or note to substantiate the suicide theory.

Foreman Rochester had one last chance. He had received a letter from Gustav Berger, a former waiter. The letter stated he had been employed at the Sidewalk Café during the summer of 1934. He had a story that Thelma had been "beaten up and thrown out into the rain."[47] Berger admitted that he had not personally witnessed the event but had only heard of it from others. Berger was a prisoner in a San Diego jail. Rochester and an investigator spoke with him, but Berger could not recall the exact date of the incident. The jailed inmate wanted to return to Los Angeles so he could ask "several of the boys" to corroborate his statement. Detectives had no faith in Berger's tale; they believed that he only wanted to get out of jail.

On January 9, 1936, silent screen star John Gilbert died. Though only 38, Gilbert had suffered a fatal heart attack. He had once been a handsome and famous screen idol, madly in love with Greta Garbo, but his career had faded with the arrival of sound. According to his friend Marlene Dietrich, he was planning a comeback, but a heart condition forced him to live as an invalid. Gilbert awaited the end in his mansion at 1400 Tower Grove Road. The tragic life of John Gilbert now filled the newspapers. The press frenzy over "the Todd mystery" faded and slipped to the back pages.

At Roach Studio there was a meeting; Hal Roach and Stan Laurel agreed that Thelma's scenes in *The Bohemian Girl* should be cut; audiences would be distracted to see Thelma singing of love and life when she was dead.

After four weeks of daily testimony and intense investigation, the grand jury could produce no evidence that Thelma had been murdered. The last hope of making a murder of Thelma's death ended when County Chemist R.J. Abernethy testified that he found no evidence of poison in her vital organs. The grand jury closed the case. Most newspapers didn't bother to print the chemist's scientific conclusion; it was an anti-climatic curtain for what had begun as a sensational event.

Thelma's estate, estimated by reporters to be valued as high as $200,000 was established in court to be $47,452.25. This was the statement of Ray Hays, appointed co-executor of the will with Alice Todd. Hays said the estate had $14,421.81 in cash; the remaining assets were in personal property, stocks, jewelry, and real estate. Thelma's expensive clothes sold for $1,071 less than the appraised value. A large portion of Thelma's wardrobe was bought by a dress shop on West Sixth Street for only $229; it consisted of 29 dresses and pajamas, 21 pairs of gloves, 37 pairs of shoes, 16 hats, and other apparel. The sale included the "blue metal evening gown" and fur coat that Thelma had worn to her last party at Café Trocadero. The sleek 1932 Lincoln Phaeton, Thelma's prize possession, now had a tragic history and, after appraisal, the automobile was sold for $550, as this was the highest and best offer made, reported Ray Hays to Alice.[48] Thelma had generously loaned $250 to Jack Luden and $386 to Catherine Hunter. Hays asked for repayment from both. Alice kept Thelma's valuable jewelry which included a platinum ring with diamond studded letters spelling "I Love You"; the ring was set with 69 diamonds and two rubies.

Alice Todd and Ray Hays settled all outstanding accounts, including $1,500 for the funeral, a dental bill of $14 owed to Dr. Cyril J. Gail for pyorrhea treatment and $175 owed to Dr. Ralph Arnold. Thelma died before her Saturday check to Dr. Arnold had cleared the bank. Watson and Son, tailors, sent a bill from their shop on Hollywood Boulevard. The owners wanted final payment for a dark grey, chalk-striped, three piece suit, delivered on March 19, 1934, to Pat De Cicco. The suit cost $125 and $3.13 for sales tax. Thelma had already paid $100. The shop wanted the remainder of $28.13.

Alice must have caught her breath when a bill arrived from a building contractor. Thelma had paid $1,500 for a lot at 17569 Castellammare Drive. The contractor asked for payment of $35 "for contemplated garage and retaining wall" on the property. Thelma had already paid $365 for excavation and grading for a planned garage where she could park her large Lincoln Phaeton. Alice dutifully paid all bills, inheritance, and income tax. The estate paid a California inheritance tax of $967.50 and $152.11 in federal taxes. Alice could no longer remain in the land of dreams. She made her last statement to the press in February, and said she planned to return to Lawrence and stay with relatives. For nine years Alice had resided with her daughter in Hollywood. Alice enjoyed the glory of Thelma's fame and kept a sharp eye on her only child. Now she was going home with Thelma's ashes in a bronze urn. The urn would remain with Alice for 34 years. She could not say goodbye; neither could the curious who felt that Thelma's untimely death was still unsolved. The public read about sinister characters who lurked in the shadows, ready to take advantage of wealthy performers. Screen stars were regarded as prey. In August 1936, the parents of child star Shirley Temple received an extortion demand of $25,000. Authorities arrested a teenager. Yet many threats remained secret, known to only the potential victims and the police. As time passed, rumors and myths circulated about Thelma. Surely her death was more than a simple accident, whispered the skeptical. Was she was murdered by Roland West, Pat De Cicco, or gangsters? Gossip would not let the memory of Thelma Todd rest in peace.

NINE

The Aftermath

Before leaving Los Angeles, Alice gave many of Thelma's personal possessions to her daughter's close friends. Though far from rich, Thelma provided a comfortable inheritance for her mother. Alice was left stock shares in AT&T, Consolidated Gas Company of New York, Standard Oil, and other blue chip companies.

At age 58, Alice started a new life. She spent several weeks in Hollywood, Florida, to recover her emotional strength. She returned to Massachusetts, where she was a guest in the home of Judge Louis S. Cox and his wife in Methuen, near Lawrence. Family and friends offered their comfort and condolences. For many years, Alice lived in the Aberdeen Apartments in Shawsheen Village in Andover. She later moved to an apartment on Bedford Street in South Lawrence, in her old neighborhood, where she once happily lived with her husband, son, and daughter. In 1956, Alice was invited to share a home with her sister-in-law, Gertrude. Over the years, Alice kept Thelma's ashes in her bedroom. Adam Todd was very fond of his elderly aunt who, despite her many personal tragedies, displayed a keen sense of humor. "She tried not to talk about Thelma," says Adam Todd, "but of course, she did, and it would be painful."[1] Except for the cherished urn and photographs, Alice kept few mementoes from Thelma's career. Alice Todd died in December 1969, at age 92. Thelma's ashes were buried with her.

And what became of Roland and Jewel?

In October 1939, Jewel Carmen was once again living in the sumptuous Castillo del Mar, but she complained that her income of $170 per month was insufficient. Roland ignored her plea for more money. After several years of emotional estrangement, Jewel felt it was time to begin a new life. Court documents reveal how Roland and Jewel ended their relationship. Jewel hired attorney Jerry Giesler to represent her. Jewel claimed that in June 1935, she advanced Roland $28,000. The amount was to be invested in stocks, bonds, and the restaurant business. Jewel wanted repayment of the money with interest. Roland responded that from June of 1933 to June of 1934, Jewel had actually given him $34,000. Jewel already had $70,000 invested in a shared annuity, from which they had both profited.

Jewel subsequently filed a complaint for separate maintenance. She asked for $635 a month and a division of all community property. She asserted that since their marriage Roland had inflicted extreme "mental cruelty."[2] According to Jewel, when she discussed the issue of divorce with Roland, he threatened to hide his assets. A court order froze Roland's cash and property. Roland protested that the separate maintenance sum was exorbitant. He informed the court that his yearly income was "at $30,000" and "the Thelma Todd Inn" operated at a loss. Jewel also wanted $10,000 for legal fees.[3] The restraining order on Roland's assets was lifted after he agreed to an immediate property settlement of $50,000 for Jewel.

Jewel filed a petition for a divorce. Her documents stated they had wed on June 1, 1918, in New York, and had separated on March 1, 1934. Roland announced that he would contest the monthly allowance on the grounds that they had actually separated in 1930 and that a division of community property was made at that time. In December 1939, Roland filed an astonishing response. West denied that he had ever been married to Jewel Carmen. The astounding news forced Jewel into silence. An out of court property agreement was arranged in November 1940. Roland agreed to a cash settlement; the details of the final arrangement were never made public. Jewel severed her legal ties with Roland, and vanished.

West was entangled in another, more serious legal case in 1941. Joe Schenck, chairman of the board of directors of 20th Century–Fox, was indicted by a federal grand jury in New York for income tax evasion. According to the U.S. attorney, Schenck had evaded taxes from 1935 to 1937. The wealthy studio magnate was investigated for submitting tax returns with false business deductions. In addition, federal agents discovered a mysterious payment of $100,000 to Willie Bioff, a union official. The "loan," as Bioff explained the sum, appeared to be extortion. Federal investigators also uncovered Schenck's penchant for gambling. He kept meticulous records of wins and losses. The studio mogul often lost thousands of dollars at poker. Schenck wrote checks to Chico Marx, Constance Bennett, Charles Boyer, and Darryl Zanuck.

One of Schenck's friends was Lou Wertheimer who, with his brother Al, had operated the fashionable Clover Club, a gambling operation frequented by the wealthy, including film stars, and studio executives. In the summer of 1935, while Schenck was in Europe, drawing his Fox salary of $2,500 per week, plus travel expenses, the Wertheimer brothers transformed Schenck's Hollywood mansion into a gambling den. They paid $2,000 to Lou Anger for the use of the residence on Sunset Boulevard. A living room on the first floor was used for private parties; the front of the house was kept dark so

Forever young (author's collection).

it wouldn't attract attention. The brothers even tore down walls to set up a roulette table. When Schenck was told of the gambling he was furious. The Wertheimers gave him a check for $2,000. Despite the Wertheimers' audacity, Schenck remained friendly with them. Schenck continued to rent a Palm Springs home from the brothers for $5,000 a year. Schenck put Lou Wertheimer on the Fox payroll in 1938, at a salary $500 per week.[4]

A heavy gambler, Schenck had even placed bets on the national election in 1936. Roosevelt's victory had won him $40,000. But in a single day in 1937, Joe Schenck had lost $30,000 in bets. Schenck was tried for defrauding the government of unpaid tax revenue. During the long trial, he appeared daily at the courtroom in Foley Square in New York City; it was revealed that Schenck used his yacht, the *Caroline*, for lavish parties. Among those entertained were Irving Berlin, Douglas Fairbanks, Countess di Frasso, Louis B. Mayer, and Charlie Chaplin. On his tax return Schenck had deducted $80,000 as a business expense to maintain the yacht. But prosecutors told jurors the *Caroline* seldom sailed the Pacific. Court testimony revealed that Harpo Marx had won $7,827 from Schenck while playing cards aboard the moored *Caroline*.[5] The yacht was used for social gatherings, not business transactions, asserted prosecutors, and the captain testified: "Most of these people get seasick at sea."[6]

Further court testimony revealed that when actress Grace Poggi, Schenck's girlfriend of eight years, performed at a dance engagement in London, Schenck paid her Savoy Hotel bill, a sum that amounted to $700. Vouchers for flowers, parties, hotel bills, and the use of the yacht were presented in tax returns as "business deductions." More serious, Schenck claimed he had lost $403,000 in the Compagnia Mexicana del Agua Caliente's hotel and casino properties and deducted the large sum. Enrique S. Neidhart, property manager, testified that Schenck paid $403,000 for 67,000 shares of the company's common stock. The government issued a decree banning gambling in 1935, and the casino property was expropriated by the Mexican government in 1938.

A government witness, Erwin Luttermoser, testified about conversations he had with Roland West in 1935, when West purchased Schenck's stock worth $403,000 in the Agua Caliente Casino and Racetrack for $50,000. At the time, Luttermoser was West's accountant. The government contended that the stock had been "sold" by Schenck at a loss, a legal transaction, prosecutors admitted. However, the stock sale was for tax deductions only and the stock was never really relinquished, an act that was illegal. The accountant proceeded to explain that West's net worth at the end of 1935 was $250,000 but his cash value was only $30,000. Joe Schenck guaranteed a bank loan of $15,000 for Roland, to allow him to make the down payment on the Agua Caliente stock. Schenck had also provided his friend Roland with the first monthly payment of $5,000, in addition to smaller sums, as stock profit. "I won't have you lose a penny," Schenck assured Roland.[7] The government believed Schenck sold the stock merely to establish a loss in order to deduct $170,000 from his 1935 income tax.[8]

Schenck argued that the stock sales were genuine because the president of Mexico had banned gambling in July 1935 and the Agua Caliente resort collapsed; as a consequence, the company's stock value plummeted. The court records revealed that Schenck had never asked West for the additional debt of $30,000, since he felt the stock was utterly worthless. Schenck did, however, deduct $170,000 from his gross income.

West's accountant explained his client's financial decline. "A misfortune for West was the death of Miss Todd," said Luttermoser. After Thelma's death, Roland had given Alice Todd a percentage of future profits from the Thelma Todd Inn, but there had been no profits.[9] Roland feared Alice would liquidate her interest in the restaurant. This meant a cash settlement for money he did not have at the time.

Schenck's former secretary took the witness stand and delivered damaging testimony. The secretary had entered Schenck's studio office and saw him sitting at a desk with Willie Bioff, counting money. When Schenck reached $100,000 he stopped and stuffed the cash in a large envelope. Schenck's story was that Bioff was merely repaying a loan. If true, noted prosecutors, Schenck had failed to declare the money as income. As the seven-week trial neared the end, character witnesses were called to verify Schenck's honesty. A short, white-haired man raised his hand and swore to tell the truth. "I'm his friend," said Charlie Chaplin, "that's why I'm here. I know his reputation for honesty and integrity thoroughly. It is good."[10] Chaplin, 52, identified himself as a motion picture actor and producer. When asked to name his own outstanding pictures, Chaplin, noted a reporter, hesitated: "Modesty forbids this, but I will try." He named *The Kid, The Gold Rush, City Lights*, and *The Great Dictator*. Chaplin said he had known Schenck since 1914 but his close friendship began with him in 1924, when he was recommended by Douglas Fairbanks and Mary Pickford to assist United Artists. "The company was organized to fight a great trust that was then forming," said Chaplin. "We independent artists could not get proper dates for our pictures because the producers were ganging up on us.... Mr. Schenck was the chairman of our company, the man who kept us together. He was an appeaser, who tried his best to appease the temperaments of the motion picture artists ... we relied on him, his judgment and his generosity." Other friends who asserted Schenck's honesty were Irving Berlin, Will Hays, and Paul S. Gibson, Chief Justice of the Supreme Court of California.

Despite the warm words of praise by Chaplin and others, Schenck was convicted of income tax fraud in federal court, found guilty of failing to pay $253,692 on income from 1935 and 1936. Schenck's income for those years was $930,787. Schenck was sentenced to serve three years in prison and pay fines totaling $20,000. He faced an indictment for perjury, accused of concealing the $100,000 payment to Willie Bioff, a sinister presence in Los Angeles. Bioff, the president of the International Alliance of Theatrical Stage Employees (IATSE), was a native of Chicago, where he achieved power as a union official who represented theatre projectionists. The union was controlled by crime figures linked to Al Capone. In response to the controversy, Schenck gave tangled accounts of the transactions. "It was a loan," Bioff insisted. "I got it to buy land in the San Fernando Valley."[11]

Willie Bioff started his rise to power in Hollywood after an unsuccessful strike in 1933 weakened the American Federation of Labor. When union strikers ran out of money, Bioff managed to gain control of the union. In December 1935, representatives of major motion picture studios met with union officials in New York and negotiated the Studio Basic Agreement. Bioff's explanations unraveled when federal tax investigators observed the discrepancy between the labor official's $7,206 yearly salary and his lavish lifestyle. Bioff and George Browne, president of IATSE, were indicted for extortion. Columnist Westbrook Pegler uncovered information that Bioff had failed to serve a jail sentence in Chicago for pandering. Chicago police arrested Bioff and put him behind bars.

Schenck's sentence was suspended in return for aiding the investigation of Willie Bioff and George Browne on extortion charges. Schenck admitted to federal agents the studio had made extortion payoffs of 1.2 million dollars. Schenck claimed that he was not aware of Bioff and Browne's connection to Chicago crime figures. Schenck pleaded guilty to one charge in the indictment of perjury and the making of false statements. He was sentenced to a year and a day. After serving four months in Danbury Prison in Connecticut, Schenck was paroled; he was later given a full pardon. Bioff and Browne admitted to federal investigators in 1943 that they had been involved with Chicago underworld figures Frank Nitti, Louis Campagna, Phil D'Andrea, Charles Gioe, and other criminals. As a result, the gangsters were prosecuted for tax evasion, racketeering, and extortion. Several years later, the mobsters got their revenge. In 1955, Willie Bioff died when he turned the ignition of his truck and it exploded.

The fall of Joe Schenck ruined any chance of Roland West to return to films. Moreover, a shadow fell on West after Thelma's death. "It was a big scandal for those days, that he was running around with Thelma." observed Lina Basquette, "If there was a scandal, they dropped you like hot potatoes." Roland remained in the restaurant business. The Thelma Todd Inn became Chez Roland.[12] Roland hired Queenie Eileen Shannon, 21, an attractive chorus girl from Toronto, to help him manage the restaurant. She had initially been hired for a song and dance routine in the nightclub above the restaurant, but her special recipes impressed Roland, so she was promoted to manager. Shannon left Chez Roland in 1946 after Roland married actress Lola Lane, one of the famous Lane Sisters who, along with Rosemary and Priscilla, had entertained movie audiences. Chez Roland continued as a posh supper club that catered to the wealthy. After developing a heart condition in the late forties, Roland and Lola spent time in Eau Gallie, Florida, where West died in March 1952, at age 67. A small group of friends gathered at the Wee Kirk o' the Heather for a memorial service, the same church where Thelma had been eulogized. The fifteen-minute service was conducted by a minister of the Christian Scientist Church, with readings from the Bible and the writings of Mary Baker Eddy. Roland was buried in a modest grave at Forest Lawn Cemetery. The marker expressed Lola's affection: "My Beloved Husband."

The reclusive Roland West had the curtain of his private life lifted when his will was presented in court; it was filed under the name of Roland Van Ziemer. Two weeks before his death, Roland had written his last will and testament. Jewel Carmen, "address unknown," was made a nominal beneficiary, and was left one dollar, to prevent her from contesting the document. A woman named Helen Knight, "who may also be known as Helen Knight West," was also left a single dollar. She was listed as living at 1774 N. Las Palmas. To Joe Schenck, "my good friend of fifty years ... being financially independent, I hereby bequeath to him my greatest esteem and affection." John Gordon, another friend, received $3,000. Harry Brand, publicity representative, and Ned Marin, theatrical agent, were left the rights to *The Unknown Purple* and other stories. Queenie Shannon was left one dollar, since "I do not leave more to her for the reason that she has squandered or wasted all previous sums given by me to her." Pat Shannon, her sister, was left $2,500. Rhea Weedon, an employee of Chez Roland, was bequeathed $1,000. The remainder, estimated at "several hundred thousand dollars" was left to Lola Lane, "my beloved wife."[13] Queenie Shannon had expected more than one dollar: "Roland told me not to worry; that he'd take care of me in his will."[14] Queenie, then employed at a Malibu restaurant, told reporters she would hire an attorney to break the will but never did so.

Just like Roland's $1.00 gifts, Thelma had left a single dollar to her ex-spouse, described in her will as "a stranger." Ronald Butts, a process server, had tried to deliver the check to Pat De Cicco's office at the Joyce–Selznick agency at 9460 Wilshire, but De Cicco always managed to dodge the humiliating gift. De Cicco remained an agent for a while, then went to work for Howard Hughes in 1935. While helping director Lowell Sherman to find a cast for *Nightlife of the Gods*, a handsome actor could not be found to play Perseus. De Cicco asked for more time. "You're just the type," said Sherman.[15] De Cicco portrayed the god. Women always found him appealing, including beautiful Gloria Vanderbilt. She was 17 when she met him at a party in the company of his friends Bruce Cabot and Van Heflin. De Cicco, then 32, came courting at the Vanderbilt home on Maple Drive in Beverly Hills. Gloria was going to inherit four million dollars on her twenty-first birthday. She fell for Pat's charm and looks. Gloria exchanged vows with "Pat Pasquale," as she called him, in a ceremony in Santa Barbara in December 1941. The best man was Bruce Cabot. The ushers were Errol Flynn, Howard Hughes, Franchot Tone, and Pat's cousin, Albert "Cubby" Broccoli. Instead of a storybook romance, Vanderbilt found her new husband handsome, self-assured, and brutal. As she wrote in her memoir *Black Knight, White Knight*: "Pat terrifies me with the rages he falls into. Yes, it's like a volcano erupts, only he's the volcano and I'm the one that falls in."[16]

At the time of their marriage, De Cicco told his wife he was employed by Howard Hughes, though in what position she wasn't sure. However, Pat worked for Hughes in various capacities, including duty as a "talent scout." Pat and Hughes searched nightclubs for a pretty face. Pat even used $10,000 of Hughes's money to buy the rights to a Hemingway literary property, something that angered Hughes. Pat arranged a job with Howard Hughes Productions for his cousin, Cubby Broccoli, as an assistant director.

At six foot one, 275 pounds, Gloria found her husband cocky and intimidating. He was content to enjoy his wife's money and expected life would be even sweeter when the inherited millions came. According to Gloria, whenever Pat lost his temper she was treated as a punching bag. One evening in New York, De Cicco attacked Harry Cohn and threatened to kill him. Gloria fell in love with conductor Leopold Stokowski. Before the divorce, their gin rummy pal, "Uncle Joe" Schenck, telephoned and tried to reconcile the couple, but Gloria refused to return to her husband. Schenck passed along the message that Pat needed an operation and $200,000 would be helpful; it was just two months before Vanderbilt received her inheritance of four million dollars, so Pat Pasquale got something after all.

De Cicco became a producer and worked with his cousin Cubby Broccoli. In 1946, they released *Avalanche*, a film directed by Irving Allen starring Bruce Cabot. Pat became president of West Coast United Artists Theatres. After he married Mary Papac in 1952, he was corporate director of a food catering organization. Pat became wealthy after he successfully marketed Bons Bons chocolates to movie theatres internationally. His marriage ended in 1959, without children. The same year, he retired. He was a communicant of Good Shepherd Church in Beverly Hills. Pat could be seen every Sunday taking up the collection, though observers like William Bakewell wondered what his percentage would be. In January 1978, while residing in Madrid, he was summoned to Texas to testify in probate court concerning the estate of Howard Hughes. Pat testified he had met Hughes at a party at the Clover Club in 1932 and began working for him in 1935 as "first assistant in the motion picture business." Pat saw Howard Hughes five or six times a week during the thirties. They watched films at 7000 Romaine. Whenever Hughes got mad, Pat asked why he just didn't return to Texas. "I am an ex–Texan," Hughes shot back. Hughes's main interests were golf, airplanes, and motion pictures. The last time they talked was in December 1967, when Hughes asked Pat to call Henry Ford and have a special Continental made as a Christmas gift for Jean Peters. When Pat asked where he was living, Hughes told him: "I am home. I am at the Desert Inn."[17] Hughes said he lived in Las Vegas for his health. Ironically, the ailing Hughes lived longer than Pat De Cicco, who died of cancer in New York in 1978.

Toward the end, De Cicco said he believed that Roland West had killed Thelma, while others felt that De Cicco, with his violent temper, was the likely culprit in murder theories. Though dead for decades, Thelma's tragic demise remained a puzzle for many in Hollywood. Suspicions of foul play circulated, kept alive by gossip in the motion picture community and in newspaper articles. There were tales of gangsters, illegal gambling, and murder. The *facts* of Thelma's death dissolved into the distant past, while whispers of murder were alleged. Fellow actress Anita Garvin believed Thelma had been murdered, as did character actor Frank McHugh, who had appeared with her in *Corsair*. There were others as well. Patsy Kelly seemed to imply foul play with her few comments about Thelma's death. Kelly, down on her luck in her last years, worked for entertainer Tallulah Bankhead. She was hired as a personal companion and assistant in Bankhead's nightclub act. In later years, Kelly lived in the shadow of the flamboyantly outrageous Tallulah and kept quiet about two things: "Patsy never discussed her own lesbianism and seldom talked about Thelma Todd," says Rena Lundigan, wife of actor William Lundigan.[18] Occasionally, however, Kelly would attest to Thelma's kindness and friendship, and their heyday with the Todd-Kelly shorts. In 1937, in an interview with *Movie Mirror Magazine*, she spoke of Thelma. She revealed a streak of bad luck involving herself and her close friends. "You see, something, darned if I know what it is, has happened to me since I came to this crazy town. Everyone I loved, turned to, needed, has gone, just like Thelma. It was Jean Malin, that swell New York actor and impersonator, first. I'd been a friend of Jean and his wife for years in New York. Then I went down to the Ship Café that night of Jean's disappearance. I glanced up at the flashing sign over the door that said, 'Jean Malin's last night,' and as clearly as I'm hearing you, a voice said, 'Be careful, it *is* his last night.' He backed the car into the ocean off the end of the pier just one hour later. We were all submerged in the water. Adrenalin worked with me. It didn't with Jean." Then came a greater loss: "Thelma. She gave me everything I needed. Got me on my feet. Gave me confidence and true friendship. And then she went. I had Ralph Farnum my agent left. He took me in hand, fought my battles, and gave me advice. He went, too, just a few weeks ago.... But Thelma is always near me."

Toward the end, Kelly made her most personal statement about Thelma's death: "She had a fight with her lover at a party that night. I wasn't there but friends of mine were and they told me about it. There were a lot of suspicious things surrounding her death that never got explained. She most certainly wasn't drunk. Thelma used to nurse one drink for a whole evening and she never touched drugs of any kind. She was a strong New England woman with a powerful sense of humor and a wonderful zest for life. I always figured God wanted another angel. She was too young and too beautiful...."[19]

Writer Nicholas Hordern reported Pat De Cicco's comment that West had killed Thelma, although unintentionally. West waited for her to come back from the Trocadero. After an argument, she went to the garage, with West following. West didn't want her to leave: "He struck her, and then closed the door, almost to eight inches in a rage. He wanted to teach her a lesson, opined De Cicco."[20]

Film scholar Scott MacQueen, an authority on the cinema of Roland West, wrote a fine profile of the director in *Between Action and Cut* in 1985. While primarily concerned with West's career, the article provided fresh research and insightful comments about West's life, though just touching on the death of Thelma Todd. MacQueen presented a story similar to Kelly's version, though given by an anonymous source. This story related that Thelma had been partying heavily and that she and Roland exchanged "angry words." West had locked her out that night, and the fight was resumed when she returned. She stormed to the garage after announcing she would attend any party she liked, such as Mrs. Wallace Ford's event. West tried to stop her, when Thelma was in the Lincoln, ready to drive off, but West locked the garage door. "Stubborn Thelma sat, the engine on, waiting for Roland to open the doors. She didn't consider in her anger, the odorless carbon monoxide filling the garage, neither did Roland." In this version, West confessed to the police, who believed him when he claimed her death was not planned. And who was the source?

The same explanation was given two years later when writers Kathleen Mader and Marvin Wolff wrote an article titled "Thelma Todd's Murder Solved!" The source of West's alleged confession was Hal Roach. According to Mader and Wolff, Roach told them that he had been visited by three "sheriff's detectives" at his studio office on December 17, 1935, the day after Thelma was found. The detectives said that under intense questioning West had confessed. West told Thelma she was to be back at 2:00 A.M. Thelma said she'd come and go as she pleased. There was "a little argument," and then Thelma left for the party. Later, When Sid Grauman called West to tell him Thelma was leaving, West went into her apartment and locked her out. He was going to teach her a lesson, claimed Roach. When Thelma came home, an argument ensued. West didn't like her attending so many parties. Thelma climbed the steps to reach the garage. West followed. Thelma entered the garage and started the engine. "He ran around and locked the garage door," said Roach, who wanted "to teach her a lesson about who was the boss." After daylight, West returned and unlocked the garage to find Thelma's body. West never intended to kill her, said Roach, who claimed the detectives visited him to solicit his opinion about what they should do concerning West's confession.[21] Roach told them to forget it, since he'd have the best lawyers and would deny everything in court. And there were no witnesses. So why cause him all that trouble? The writers found Roach's comments "very unsettling." Was Roland West responsible for Thelma's death, as Pat De Cicco claimed in 1976? As Hal Roach claimed in 1987?

The most significant evidence in examining the death of Thelma Todd is the testimony in the Coroner's Inquest where important figures in Thelma's life were questioned under oath and under the critical eye of the sharpest reporters in Los Angeles. Roach publicly withheld his story until 1987 when, at age 95, he revealed how three detectives had visited *him*, claiming to have a confession from Roland West. They asked his opinion about what to do. Is this credible? Why would investigators confide anything to Hal Roach? If West confessed, wouldn't they tell Alice Todd? Did Roach have a score to settle with Roland West? Yes, he did. There are glaring errors of fact in Roach's tale. It was incorrectly reported in many articles that Thelma and Roland had "argued" before the party, exchanging heated words about what time she should be home. But a close examination illuminates what occurred. Alice Todd and Ernest O. Peters *witnessed* the bantering and Roland West testified "it was laughing." Roach said that West purposely "locked her out" after Sid Grauman telephoned. Why would West lose his temper if she came home late? It would be understandable if she had to work before the camera with only a few hours sleep, but she didn't have to work; it was Saturday night — party night.

The testimony of Mae Whitehead is *conclusive*. She explained in her testimony that Thelma did not want a lot of keys in her purse that evening, so only a single key was placed in it, unknown to Roland, who thought Thelma had her passkeys. Is it credible that West, who seldom left the café, would have a heated argument with Thelma and pursue her through the neighborhood to the garage at 4:00 A.M., lock two garage doors, then walk off and leave her in the locked garage? West testified the garage doors were never locked. The information was corroborated by Mae Whitehead and Robert Anderson.

West never budged from his story that he felt Thelma was unable to enter the apartment due to the fact she only had a single key. He suggested that she likely went to the garage to wait until the porters arrived. Roach claimed that Roland West confessed on January 17, but West stated publicly: "Police detectives and investigators plied me with questions. They have taken five statements from me so far." If Roland West had "confessed," the officers would have revealed the information to reporters. No leaks about an alleged confession ever surfaced in print. In fact, Captain Bruce F. Clark testified at the Coroner's Inquest on December 18 that West had not altered his story in any way.

Randy Skretvedt's *Laurel and Hardy* exposes a tall tale repeated over the years by Hal Roach; specifically, film lore pertaining to the 1928 *Big Business*, a comedy short where Stan and Ollie demolish a house. For years Roach claimed the production crew inadvertently wrecked the wrong home. "So we had to pay for that house," said Roach in 1981, "as well as pay for the house that nobody used." In the sixties, Roach had told the same story on *The Les Crane* television show. It was contradicted by Stan Laurel as "definitely not true." Skretvedt, an authority on Laurel and Hardy, revealed that the home used in the 1928 production was rented by the studio and was still in existence.

Either Roach exaggerated the story to the point of deluding himself or he simply wanted to damn Roland West, a producer who convinced Thelma to change her name and abandon comedy. At the time of her death, Roland was about to arrange a major contract for Thelma with Joe Schenck. Roach's claim that West was very possessive and controlling is without merit. Would an insecure, jealous lover, permit his girlfriend to attend a party alone, until the early hours? Or would he keep her under scrutiny and accompany her everywhere? Thelma had asked Roland to attend the Trocadero party as her escort; she hoped that Roland would eventually marry her, so she could fully share her life with him. Roach had a long-standing grudge against West. Roland had tried to transform Thelma into a dramatic actress. Such a transformation would have fulfilled Thelma's publicly stated goal — to achieve her dream to be a serious actress. Thelma was reinvented as Alison Loyd. At the time, Roach publicly criticized Thelma's career change and even threatened legal action. Roach's business response is understood. Roach was a great producer who valued and appreciated Thelma's fine comedic skill. He also had a contract with Thelma for the Todd-Pitts-Kelly shorts. West publicly stated that Thelma was going to sign a contract with Joe Schenck once the Roach contract ended. Did Roach have a motive for disliking Roland West to the point of telling a story without substance? Would Roland lock her in a garage because she came home late?

Thelma Todd was in love with Roland West. This is confirmed by Lina Basquette and others. Thelma had long loved Roland. She fell in love with him during *Corsair*. Thelma married Pat De Cicco on the rebound. When Thelma's life was threatened by the extortion letters, she turned to Roland West, the person she trusted the most. Although she had a home on Tramonto Drive, near Roland, Thelma and Roland shared adjoining apartments and a life together. Thelma could have lived anywhere.

"Will I marry this year?" she asked numerologist Patricia D' Este.

There was never any testimony that the relationship between Roland and Thelma was disintegrating. In fact, Catherine Hunter and Marion Wilkinson, both intimate friends of Thelma and Alice, confirmed that she was happy in both her professional and personal life. But most significant is the testimony and behavior of Alice Todd. Alice spoke with her daughter nearly every day and knew intimate details of Thelma's personal life. Alice not only spoke admirably of Roland West publicly, but he was her escort at Thelma's funeral. If Alice suspected that Roland had been involved in her daughter's death she would have moved heaven and earth to prosecute him.

Moreover, it was not in West's nature to argue. He did not have the fiery temperament of Pat De Cicco. If Thelma had knocked to awaken Roland, it is likely that he simply would have let her inside. They were partners and lovers. Both enjoyed the café business, and it gave her the opportunity to be close to Roland, to make him happy. If it wasn't in West's personality to be foul tempered, like De Cicco, it was indeed in Thelma's nature to be kind, gracious, and considerate, as Alice, Roland, and others verified. This kindness made her "loved by all," said her close friend Catherine Hunter. On the last day of her life, Thelma shopped for Christmas gifts with Alice. Rather than accompany her mother home the night of the party, she thought it was best to go inside, since the Lupinos, her hosts, expected her. This was correct social etiquette. After De Cicco got himself invited to the party, but showed up with Margaret Lindsay, Thelma did not verbally embarrass him, though he rudely ignored her. Thelma spoke to him with courtesy and suggested that he send a note of apology to the Lupinos, as good manners would dictate, as she would have done. Indeed, Thelma sent a thoughtful handwritten cancellation note to her tutor in French. Thelma always displayed kindness and good manners; she possessed a sparkling personality and charm. In essence, Thelma had *class*. Thelma wasn't idling late at the Trocadero, she sat and engaged in a business discussion with Stanley Lupino. Moreover, she was working. She cleverly made a bet with the Skouras brothers to challenge them to dine at the café the next day—and they showed up.

The day of Thelma's funeral, Alice confirmed that Thelma "never worried about time." She liked people and parties. While she may have been somewhat heedless of time, she was thoughtful to the point of having Sid Grauman telephone Roland, informing him that she was "leaving immediately," just as a dutiful wife would notify a concerned husband. But Thelma remained longer, deep in her business talk with Stanley Lupino. And time passed. To assert that Roland West would lock her in the garage for simply coming home late is absurd. There were no locks on the garage doors. According to Roach's tale, West would have had to have two locks in his pocket when he followed Thelma. Roach's explanation is, to put it charitably, fallacious. De Cicco's similar story is also suspect.

So what exactly occurred in the pre-dawn hours? Was she murdered? No. Did she commit suicide? No. Her death was an accident. This is what likely happened, in my view.

When she arrived at the café, around 3:45 A.M., she tried to enter her apartment with the single the key but realized the door was bolted; a logical conclusion is that she then walked to the garage. Realizing she was late, with only a single key, and not wishing to awaken Roland, who had supervised the café while she had gone to the party, Thelma likely felt at fault. She had told Mae Whitehead to place a single key in her purse; moreover, she had asked Sid Grauman to tell Roland she was on her way home, but she arrived late and was unable to enter, so why wake Roland? She had also been drinking, another reason not to awaken Roland. Thelma had consumed several drinks, since her blood alcohol level was 0.13, a high level. She likely intended to doze for a few hours in the Lincoln Phaeton, until the restaurant staff arrived, then drive to the café or to Alice's residence.

Thelma could have ascended the steep steps directly behind the café to reach Posetano Road or, most likely, she simply walked along Castellammare Drive to Stretto Way, to the garage where the Lincoln Phaeton was parked. Mae Whitehead had walked from the café to the garage to get the Lincoln for Thelma on Saturday morning. Bob Anderson, the bartender, drove the Lincoln to the garage after the café closed Saturday night, and he walked back to the café. This was standard procedure, so the residents were used to seeing Anderson walk in the street late at night. Thelma knew the routine. Thelma had a good reason to go to the garage: the key was in the ignition of the Lincoln. All she had to do was start the car and drive away but, perhaps, she changed her mind and decided to simply stay, so she closed the garage door and fell asleep in the automobile. When she awoke, between six and eight A.M., she then started the car, ready to depart, but before she could leave the Lincoln to slide open the garage door, she was overcome by the odorless and deadly fumes. When Whitehead found her, the driver door was open, as if she intended to step out. Thelma's death was an accident, just as the police concluded, just as Roland West theorized, just as Alice Todd agreed. Captain Bruce F. Clark told the grand jury, under oath: "We were convinced at 4:30 P.M., the day of the discovery of the body, that death was entirely accidental." But at every point when the tragic death seemed logically explained, a bizarre twist occurred. However, it is a fact that she could not enter her apartment without a second key. The simple lockout was overshadowed by the sensational kidnapping threats. Yet, Thelma no longer feared the extortionist because he had been caught. The accidental death was sensationalized by several accounts.

Martha Ford was certain she had spoken with Thelma on Sunday afternoon, but Dr. Wagner ultimately concluded that death had taken place between 6:00 and 8:00 A.M. When Ford was asked by authorities if Thelma would wear a faded camellia on her dress Sunday afternoon, she responded, "I think not." Then she admitted: "I think I may be a little confused or mixed up on what the maid said." Ford's credibility was shattered when Mae Whitehead verified that Thelma *disliked* being called "Hot Toddy." Whitehead stated: "She became very angry one time, when one of her friends called her that in a joking way." Ford was not as close a friend, as she claimed.

Jewel Carmen's tale of seeing Thelma riding in the Lincoln Sunday evening was also demolished by the facts. Thelma wore no hat to the party, and it is hard to believe she would have ridden through Hollywood in the same clothes she had worn Saturday evening with the wilted camellia on her evening gown. Most significantly, Jewel later admitted she had been mistaken.

Ida Lupino further sensationalized the case with her revelation about "the man in San

Francisco." This provided the grand jury, as well as the press, with the possibility that there was a love triangle, and perhaps Roland West was murderously jealous. A frantic effort was made to find the mystery man in Thelma's life. But did such a person exist? Stanley Lupino directly refuted his daughter's version. He said that Thelma had made the remarks in "a hasty joking way." It was clear to him that she was merely entertaining Ida. No mystery man ever turned up. In fact, Thelma had made a similar comment in January 1935. Wrote Louella Parsons: "Thelma Todd back from San Francisco, where she saw the object of her affections and where she bought fish for her restaurant; what a combination."[22] Is it credible that Thelma would *publicly* mention a romantic interest in San Francisco, while she shared a life with Roland West? It is highly unlikely. The remark was made in jest to Louella Parsons and the Lupinos.

Ida Lupino was an intense young woman who was to become one of the great dramatic actresses of the forties and later a distinguished director. Before the grand jury, discussing Pat De Cicco, Ida said that Thelma had "bawled him out" at the Trocadero. But Margaret Lindsay and Stanley Lupino, both witnesses to the incident, denied that Thelma had lashed out at her boorish ex-husband but reprimanded him courteously; it was Ida who was steamed at De Cicco for getting himself invited to the party, then ignoring Thelma. Throughout her life Lupino had a tendency to dramatize events, as friends and even Lupino herself acknowledged.

And what about the gambling stories? According to Rudolph Schaefer, Thelma had been approached by "gambling interests."[23] They had asked her to install gaming equipment in the café, but she had met the offer with a vehement refusal. The request was several months before her death. A. Ronald Button, Thelma's attorney, also related his story of gamblers wanting to operate in the café. The gamblers were never identified. And who were the "gambling interests"? Is it possible that they were Joe Schenck's cronies, Al and Lou Wertheimer, who had operated the Clover Club? No, the gamblers who approached Thelma were unlikely members of Schenck's gambling circle. Roland West owned the café property, so why ask Thelma? The final decision would have been his to make. So if professional gamblers truly wanted Thelma Todd's Sidewalk Café, they would have approached West, to threaten him or make an offer for the building. But the gambling angle is not as sinister as some have made it. Apparently, gambling had been permitted for Thelma's friends who threw parties, as part of the fun, but authorities were arresting owners of illegal gambling clubs, so any nightly high stake gambling with professionals present would have caused serious problems for everyone.

As previously mentioned, in 1932 a drive was launched to "clean up Hollywood" before the Olympic Games. The drive resulted in raids on gambling dens.[24] Even exclusive nightclubs that catered to the elite film community were raided, despite the protests that they were "private clubs." In January 1934, sheriff's deputies struck at the heart of high-class gambling. They raided the fashionable Colony Club on North Alta Loma Drive where "at least 500 patrons were gambling."[25] Also raided were the nearby Club La Boheme and the Clover Club, where deputies arrested card dealers and seized a roulette table and craps table. The next month, the vice squad staged another series of raids and used a battering ram to smash the doors of illegal gaming houses. Authorities raided the water taxis off Long Beach and 400 gamblers were stranded on the *Monte Carlo,* a ship casino at sea. Consequently, it is logical to assume that Thelma's fear was based on the obvious: nightly gambling would bring arrests and closure of the café. Furthermore, why would gamblers kill Thelma? After all, she was the draw to the café, the lovely actress with rich friends. The restaurant prices at the Sidewalk Café were even higher than the chic Trocadero.

There was sensational information in print during the daily coverage of Thelma's death. Accusations were raised, such as: "Thelma had been purposely locked out.... Thelma meant to leave Roland.... How did she open the heavy door of the garage?" There was never any evidence that Thelma was leaving Roland, and he explained that he never meant to lock her out. As for the garage doors, Mae Whitehead and Captain Clark testified they were quite easy to open. And there were no locks on them. With all the suspicious eyes prying into the life of Roland West, it is important to note that no incriminating evidence was ever brought forward that he had harmed Thelma. He was queried by the police, press, coroner's office, and grand jury. Roland was always consistent in his story. But Roland was a private, reserved man. He also made clever mystery pictures whose theme was the thin line between illusion and reality. It was apparent that he and Thelma were romantically involved, especially after Jewel finally admitted the truth, but Roland refused to discuss his private relationship with Thelma. In addition, Roland kept secrets, such as the fact that he and Jewel were never legally married, though they had lived together as husband and wife. Roland later claimed that they had separated in 1930, though Jewel gave the year as 1934. If Roland had publicly admitted that he and Thelma were in love, less suspicion, and more sympathy would have gone to him. Close friends knew that Thelma was deeply in love with Roland, and he returned her affection, though he said he had no plans to marry her. He believed that his private life was his own affair and described Thelma as his "best friend," a comment that many viewed as a rather casual remark; nevertheless, there seems to have been a fatherly role in Roland's care of Thelma. Only West had believed in her long cherished desire to be a dramatic actress. They had gambled on *Corsair* together and lost. She was his Alison, the high-class, serious *artiste*, not the comedic actress. If Thelma drank too much and stayed out too late, Roland was the father-figure who reminded her to come home early for the proper rest she needed to sustain her career. The experience of receiving the extortion threats had frightened Thelma. The failure of *Corsair* may have led to a loss of self-confidence. If she did visit a psychiatrist, the psychological issue could have been the loss of professional self-esteem. Thelma had often voiced her belief that beauty was nice but not enough; intelligence was also necessary. The comment has a truthful tone: "He told me I hadn't, for the last year or so, made the right use of my brilliant brain and my youth and beauty." But with Roland's help, she became a businesswoman. She was given the opportunity to have her own high-class restaurant, at Roland's expense. Her self-identity was enhanced; she was more than a screen clown.

Roland West was a businessman at heart. As his friend Bill Clifford had told him: "I often think of you, and wonder if you are *happy* making money...." Yes, indeed, Roland was very happy making money. Yet, despite his efforts, the café never earned a real profit, but it gave the lovers a chance to be together. Furthermore, when Roland fell in love with Thelma, and started the café, he wrecked his relationship with Jewel. Roland's will reveals that he may have had an estranged wife or girlfriend, a woman identified as Helen Knight West. To prevent a claim against his estate, he only left her $1.00. Who was she? Was she part of his life after Thelma and before Lola Lane?

Film historian William Studer interviewed Lola Lane in 1978. Studer was impressed by her knowledge of the Thelma Todd controversy. Lola Lane had not only read the Coroner's Inquest, but she adamantly defended her deceased husband: "I would never have married Roland had I felt he was guilty. He was the most innocent man you ever met."[26] She blamed the press for casting a shadow on Roland with its photographs and articles. Lane said that West regarded his relationship with Thelma as a romance. At one point, said Lane, Roland had told Thelma that the romance would end if she didn't stop drinking. Roland had said during the investigation that Thelma's work and beauty were his main concern: "I often told her she should watch her hours. I know she drank very little the last few weeks. Her beauty was her career, and I wanted her to keep her independence." Thelma must have enjoyed West's genuine interest. He was not a dashing or lively man, but Roland had deep charm that made Thelma fall in love with him.

After Roland died in 1952, a rumor circulated that he had made a deathbed confession. That such an incident never took place is verified by Lola Lane's staunch belief in his innocence. She inherited the café and refurbished the apartment on the third level, where she resided. She later married businessman Robert Hanlon, her fifth husband. Lola frequented St. Paul's Catholic Church in Westwood and, discovering the overcrowded condition in the rectory, offered assistance to the Paulist priests. "She invited us to come down and use the first floor," said Father Ellwood Kieser.[27] The former café became the headquarters of *Insight*, an award winning television dramatic series. Lola Lane died at her Santa Barbara home at age 75. Before her death, she informed the Paulist priests that they would inherit the former Sidewalk Café, but there was one request: they "could not destroy the walk-in iceboxes in the downstairs kitchen." Respecting her request, Paulist Productions made the large spaces a film vault. The religious order occupied the building and produced religious films and the highly-praised feature film *Romero,* starring Raul Julia. Where Thelma and Roland once shared their lives, operating the café "where Epicureans dine in seclusion," a religious message and humanitarian program were planned. Halfway up the wide staircase, which led to the apartments of Thelma and Roland, the priests placed a red neon sign — *Ole Jesus.*

In 1972, an unannounced caller came to the Academy of Motion Pictures Arts and Sciences with a box of material from the personal file of Roland West. The man gave the documents to the Academy and expressed the view that they were historically significant. The donor requested anonymity. The documents seem to have been left by West at United Artists Studios. Although West was an independent producer, he kept an office at UA until 1931. The items provide insight into his life and career. The discovery was a fortuitous donation, quite mysterious, and not unlike the lives of Roland and Jewel. The documents shed considerable light on the private life of the Wests. Roland was a man who kept meticulous records, recording every expense and saving all correspondence. One can only wish that other personal documents were available from the later years, but these seem to have disappeared. While Roland was the main suspect in suspicions of murder, there was another person who surfaced as the culprit in later years. And who was he? Lucky Luciano, claimed writers.

In 1976, Nicholas Hordern put in print a long-whispered rumor that Luciano was the man Thelma was seen with all day and would have made Martha Ford "drop dead" with surprise if she'd brought him to the party. Hordern provides no documentation except Jewel's description of a "dark complexioned man, probably a foreigner ... a dark, handsome man" riding with Thelma. Of course, Jewel later admitted she was mistaken; factual evidence demonstrates that Thelma was dead by Sunday morning and the Lincoln was parked exactly where Robert Anderson drove it in the early hours. And Lucky Luciano was hardly handsome.

The Luciano tale was expanded by author Andy Edmonds in the biography of Thelma Todd, *Hot Toddy: The True Story of Hollywood's Most Sensational Murder.* Edmonds wrote that Thelma and Lucky were lovers. When Thelma resisted his takeover of the Sidewalk Café, Luciano had her murdered. The biography lacks documentation. Intimate conversations are presented throughout the book without any identifiable source and with only a handful of acknowledgements, such as "Chicago P.D. Detective Bald Eagle." Thelma's cousins and friends were appalled by the book.

"There are so many untruths that I was highly incensed," said Bill Todd.[28] He scoffed at Edmonds's claims that John Todd was a political power. Thelma's father was described as one of the most important men in the East and director of health and welfare for Massachusetts. The author presents a narrative that John Todd's crooked cronies impressed his eight-year-old daughter, leading to a "compulsion that dragged her through the depths of drugs and the underworld."

"Preposterous and offensive," concluded Bill Todd.

"Thelma had a drinking problem," stated Lina Basquette. Lina admitted her own addiction to morphine. "I went to the desert and went cold turkey," she said. But, as for Thelma: "I never knew her to use narcotics." Thelma did tell her aunt about demands from the Mafia for protection money, but Bill Todd could offer no details, other than that demands were made.

Edmonds portrays Lucky as a shrewd killer with a magical ability to corrupt, not only the police but the coroner's office as well. Edmonds writes: "Only Luciano could have achieved the unbelievable ending to such a macabre murder." However, there is no evidence that Thelma Todd and Lucky Luciano ever met. After Dutch Schultz was murdered, Luciano hurriedly left New York City. Police wanted to question him. There is also no evidence that Luciano had ever visited Los Angeles. The scenario for the murder has been that Thelma was beaten and placed in the garage to die from carbon monoxide fumes. If Thelma had been struck by anyone, either outside or inside the garage, there would have been noticeable wounds and bloodstains without traces of carbon monoxide. The autopsy surgeon concluded: "There were no marks of violence anywhere upon or within the body." As he stated: "A superficial contusion on the lower lip did not penetrate beneath the skin." Detectives concluded the light lip abrasion was consistent with Thelma slumping forward, striking the steering wheel as the fumes made her drowsy. Dr. Wagner explained at the Coroner's Inquest that blood droplets were a symptom of death: "The blood that was seen around this case had no significance other than just the poisoning of the gas. It did not mean that it was due to any bruise or any fall or any violence at all." Edmonds claims that Luciano corrupted numerous people, all within a few days. The historical record and evidence reveals otherwise.

On October 23, 1935, "Dutch Schultz" Flegenheimer, a notorious beer baron and gangster, was shot in the Palace Chop House in Brooklyn. Schultz died, along with three gang members. As the body of Dutch Schultz lay unclaimed in Coughlin Brothers Mortuary on Tenth Avenue, Lucky Luciano, a prime suspect, left town. *The New York Times* spread the word across the nation: "The police, however, were still holding to the belief that Schultz and his men may have been wiped out by an Italian organization headed by Charles 'Lucky' Luciana [*sic*] of Manhattan."[29] By November 2, detectives had traced Lucky to the Waldorf, but he was gone. They watched Jamison's Bar and Grill and other places he frequented. However, news reports relayed the information that Luciano was in Miami and had gone to the police in compliance with a city ordinance "requiring persons convicted of felonies to register within twenty-four hours after reaching the city."[30] Lucky registered with the police and was photographed and fingerprinted. Detective Charles Brennan was immediately sent to Miami to watch Luciano, while the Schultz murder case was under investigation. Brennan kept an eye on Luciano while investigators in New York City watched Luciano's hangouts in case he returned. Thomas E. Dewey also wanted Luciano. From his vast suite of offices on the fourteenth floor of the Woolworth Building, Dewey worked tirelessly with his staff to prosecute the extortionists and the illegal rackets that permeated the city. By October, reports reached Dewey that Luciano was involved in extorting money from prostitutes in New York City. Archival police reports confirm that Detective Brennan kept Luciano under surveillance from November 1935, starting in Miami, to the day when Luciano's luck ended with his arrest on April 2, 1936, in Hot Springs, Arkansas, where he was publicly enjoying the mineral baths and thoroughbred racing. A warrant was served on Luciano for "compulsory prostitution." After months of painstaking investigation and interviewing prostitutes, Thomas E. Dewey built a solid case against Luciano. According to *Hot Toddy*, Thelma and Lucky drove around Los Angeles the day before her death. They had already visited Santa Barbara. Now, according to Edmonds, they went Christmas tree shopping together. Eventually, tired of driving, Lucky dropped Thelma off at the Sidewalk Café. They said farewell, then he drove off into the night. From the shadows, Lucky's assassin supposedly grabbed her, beat her, and ended her life in the garage. However, factual evidence demonstrates that Luciano was under police surveillance at the time. Detective Brennan had followed him from Florida to Arkansas: "On the afternoon of November 20, 1935, a report came to the New York police that subject is at this time in Hot Springs, Arkansas, and that he intends to remain there until the opening of the winter season in Miami."[31] Indeed, Luciano's own testimony establishes he was watched by police, and knew it: "When I left New York the latter part of last year, I went to Miami. I conferred with the chief of police in that city, telling him who I was and that I would be in Miami. The New York authorities knew that. They also knew that I had come to Hot Springs and was here before Christmas, then I went back to Miami and later returned to Hot Springs."[32] Any trip by Lucky Luciano to Los Angeles to meet Thelma Todd would have been observed by police surveillance. In *Lucky Luciano: The Rise and Fall of a Mob Boss*, I examined over 40,000 archival documents to investigate Thomas E. Dewey's prosecution of the Luciano gang. Although Luciano did gamble with celebrities in Saratoga in New York state, the extensive file makes no reference whatsoever to Thelma Todd or Pat De Cicco. Luciano was in the news soon after her death; in June 1936, he was sentenced to prison. Rumors circulated about his underworld activity.

Will Fowler wrote in *Reporters*, his memoir, that Agness "Aggie" Underwood had learned that Thelma had met and talked with Luciano. He wanted to transform the Sidewalk Café into a nightclub where he could sell narcotics. Fowler had started as a reporter for the *Los Angeles Examiner* in the forties. In 1947, he was one of the first journalists on the scene of the infamous Black Dahlia murder case. Fowler knew Underwood when they both worked for Hearst newspapers. I came to know Will Fowler well. I was skeptical about the Todd–Luciano tale. When I asked Will for additional details, he could offer nothing. After I conducted research concerning Luciano, I informed Fowler of my findings. I proved Luciano had never been in Los Angeles at the time of Thelma's death and no evidence exists that they had even met. So where and when did the alleged meeting occur? If Lucky had never even seen the Sidewalk Café, why did he want it? The story is a fanciful tale without substance. Underwood, a crime reporter and later a prominent editor, covered Thelma's death in 1935, as well as her funeral. However, in *Newspaperwoman*, her autobiography, Underwood states that despite various theories of foul play, nothing was ever substantiated. Why would she withhold such information, if it even existed? After Will Fowler saw my research, he acknowledged that the story of Luciano's involvement with Thelma Todd was a myth.

Hot Toddy makes numerous unsubstantiated claims, including the tale that whenever the name of Lucky Luciano was mentioned, Alice became frightened and avoided people. This is disputed by the Todd family, for in the 34 remaining years of her life, Alice never displayed such behavior with relatives as her nephew, Adam Todd, with whom she resided, confirmed. Alice Todd was an incredibly strong woman who endured terrible tragedies in her life.

In recent years, a new killer has emerged: Ben "Bugsy" Siegel. According to Donald H. Wolfe, it was Bugsy Siegel who had beaten and murdered Thelma Todd, put together a suicide scenario, and paid off District Attorney Fitts. So claims Wolfe in *The Black Dahlia Files*. Wolfe writes that Thelma and De Cicco opened the Sidewalk Café, and the Joya Room was a "clandestine Syndicate gambling den on the third floor." On December 11, Thelma complained to Fitts, fed up with the mobsters who had taken over her café. Fitts, on the mob's payroll, told Bugsy, so the gangster killed her. Wolfe offers no documentation. The facts prove that Roland and Thelma opened the Sidewalk Café. West owned the property and business; it had nothing to do with De Cicco. As previously stated, anyone who asked Thelma about gambling assumed the restaurant belonged to her and would have been unaware that it was actually West's operation. West explained the business arrangement under oath. The Siegel theory also collapses.[33]

As time went by, those who knew or worked with Thelma passed into the great beyond. Though most of the fascinating youth who sought stardom never achieved fame, they had normal lives, like that of Greg Blackton, who had danced the tango on tour with Thelma. Blackton left Hollywood and became a businessman who owned a chain of clothing stores. In later years, Blackton became a renowned artist. "*Hot Toddy* infuriated me," he said in an interview in September 1991. "Thelma had a heart. She was a beautiful lady in soul and spirit." Blackton remained a close friend of Buddy Rogers, who married Mary Pickford. Most of the Paramount Class of 1926 lived quiet but happy lives. But there was a tragic exception. Film scholar Luther Hathcock uncovered the sad end of Jack Luden. Once a handsome actor, Luden's career faded. By the late thirties, Luden appeared in minor cowboy films. He died in 1951, at age 49, in San Quentin State Prison, where he had been sentenced the previous year. Hathcock discovered the actor went to prison after a conviction in Los Angeles Superior Court for writing bad checks and possession of narcotics.[34] Luden had written checks with insufficient funds over the Christmas holidays and was convicted of possession of heroin. It was a sad end for the man who had escorted Thelma to her funeral pyre.

And what became of Jewel? Government social security records indicate she died in 1984 at age 86. Her birth date is given as July 13, 1897. To collect social security, Jewel must have worked after turning her back on Roland West and Hollywood in 1940. Jewel West maintained a private life for 45 years and died in El Cajon, a small city in San Diego County, California. Jewel chose to keep the door closed on the past.[35] Alberta, her sister, was just as reclusive.

Benny Drinnon exchanged correspondence with Rudy Schafer, the son of Rudolph H.W. Schafer, the manager of the Sidewalk Café. Rudy's stepmother, Alberta Schafer, had worked as a cashier at the café. At the time he provided his memories, Rudy was 72. His father passed away in 1967, at age 62, but Alberta lived decades longer. Drinnon asked him about gambling devices in the upper room of the café. Rudy's response: "Well, it's been years and the memory grows dim. I do recall, however, my dad taking me to the upstairs room and telling me that this is where Thelma's friends played various games of chance. I don't remember his exact words, but that is the idea I gained from the visit. I'm not sure, but I believe there was a roulette wheel along with card tables of various kinds. As mentioned earlier, my stepmother, Alberta Carmen Schafer, would not talk about any of the gambling operations, or a lot of other mysterious goings on to her dying day. She said she had been warned by parties she would not name, that terrible things would happen to her if she told anything she knew." In later correspondence Rudy explained the gambling: "My understanding was that the casino was an informal kind of thing for Thelma and her guests, but later on the 'baddies' wanted in. L.A. was notoriously corrupt in those days. My stepmother, cashier at the café, was terrorized by some unsavory character or characters somewhere along the line, and to her dying day would not talk about that side of things. My dad showed me the upstairs room during the daytime once, but I never saw any of the action. I don't know for sure if Roland West was involved, but it is hard to believe that he was not. As for Joe Schen[c]k I know nothing of his involvement, but I heard his name mentioned often by my dad, usually preceded by the expression SOB."[36]

Lina Basquette in Los Angeles in 1991 (author's collection).

Rudy, a boy of eight, recalled seeing slot machines at the café, on the first level, but wasn't sure who installed them. Although only a boy, he was asked to pull the handle for luck by people who knew him. Alberta had died several years earlier, but she was silent to the end. He clarified Alberta's fears: "Now that I think about it, I would have to say that I don't recall her stating her fears were specifically based on her knowledge of gambling at SWC [Sidewalk Café] it was over all that happened there at the time. I tried several times to get her to talk about Thelma, her death, the café, etc., but she would just freeze up and get this frightened look on her face." Rudy met his relatives at family gatherings. Jewel's mother was an American Indian, Rudy believed, something he perceived from her appearance and family comments.

Rudy recalled the garden parties on the Wests' lawn. On one occasion his father introduced him to Stan and Ollie, who were "like gods to me." The Wests' dog would jump on him and frighten him. Rudy had no kind words for his uncle: "As for Roland West, he was a sinister, sneaky kind of guy and not liked by most people. I feel that there was

William Donati and Ida Lupino, Thanksgiving 1983 (author's collection).

something sinister going on, but can't contribute anything but what the lawyers call hearsay evidence." But Jewel was different: "I would describe her as beautiful and exotic. Something like Garbo." Jewel was quiet, reserved, and sophisticated. Rudy observed that his aunt liked to read. "I have one of her books—*Elmer Gantry.* There were lots of books around the Wests' home, but I didn't take much note of them. Remember, I was just a kid then. It seemed to me that Jewel quite often had a book in hand—something which looked 'arty.' I don't recall seeing any murder mysteries or similar material." As for Jewel's relationship with Thelma, Rudy never saw them together, so he was unaware how they got along. Rudy's father later opened a restaurant with Stanley Krantz, the Viennese head chef of the Sidewalk Café, a temperamental man, but a true artist with steaks. Rudy never forgot Thelma's customary drink order, as reported by his father: "three fingers of rye." Alberta lost touch with Jewel but occasionally received a card from her. However, Alberta kept memorabilia from the café days: "Menus from the café, pictures of my dad, pictures of Alberta, and others taken on Roland's boat, etc. I tried to get all this material from Alberta, but she wouldn't give it up." Alberta suffered from Alzheimer's disease in later years. After her death Rudy was shocked to discover her caregiver had supposedly thrown the memorabilia away: "'Threw it in a trash can!' she said. I raised hell." Rudy did manage to retrieve the .25 Colt automatic pistol Thelma had given his father to carry at the restaurant while on duty.

Thelma's attorney, A. Ronald Button, had started his legal career in 1928, after attending Stanford University and Harvard School of Law. Button had numerous celebrity clients before he concentrated on corporate, business law, and a political career. During World War II Button served as a major in the Army Signal Corps' motion picture division. He spent time at Hal Roach Studios working alongside Ronald Reagan, who served in the Army Air Force Motion Picture Unit, producing and narrating training films. Button was a major developer of Rancho Mirage near Palm Springs.[37]

The actress who starred with Thelma in *The Noose* in 1928, a woman whose fast-paced life seemed to presage a fast burnout, managed to survive. "I went to the dogs," quipped Lina Basquette. For decades, Basquette raised champion Great Danes and traveled the nation as a prestigious judge for the American Kennel Association until her death in 1994, at 87. While in her eighties, Basquette published her memoirs, *Lina: DeMille's Godless Girl,* a steamy and controversial account of her eventful life. Only after Jack Warner's death did Lina truly get to know her daughter, Lita, who had been raised by Harry and Rhea Warner. Married seven times, Basquette had romances with Jack Dempsey and Johnny Roselli, the Chicago mob representative whose job was "keeping the labor peace." Roselli wore a shoulder holster and was reputed to be a Mafia hit man, said Lina. However, during her romance with Roselli, Lina never heard any talk whatsoever of an affair between Thelma and Luciano or any gangster. "Thelma's great love was Roland West," asserted Lina Basquette. Lina always wondered if Thelma, in a moment of depression, simply gave up: "I once attempted suicide, maybe Thelma succeeded." However, the evidence negates the idea. Close friends who saw her in recent weeks believed she was quite happy.

Forty-eight years after the Trocadero party, Ida Lupino reminisced about the death of Thelma Todd. In the den of her ranch-style home in Brentwood, she lit a Carlton and her thoughts returned to the past. She recalled how, during the Trocadero party, Thelma had invited her family to dine at the Sidewalk Café the following day. During the interview it was apparent that Lupino was still angry at De Cicco for wrangling an invitation to the party and then showing up with Margaret Lindsay. Lupino was also still miffed about Alice Todd. Alice had publicly challenged Ida's comment that Thelma displayed a morbid streak. Ida and her parents believed Thelma suffered from a serious heart condition, since Thelma had collapsed during *You Made Me Love You.* Ida wondered if Thelma may have suffered a heart attack and was unable to leave the garage. "She knew she was booked," Ida insisted. "Thelma believed she didn't have much time left," said Lupino in 1983. Lupino's voice became intense, filled with the drama which made her famous as an actress: "Certain people were incriminating a man who did not murder her at all, and she did not commit suicide ... she had just gone into the garage ... you get carbon monoxide and you go...."[38]

The last time Bill Todd saw his famous cousin was in 1935, the year of her death.

Bill, then 22, had accompanied her with friends on a trip to June Lake. On the drive, Bill sat in a rumble seat with her: "She was very affectionate, loveable...."[39]

Epilogue

On a snowy winter day I arrived in Lawrence, to retrace Thelma's footsteps. I wanted to meet those who remembered the lovely blonde, the famous actress who made the city famous. I also wanted to see for myself the city that had nurtured Thelma Todd. What surprised me most was the size of the town; it was much smaller than I had expected. Thelma had once considered opening a theatre in her hometown but, after her death, her popularity and acclaim faded. The neighborhood where Thelma grew up still conveyed her era. Her birthplace at 306 South Broadway still stood, as did many of the homes where she lived. It is easy to imagine Thelma riding her bicycle down Bowdoin Street or excitedly descending the steps at 592 Andover Street, on her way to the Paramount School in Astoria. Thelma is remembered at the neighborhood church where she sang in the choir. The original South Congregational Church was destroyed by fire in 1938. Alice Todd, a loyal member, donated funds for a stage that was built in the meeting room in honor of Thelma. The stage was designed for church activities but also as a place where the needy receive assistance.

"The Queen City of the Merrimack" was a city whose glory disappeared with the demise of woolen manufacturing, an industry it once dominated. Textiles produced in Lawrence were once exported for worldwide consumption. Over time, however, the thriving industry had been eliminated by cheap, foreign competition. The great mills disappeared. Theatre Row was gone. But the echoes of prosperity still linger. The Common remains a beautiful park, and one can imagine a beautiful blonde on her way home from Lawrence High School, male admirers trailing behind her.

On a cold morning I met Rosario Drago, Thelma's screen partner. Drago, 92, was still dapper. He sported a pencil-thin moustache and looked much younger than his actual age. In Catalano's Market he reminisced about Thelma, the Contarino brothers, and the road he had not taken. "Thelma was so beautiful," he said quietly, with a strong Italian accent. "Fox wanted me, but I was a parrot, my English was so poor." Rather than take a chance on Hollywood, Drago opened a pastry shop and later worked in the grocery business. Outside the market, he tightened his scarf and buttoned his overcoat. Gazing down Newbury Street, he pointed to where the Contarino family had operated the magical theatre that had entranced him so long ago. He spoke of Lawrence's golden years, when thousands had arrived to begin a new life in the mill town. "Then the mills closed..." he said with sadness.

He complained about the decline of the city, then said quietly in his native Italian, "Tutti sono morti." *Everyone's dead.* Drago's wife arrived to drive him home after his morning visit with his friends at the market. "It won't be long for me," he smiled.

Where Thelma was best remembered in Lawrence was among the Todd family. The famous cousin was discussed with pride and warmth. The oldest cousin, Bill Todd, knew his cousin and recalled conversations with uncles and aunts. Bill Todd was 22 when he last saw Thelma. They rode in the rumble seat of a roadster; pedestrians stared and waved at lovely Thelma Todd. Edna, Bill's sister, was just a child when the town fell in love with the girl from South Lawrence. Yet, in her meticulously neat, white-frame home Edna removed an edition of *Pinocchio* from a bookcase. "This is one of my dearest treasures," she said. Edna showed me the inscription in Thelma's hand.

December 25, 1926
To Edna,
Hope you like him
as much as I did
when I was your age.
Love, Thelma

What Bill Todd remembered most about his cousin was her laughter, her vivacious spirit, and generosity. "I could never really believe in my own heart that Thelma was dead," he said. "She had too much going for her. Even today, 50 years later, it's hard to believe."

In the older section of the Bellevue Cemetery, John Todd lies buried in a family plot, along with his father, mother, son, and relatives. In another section, situated on Tower Hill, the highest point in the city, Thelma's ashes are interred with Alice Todd. A red granite marker simply states her name, year of birth, and death. In her brief 29 years, Thelma Todd dazzled everyone. All too soon she disappeared. She made her dream of stardom come true; she

Thelma proudly stands before her restaurant, date unknown.

Thelma's grave in Bellevue Cemetery, 1991.

achieved what spectators around the world wanted, to be on the silver screen, to be a star. Thelma Todd had accomplished so much, then, as Ida Lupino said: "You get carbon monoxide and you go." And she was gone at 29. Thelma Todd was truly an American tragedy. She had it all, then she vanished. As I stood before Thelma's grave Shelley's "Mutability" came to mind.

> We are as clouds that veil the midnight moon;
> How restlessly they speed, and gleam and quiver,
> Streaking the darkness radiantly — yet soon
> Night closes round, and they are lost forever...

Although Thelma died before her time, she remains forever young. Even today her warm smile and beautiful face radiate in photographs and films. Roland West was captivated by her gorgeous looks, just like her fans. She had something magical, a lovely face and smile that exuded charisma and charm.

On a cold December night, when the surf crashes and strong winds sweep across the coast highway, the imagination can see a lovely blonde proudly surveying Thelma Todd's Sidewalk Café. Roland's precious gift meant more than diamonds. *The years are not going to bother me...*

Documents

The Last Will and Testament of Thelma Todd De Cicco

September 19, 1933

I, Thelma Todd De Cicco, of the City of Los Angeles, County of Los Angeles State of California, being of lawful age and of sound and disposing mind and memory, and not acting under duress, menace, fraud or undue influence of any person or persons whomsoever, do hereby make, publish and declare this my last Will and Testament in the manner following, that is to say:

Article First: I hereby revoke any and all wills and Codicils by me at any time heretofore made.

Article Second: I direct my executrix hereinafter named to pay the expenses of my last illness, my funeral expenses and all of my just debts and liabilities as soon after my death as practicable.

Article Third: I give and bequeath to my husband Pasquale De Cicco the sum of one dollar ($1.00) in cash.

Article Fourth: I give, devise and bequeath to my mother Alice Elizabeth Edwards Todd of Los Angeles, California, all the rest, residue and remainder of my property and estate of every kind and nature whatsoever whether real, personal or mixed and wheresoever situated, to have and to hold the same as her sole, separate and absolute property.

Article Fifth: I hereby nominate, constitute and appoint my said mother Alice Elizabeth Edwards Todd and Ray Hays, of Los Angeles, California, Executors of this, my Last Will and Testament, and I hereby authorize and empower my said executors to sell, lease, mortgage, or encumber the whole or any part of my estate, and to sell, at either public or private sale, and to sell, lease, mortgage, or encumber, with or without notice, and with or without securing any previous order or authorization of court therefore, and upon such terms and conditions as to them may seem best, but subject, however, to such confirmation as is or may hereafter be provided by law.

In witness whereof, I, the said Thelma Todd De Cicco have hereunto set my and at Los Angeles, California, this 19th day of September, 1933.

Thelma Todd De Cicco

The foregoing instrument, consisting of two (2) pages, including the page signed by the testatrix, was, at the date hereof by the said Thelma Todd De Cicco, subscribed and published as and declared to be her Last Will and Testament in the presence of us, who at her request and in her presence and in the presence of each other have signed the same as witnesses thereto.

Ronald Button

Delma Rapp

Albert Mosher

Autopsy Documents

Office of County Coroner — 59739

I performed an autopsy on Thelma Todd Dec. 17, 1935, at the Los Angeles County Coroner's Mortuary and found the extent of the body presenting a red discoloration and on examination of the blood, I found it to contain 75 to 80% carbon monoxide saturation.

On opening the head, the brain showed a scarlet red color of the blood and the organs were similarly colored.

On opening the body I found all the vital organs normal, that is free from organic disease. There were no marks of violence anywhere upon or within the body. A superficial contusion on the lower lip did not penetrate beneath the skin. The cause of death was carbon monoxide poisoning.

A.F. Wagner

Los Angeles County

Autopsy Surgeon

Coroner's Office

Room 102 Hall of Justice

Los Angeles County Health Department: Sample No. 4518
County Department regular examination Dr. A.F. Wagner
Date submitted, Dec. 16, 1935, Time 5:10 P.M.
Material presented Thelma Todd brain (not embalmed)
Tests desired: alcohol
Laboratory Findings: Examination of the brain show the presence of 0.13 percent ethanol
Examined by R.J. Abernethy Dec. 17, 1935

Dec. 18, 1935
Verdict of Coroner's Jury

Death caused by carbon monoxide poisoning. The deceased was found Dec. 16, 1935, in a garage at 17531 Posetano Rd. near Santa Monica, Ca., and from the evidence submitted to the jury the death of the deceased appears to have been accident but we recommend further investigation in this case, by the proper authorities.

Dec. 19, 1935 10:30 A.M.
Thelma Todd: stomach, liver, kidney (embalmed)

No poisons found. Jan. 1936

The Jewelry of the Estate of Thelma Todd De Cicco (valued at $1,850)

1. Cushion of miscellaneous costume jewelry — six pieces
2. Cushion, having affixed thereto:
    1 stickpin, 1 horse pin (gold color), 1 octagonal, black base, white figure pin
    1 tie pin, having blue stone surrounded by diamond-like stones
3. One oval-shaped bracelet, open on one side and on the other side having seven groups of three each, alternating, blue and diamond-like stones (bracelet seems to have been enlarged by one group)
4. One white gold-looking ring, having 18k on the inside and orange-like colored stone with face of Grecian warrior
5. One crystal-like bar pin, encased in gold, having a pendant with link and gold initials "TAT" in middle of crystal-like pendant
6. One bracelet, alternating in groups of eight, links of gold, with bar of black and green, having about seven of such
7. Amber-colored faced ring
8. One pin, anchor-shaped, gold-tipped, and rope entwining
9. One pair costume earrings, five crystal stones in each
10. One small wrist watch
11. One platinum bracelet, having plate with TT in printing on back
12. One guard ring, diamonds encircling
13. One platinum, diamond and sapphire circle brooch, consisting of sixty-two diamonds, approximate weight three carats. seventeen genuine sapphires
14. One platinum pendant, seventy-two small diamonds, seventeen onyx, one oriental pearl with platinum chain
15. One 14k gold ladies' wrist watch, with platinum ornaments on the lid, cat, mouse, and lamb chop set with genuine ruby 17J Hamilton movement
16. One ladies' platinum ring, set with one emerald cut diamond about three carats
17. One ladies' platinum ring, set with one cabochon oriental sapphire about ten carats
18. One ladies' flexible platinum ring with diamond studded letters, "I Love You," set with sixty-nine diamonds and two rubies
19. One ladies' platinum wrist watch with gold back with seventeen jewel Longine movement No. 3077848, set with thirty-six small diamonds
20. One ladies' platinum ring with one emerald cut aquamarine
21. One gold chain bracelet with eight gold charms; one gold charm bracelet with six silver charms; one gold bracelet with nine gold charms; one gold charm bracelet with ten gold charms; one silver chain bracelet with eight gold charms, all combined as one bracelet
22. Miscellaneous rings, pins, bracelets, earrings, chains, necklaces and other asserted jewels both costume and what appears to be of precious metal

Filmography

1924

Tangled Hearts   Aurora Film Corporation; producers, Peter and Rosario Contarino; director, Peter Contarino; director of photography, Rosario Contarino. From a book by William Galt. Cast: Eva McKenna, Thelma Todd and other cast members.

The Life of St. Genevieve   Aurora Film Corporation; producers, Peter and Rosario Contarino. Cast: Thelma Todd, Rosario Drago and other cast members.

1926

Fascinating Youth   Famous Players–Lasky, Adolph Zukor, Jesse Lasky; Sam Wood Production, presented by Famous Players, Adolph Zukor, Jesse Lasky; director, Sam Wood; director of photography, Leo Tover; story, Byron Morgan, adapted by Paul Schofield; features the Paramount School Junior Stars of 1926; distributor, Paramount Pictures; 79 minutes. Cast: Charles Rogers, Ivy Harris, Jack Luden, Robert Ward, Claude Buchanan, Mona Palma, Thelma Todd.

God Gave Me 20 Cents   Famous Players–Lasky, Adolph Zukor, Jesse Lasky; Herbert Brenon Production; director, Herbert Brenon; assistant director, Ray Lissner; director of photography, Leo Tover; story, Dixie Willson, adapted by John Russell; script, Elizabeth Meehan; distributor, Paramount Pictures; 72 minutes. Cast: Lois Moran, Lya de Putti, Jack Mulhall, William Collier, Jr., Adrienne d'Ambricourt, Leo Feodoroff, Rosa Rosanova, Claude Brooke, Tommy Madden, Phil Bloom, Eddie "Spider" Kelly, Jack "Young" Sharkey, Harry Lewis, Thelma Todd.

The Popular Sin   Famous Players–Lasky; associate producer, William Le Baron; director, Malcolm St. Clair; director of photography, Lee Garmes; story, Monta Bell, adapted by James A. Creelman; 68 minutes. Cast: Florence Vidor, Clive Brook, Greta Nissen, Phillip Strange, Andre Beranger, Iris Gray, Thelma Todd.

1927

The Gay Defender   Paramount Famous–Lasky, presented by Adolph Zukor, Jesse L. Lasky; director, Gregory La Cava; director of photography, Edward Cronjager; story, Grover Jones, adapted by Ray Harris, Sam Mintz, Kenneth Raisbeck; 65 minutes. Cast: Richard Dix, Thelma Todd, Fred Kohler, Jerry Mandy, Robert Brower.

Fireman, Save My Child   Paramount Famous–Lasky, Adolph Zukor, Jesse Lasky; associate producer, B.P. Schulberg; director, Edward Sutherland; director of photography, H. Kinley Martin; story and screenplay, Monty Brice, Tom Geraghty; 60 minutes. Cast: Wallace Beery, Raymond Hatton, Josephine Dunn, Tom Kennedy, Walter Goss, Joseph Girard, Thelma Todd.

Rubber Heels   Paramount Famous Lasky, Adolph Zukor, Jesse Lasky; associate producer, William Le Baron; director, Victor Heerman; director of photography, J. Roy Hunt; screenplay, J. Clarkson Miller, Ray Harris, Sam Mintz, Thomas J. Crizer; 60 minutes. Cast: Ed Wynn, Chester Conklin, Thelma Todd, Robert Andrews.

Nevada   Paramount Famous Lasky, Adolph Zukor, Jesse Lasky; director, John Waters; director of photography, C. Edgar Schoenbaum; screenplay, John Stone, L.G. Rigby, from a Zane Grey story; 60 minutes. Cast: Gary Cooper, Thelma Todd, William Powell, Philip Strange.

Shield of Honor   Universal Pictures, Carl Laemmle; director, Emory Johnson; director of photography, Ross Fisher; story, Emilie Johnson, adapted by Leigh Jacobson, Gladys Lehman; 67 minutes. Cast: Neil Hamilton, Dorothy Gulliver, Ralph Lewis, Nigel Barrie, Claire McDowell, Fred Esmelton, Harry Northrup, Thelma Todd.

1928

The Noose   First National Pictures, Richard A. Rowland; producer, Henry Hobart; director, John Francis Dillon; director of photography, James C. Van Trees; screenplay, H.H. Van Loan, Willard Mack, from their stage play, adapted by James T. O'Donohoe; 75 minutes. Cast: Richard Barthelmess, Montagu Love, Robert E. O'Connor, Jay Eaton, Lina Basquette, Thelma Todd.

Vamping Venus   First National Pictures, Richard A. Rowland; director, Eddie Cline; director of photography, Dev Jennings; story, Bernard McConville, adapted by Howard J. Green; editor, Paul Weatherwax; 60 minutes. Cast: Charley Murray, Louise Fazenda, Thelma Todd, Joe Bonomo, Big Boy Williams, Yola D'Avril.

Heart to Heart   First National Pictures; director, William Beaudine; director of photography, Sol Polito; story, Juliet Wilbur Tompkins; editor, Frank Ware; 63 minutes. Cast: Mary Astor, Lloyd Hughes, Louise Fazenda, Lucien Littlefield, Thelma Todd, Virginia Grey.

The Crash   First National Pictures, Richard A. Rowland; director, Edward Cline; director of photography, Ted McCord; story, Frank L. Packard, adapted by Charles Kenyon; editor, Al Hall; 59 minutes. Cast: Milton Sills, Thelma Todd, Wade Boteler, William Demarest.

The Haunted House   First National Pictures, Richard A. Rowland; producer, Wid Gunning; director, Benjamin Christensen; director of photography, Sol Polito; screenplay, Richard Bee, Lajos Biro, from a play by Own Davis; editor, Frank Ware; 65 minutes. Cast: Larry Kent, Thelma Todd, Edmund Breese, Sidney Bracy, Chester Conklin, William V. Mong, Montagu Love.

1929

Naughty Baby   First National Pictures, Richard A. Rowland; director, Mervyn LeRoy; director of photography, Ernest Haller; story, Charles Beahan, Garrett Fort; screenplay, Tom Geraghty; editor, Leroy Stone; 70 minutes. Cast: Alice White, Jack Mulhall, Thelma Todd, Doris Dawson, James Ford, Andy Devine.

Seven Footprints to Satan   First National Pictures, Richard A. Rowland; producer, Wid Gunning; director, Benjamin Christensen;
director of photography, Sol Polito; screenplay, Richard Bee; editor, Frank Ware; 60 minutes. Cast: Thelma Todd, Creighton Hale, Sheldon Lewis, William V. Mong, Sojin, Laska Winters, Ivan Christy.

Trial Marriage   Columbia Pictures; producer, Harry Cohn; director Erle C. Kenton; assistant director, Charles C. Coleman; director of photography, Joe Walker; art director, Harrison

Wiley; screenplay, Sonya Levien; editor, William Hamilton, Pandro S. Berman; 70 minutes. Cast: Norman Kerry, Sally Eilers, Jason Robards, Thelma Todd.

The House of Horror First National Pictures, Richard A. Rowland; director, Benjamin Christensen; director of photography, Ernest Haller, Sol Polito; screenplay, Richard Bee; editor, Frank Ware; musical score, Louis Silvers; 65 minutes. Cast: Louise Fazenda, Chester Conklin, James Ford, Thelma Todd, William V. Mong, Yola D'Avril.

Her Private Life First National Pictures, Richard A. Rowland; producer, Ned Marin; director, Alexander Korda; director of photography, John Seitz; screenplay, Forrest Halsey; editor, Harold Young. Cast: Billie Dove, Walter Pidgeon, Holmes Herbert, Montagu Love, Thelma Todd, Roland Young, ZaSu Pitts.

Careers First National Pictures, Richard A. Rowland; producer, Ned Marin; director, John Francis Dillon; director of photography, John Seitz; screenplay, Forrest Halsey, from a play by Alfred Schirokayer and Paul Rosenhayn; editor, John Rawlins; 92 minutes. Cast: Billie Dove, Antonio Moreno, Thelma Todd, Noah Beery, Holmes Herbert, Carmel Myers.

Bachelor Girl Columbia Pictures; producer, Harry Cohn; director, Richard Thorpe; assistant director, George Rhein; director of photography, Joseph Walker; story, Jack Townley; art director, Harrison Riley; editor, Ben Pivar; 65 minutes. Cast: William Collier, Jr., Jacqueline Logan, Edward Hearn, Thelma Todd.

Shorts: *Unaccustomed As We Are, Snappy Sneezer, Crazy Feet, Stepping Out, Hotter Than Hot, Sky Boy, Players at Play*, Pathé Picture

1930

Her Man Pathé Exchange; producer, E.B. Derr; director, Tay Garnett; assistant director, Robert Fellows; director of photography, Edward Snyder; story, Howard Higgin, Tay Garnett; art director, Carroll Clark; editor, Joseph Kane, Doane Harrison; costumes, Gwen Wakeling; 83 minutes. Cast: Helen Twelvetrees, Marjorie Rambeau, Ricardo Cortez, Phillip Holmes, James Gleason, Harry Sweet, Thelma Todd, Franklin Pangborn.

Follow Thru Paramount Pictures; producer, Laurence Schwab, Frank Mandel; director, Laurence Schwab; director of photography, Henry Gerrard, Charles Boyle; screenplay, Laurence Schwab, Lloyd Corrigan, from the musical; editor, Alyson Shaffer; 93 minutes. Cast: Charles Rogers, Nancy Carroll, Zelma O'Neal, Jack Haley, Eugene Pallette, Thelma Todd.

Shorts: *Another Fine Mess, The Real McCoy, Whispering Whoopee, All Teed Up, Dollar Dizzy, Looser Than Loose, High C's, The Head Guy, The Fighting Parson, The Shrimp, The King*

1931

Command Performance James Cruze productions; producer, Samuel Zierler; director, Walter Lang; director of photography, Charles Schoenbaum; screenplay, Maude Fulton, Gordon Rigby, based on the play by C. Stafford Dickens; 72 minutes. Cast: Neil Hamilton, Una Merkel, Helen Ware, Albert Gran, Lawrence Grant, Thelma Todd, Mischa Auer.

Swanee River Sono Art–World-Wide Pictures, George W. Weeks; director, Raymond Cannon; director of photography, William Nobles; story, Barbara Chambers Woods; editor, Harry Webb-Douglas; 58 minutes. Cast: Grant Withers, Thelma Todd, Philo McCullough, the Jubilee Singers.

Hot Heiress First National Pictures; director, Clarence Badger; director of photography, Sol Polito; story, Herbert Fields; art director, Jack Okey; editor, Thomas Pratt; music director, Erno Rapee; 81 minutes. Cast: Ben Lyon, One Munson, Walter Pidgeon, Tom Dugan, Holmes Herbert, Inez Courtney, Thelma Todd.

Aloha Rogell Productions; director, Al Rogell; assistant director, Edgar G. Ulmer; director of photography, Charles Stumar; screenplay, Thomas H. Ince, J.G. Hawks, based on their

1915 script; editor, Richard Cahoon; 85 minutes. Cast: Ben Lyon, Raquel Torres, Robert Edeson, Alan Hale, Thelma Todd.

Monkey Business   Paramount Pictures; associate producer, Herman J. Mankiewicz; director, Norman McLeod; assistant director, Charles Barton; director of photography, Arthur L. Todd; screenplay, S.J. Perelman, Will B. Johnson; 78 minutes. Cast: The Marx Brothers, Thelma Todd, Tom Kennedy, Ruth Hall.

The Maltese Falcon   Warner Brothers Pictures; director, Roy Del Ruth; director of photography, William Rees; screenplay, Maude Fulton, Brown Holmes, based on the novel by Dashiell Hammett; art director, Robert Haas; editor, George Marks; 80 minutes. Cast: Bebe Daniels, Ricardo Cortez, Dudley Digges, Una Merkel, Robert Elliott, Thelma Todd, Walter Long, Dwight Frye.

Broadminded   First National Pictures; director, Mervyn LeRoy; director of photography, Sid Hickox; screenplay, Bert Kalmar, Harry Ruby; art director, Anton Grot; editor, Al Hall.; 65 minutes. Cast: Joe E. Brown, One Munson, William Collier, Jr., Marjorie White, Holmes Herbert, Margaret Livingston, Thelma Todd, Bela Lugosi.

Corsair   United Artists; director, Roland West; assistant directors, Robert Ross, Rollo Lloyd, Robert D.W. Webb; director of photography, Ray June; screenplay, Roland West, Josephine Lovett, based on the novel by Walter Atwater Green; music score, Alfred Newman,; editor, Hal C. Kern; 75 minutes. Cast: Chester Morris, Alison Loyd, Fred Kohler, Ned Sparks.

Shorts: *Chicken Come Home, The Pip from Pittsburgh, Rough Seas, Love Fever*
Thelma Todd–ZaSu Pitts Shorts: *Let's Do Things, Catch As Catch Can, The Pajama Party, War Mammas, On the Loose*

1932

The Big-Timer   Columbia Pictures; director, Eddie Buzzell; director of photography, L. William O' Connell; screenplay, Robert Riskin; 74 minutes. Cast: Ben Lyon, Constance Cummings, Thelma Todd, Charles Grapewin.

Speak Easily   Metro-Goldwyn-Mayer; director, Edward Sedgwick; assistant director, Earl Taggart; director of photography, Harold Wenstrom; based on *Footlights*, a novel by Clarence Kelland; art director, Cedric Gibbons; editor, William Levanway; 78 minutes. Cast: Buster Keaton, Jimmy Durante, Ruth Selwyn, Thelma Todd. Hedda Hopper.

Klondike   Monogram Pictures; director, Phil Rosen; assistant director, Harry P. Crist; director of photography, James Brown; screenplay, Tristram Tupper, based on the play *Pouche*; editor, Carl Pierson; 65 minutes. Cast Lyle Talbot, Captain Frank Hawks, Thelma Todd, Jason Robards, Henry B. Walthall.

This Is the Night   Paramount Pictures; associate producer, Benjamin Glazer; director, Frank Tuttle; director of photography, Victor Milner; screenplay, George Marion, Benjamin Glazer; 73 minutes. Cast: Lily Damita, Charlie Ruggles, Roland Young, Thelma Todd, Cary Grant, Irving Bacon.

Horse Feathers   Paramount Pictures, Adolph Zukor; director, Norman McLeod; assistant director, Charles Barton; director of photography, Ray June; screenplay, Bert Kalmar, Harry Ruby, S.J. Perelman, Will B. Johnstone; 70 minutes. Cast: The Marx Brothers, Thelma Todd, David Landau, Florine McKinney, James Pierce, Nat Pendleton.

Call Her Savage   Fox Film Corp; associate producer, Sam E. Rork; director, John Francis Dillon; assistant director, Jack Boland; director of photography, Lee Garmes; screenplay, Edwin Burke, based on the novel by Tiffany Thayer; editor, Harold Schuster; musical director, Louis De Francesco; 82 minutes. Cast: Clara Bow, Gilbert Roland, Thelma Todd, Monroe Owsley, Estelle Taylor.

Short: *Voice of Hollywood*

Thelma Todd–ZaSu Pitts Shorts: **Seal Skins, Red Noses, Strictly Unreliable, The Old Bull, Show Business, Alum and Eve, The Soilers, Sneak Easily**

1933

Deception   Columbia Pictures; producer, Bryan Foy; director, Lew Seiler; assistant director, Sam Katzman; director of photography, Chet Lyons; story, Nat Pendleton; screenplay, Harold Tarshis; editor, William Austin; 67 minutes. Cast: Leo Carillo, Dickie Moore, Nat Pendleton, Thelma Todd.

Air Hostess   Columbia Pictures; director, Al Rogell; assistant director, Arthur Black; director of photography, Joseph Walker; screenplay, Milton Raison, Keene Thompson; editor, Richard Cahoon; 67 minutes. Cast: Evalyn Knapp, James Murray, Arthur Pierson, Thelma Todd.

Cheating Blondes   Equitable Pictures; director, Joseph Levering; assistant director, J.A. Duffy; director of photography, James S. Brown, Jr.; screenplay, Lewis R. Foster, Islin Auster, based on the novel *House of Chance* by Gertie De S. Wentworth-James; editor, Dwight Caldwell; musical director, Lee Zahler; 61 minutes. Cast: Thelma Todd, Ralf Harolde, Inex Courtney, Mae Busch, Dorothy Gulliver.

Devil's Brother   Hal Roach Studios; producer, Hal Roach; director, Hal Roach and Charles Rogers; director of photography, Art Lloyd, Hap Depew; from the opera *Fra Diavolo,* adaptation by Jeanie MacPherson; editor, William Terhune, Bert Jordan; musical director, LeRoy Shield; 88 minutes. Cast: Stan Laurel, Oliver Hardy, Dennis King, Thelma Todd, James Finlayson, Lucille Browne.

Mary Stevens, M.D.   Warner Bros. Pictures; executive producer, Hal B. Wallis; director, Lloyd Bacon; assistant director, Chuck Hansen; director of photography, Sid Hickox; story, Virginia Kellogg; art director, Esdras Hartley; editor, Ray Curtiss; screenplay, Rian James, Robert Lord; 71 minutes. Cast: Kay Francis, Lyle Talbot, Glenda Farrell, Thelma Todd, Una O'Connor.

Son of a Sailor   First National Pictures; director, Lloyd Bacon; director of photography, Ira Morgan; screenplay, Al Cohn, Paul Gerard Smith; art director, Anton Grot; editor, James Gibbon; 70 minutes. Cast: Joe E. Brown, Jean Muir, Frank McHugh, Thelma Todd, Johnny Mack Brown.

Counsellor at Law   Universal Pictures; producer, Carl Laemmle; director, William Wyler; director of photography, Norbert Brodine; screenplay, Elmer, based on his play; art director, Charles D. Hall; editor, Daniel Mandell; 80 minutes. Cast: John Barrymore, Bebe Daniels, Doris Kenyon, Isabel Jewell, Melvyn Douglas, Onslow Stevens, Thelma Todd, Vincent Sherman.

Thelma Todd–ZaSu Pitts Shorts: **Asleep in the Feet, Maids a la Mode, The Bargain of the Century, One Track Minds**

Thelma Todd–Patsy Kelly Shorts: **Beauty and the Bus, Backs to Nature, Air Fright**

1934

Palooka   Reliance Pictures; producer, Edward Small; director, Benjamin Stoloff; assistant director, Joe Cooke; director of photography, Arthur Edeson; screenplay, Jack Jevne, Gertrude Purcell, Arthur Kober; art director, Alberto D'Agostino; musical director, Constantine Bakaleinikoff; editor, Grant Whytock; 80 minutes. Cast: Jimmy Durante, Lupe Velez, Stuart Erwin, Marjorie Rambeau, Robert Armstrong, Mary Carlisle, William Cagney, Thelma Todd.

Bottoms Up   Fox Film Corp., Winfield Sheehan; producer, B.G. DeSylva; director, David Butler; assistant director, Ad Schaumer; director of photography, Arthur Miller; screenplay, B.G. DeSylva, David Butler, Sid Silvers; art director, Gordon Wiles; musical director, Constantibe Bakaleinikoff; 85 minutes. Cast: Spencer Tracy, John Boles, Pat Patterson, Herbert Mundin, Sid Silvers, Thelma Todd.

The Poor Rich Universal Pictures; producer, Carl Laemmle, Jr.; associate producer, Dale Van Every; director, Edward Sedgwick; assistant director, Edward Woehler, Fred Frank; director of photography, John J. Mescall; screenplay, Dale Van Every, Ebba Havez; art director, Charles D. Hall; editor, Robert Carlisle; 76 minutes. Cast: Edward Everett Horton, Edna May Oliver, Andy Devine, Leila Hyams, Grant Mitchell, Thelma Todd, Une O'Connor, Ward Bond.

Take the Stand Liberty Pictures; associate producer, M.H. Hoffman; director, Phil Rosen; director of photography, Harry Neumann; screenplay, Albert DeMond; musical supervisor, Abe Meyer; editor, Mildred Johnston; 78 minutes. Cast: Jack La Rue, Thelma Todd, Gail Patrick, Vince Barnett, Jason Robards.

Hips, Hips, Hooray RKO Pictures; executive producer, Merian C. Cooper; associate producer, H.N. Swanson; director, Mark Sandrich; assistant director, Edward Killy; director of photography, David Abel; screenplay, Bert Kalmar, Harry Ruby, Edward Kaufman; art director, Van Nest Polglase, Carroll Clark; editor, Basil Wrangell; 68 minutes. Cast: Bert Wheeler, Robert Woolsey, Ruth Etting, Thelma Todd, Dorothy Lee.

You Made Me Love You British International Pictures; director, Monty Banks; director of photography, John J. Cox; story, Stanley Lupino, adapted by Frank Launder; editor, A.S. Bates; 70 minutes. Cast: Stanley Lupino, Thelma Todd, John Loder.

Cockeyed Cavaliers RKO Pictures; executive producer, Pandro S. Berman; associate producer, Lou Brock; director, Mark Sandrich; director of photography, David Abel; screenplay, Edward Kaufman, Edward Garrett; art director, Van Nest Polglase; editor, Jack Kitchin; 72 minutes. Cast: Bert Wheeler, Robert Woolsey, Thelma Todd, Dorothy Lee, Noah Beery, Franklin Pangborn, Billy Gilbert.

Thelma Todd–Patsy Kelly Shorts: ***Babes in the Goods, Soup and Fish, Maid in Hollywood, I'll Be Suing You, Three Chumps Ahead, One Horse Farmers, Opened by Mistake, Done in Oil, Bum Voyage***

1935

Lightning Strikes Twice RKO Pictures; associate producer, Lee Marcus; director, Ben Holmes; assistant director, Gene Yarborough; director of photography, Edward Cronjager; story, Marion Dix, Ben Holmes; art director, Van Nest Polglase; musical director, Arthur Roberts; editor, Arthur Roberts;65 minutes. Cast: Ben Lyon, Thelma Todd, Pert Kelton, Laura Hope Crews, Skeets Gallagher, Chick Chandler.

Two for Tonight Paramount Pictures, Adolph Zukor; executive producer, Henry Herzbrun, producer, Douglas MacLean; director, Frank Tuttle; director of photography, Karl Struss; screenplay, George Marion, Jr., Jane Storm; editor, William Shea; 60 minutes. Cast: Bing Crosby, Joan Bennett, Mary Boland, Lynne Overman, Thelma Todd.

After the Dance Columbia Pictures; director, Leo Bulgakov; assistant director, Cliff Broughton; director of photography, Joseph August; screenplay, Harold Shumate; editor, Otto Meyer; 70 minutes. Nancy Carroll, George Murphy, Thelma Todd, Jack La Rue.

Short: **Screen Snapshots #3**

Thelma Todd–Patsy Kelly Shorts: ***Treasure Blues, Sing, Sister, Sing, The Tin Man, The Misses Stooge, Slightly Static, Twin Triplets, Hot Money, Top Flat***

1936

The Bohemian Girl Hal Roach Studios; director, James W. Horne, Charles Rogers, Hal Roach; assistant directors, Dan Sandstron, Chet Brandy; director of cinematography, Art Lloyd, Francis Corby, Walter Lundin; story, based on the opera by Michael Balfe; musical director, Nathaniel Shilkret; editors, Bert Jordan, Louis McManus; 80 minutes.

Thelma Todd–Patsy Kelly Short: ***All-American Toothache***

Notes

Prologue

1. Autopsy. Agness Underwood, *Newspaperwoman* (New York: Harper and Brothers, 1949). Will Fowler, interview, January 10, 1991.
2. "Thelma Todd's Bright Future." *Los Angeles Times,* October 5, 1927.
3. "They'll never get...." William Todd, interview, February 12, 1991.

Chapter One

1. "The only son who...." William Todd, family history interview, February 12, 1991.
2. "Your treasury...." *Evening Tribune,* December 6, 1912. Lawrence history and the strike account are from newspaper reports and John Dorgan's *History of Lawrence* (Lawrence: Dorgan, 1924).
3. "While I am...." *Evening Tribune.* November 13, 1914.
4. "The city treasury...." Ibid. December 5, 1914.
5. "Maloney surrenders...." Ibid. December 7, 1914.
6. "The people have...." Ibid. December 9, 1914.
7. "Keep out of...." William Todd, interview, February 12, 1991.
8. "Best Moving Pictures...." *Evening Tribune,* November 23, 1912.
9. "Come on...." William Todd, interview, February 12, 1991.
10. "She always got...." Almeda King, interview, May 18, 1991.
11. "Justly proud." *Evening Tribune,* June 18, 1923.
12. "If you put...." Rosario Contarino interview by Kathy Flynn, April 20, 1988, Collection of the Lawrence History Center, Lawrence, MA. Flynn's interview provides the narrative for the Contarinos' story, along with my Rosario Drago interview and an article in the *Eagle Tribune,* August 1, 1988. Rosario Contarino was 92 when Kathy Flynn interviewed him. The interview is an invaluable document and provides a unique look at independent filmmaking in the twenties. Peter Contarino died years earlier. Rosario Contarino said he never saw Thelma Todd again after *Tangled Hearts.* Their films have disappeared. The Cosmopolitan became a store. The studio in Memphis was likely due to the city's importance as a film distribution center. See Richard J. Alley's "Hidden Memphis: On Film Row," (*Commercial Appeal,* April 3, 2011).
13. "The Mafia took...." Ibid. Rosario Contarino interview, Kathy Flynn.
14. "Ably and logically." *Evening Tribune,* December 16, 1935.
15. "Miss Todd is a young lady...." Ibid., June 2, 1925.
16. "Our aim...." *New York Times,* April 5, 1925.
17. "The girl is sent...." *Boston Evening Tribune,* undated, 1931, Bill Todd scrapbook.
18. "Two lovers...." Ibid.
19. "There was more...." Ibid.
20. "I hate people...." Ibid.
21. "I have seen...." *New York Times,* July 21, 1925.
22. "If the slightest...." *Motion Picture Classic,* June 1927.
23. "A veritable...." *Evening Tribune,* February 20, 1926.

24. "Sixteen Lucky Students." *New York Times,* October 18, 1925. J.B. Kaufman's "Fascinating Youth" in *Film History* (1990) is an excellent look at the Paramount Pictures School."
25. "The whole world...." *Photoplay,* August 1926.
26. "Personality galore." Lasky, *I Blow My Own Horn* (New York: Doubleday, 1959).
27. "I want you...." *Boston Evening American,* undated,1931, Bill Todd scrapbook.
28. "I expect to...." *Evening Tribune,* February 20, 1926.
29. "One of the outstanding...." Ibid. May 22, 1926.
30. "Thelma had a heart...." Greg Blackton, interview, September 8, 1991.
31. "Get Into the Movies." *Chicago Tribune,* June 8, 1926.
32. "The Talk...." *Commercial Appeal,* July 26, 1926.
33. *My John. Lawrence Telegram,* August 3, 1926.
34. "Thelma Todd Out...." *Evening Tribune,* August 7, 1926.
35. "Death Claims Valentino...." International News Service, August 13, 1926.
36. "If you knew...." Ibid. August 29, 1926.

Chapter Two

1. "There is a town...." Palmer, *History of Hollywood* (Hollywood: Palmer, 1938).
2. "The name of Hollywood...." Ibid.
3. "Well, boys...." Sullivan, *Chaplin Vs. Chaplin* (Los Angeles: Miller Enterprises, 1965).
4. "Girls who have...." *Los Angeles Times,* May 7, 1927.
5. "I had always...." *Picture Play,* March 1929.
6. "I discovered that...." *Photoplay,* August 1926.
7. "Never buy...." *Photoplay,* January 1927.
8. "If Wynn had a...." *Variety,* June 29, 1927.
9. "Miss Todd is already...." *Los Angeles Times,* October 5, 1927.
10. "There she recognized...." *Photoplay,* February 1932.
11. "She didn't like...." William Todd, interview, February 12, 1991.
12. "His reputation for...." Paris, *Louise Brooks* (New York: Knopf, 1989).
13. "While the studio...." Lasky, *I Blow My Own Horn* (New York: Doubleday, 1959).
14. "They'll never get me...." William Todd, interview, February 12, 1991.
15. "Every stunt...." *American Cinematographer,* January 1930.
16. "A sinister graveyard." *Photoplay,* December 1927.
17. "One of the dreariest...." *Variety,* July 4, 1928.
18. "The artist...." Contract, Warner Archives, University of Southern California.
19. "If you want...." *Picture Play,* March 1929.
20. "Crooked lawyers...." Lina Basquette, interview, December 17, 1990.
21. "Thelma and I were...." Ibid.
22. "Biggest Little Town...." Undated article, Bill Todd scrapbook.
23. "Synchronization...." *Variety,* December 19, 1928.
24. "How it was ever...." *Boston Evening American,* 1931.
25. "The public is demanding...." *Reno Evening Gazette,* July 7, 1928.
26. "I haven't done...." *Motion Picture,* June 1929.
27. "Thelma Todd is...." *Variety,* April 27, 1929.
28. "You never...." Greg Blackton, interview, September 8, 1991.
29. "Men in Hollywood...." *Motion Picture,* June 1929.
30. "Sounded like a fairy." Skretvedt, *Laurel and Hardy* (Beverly Hills, CA: Moonstone, 1987).
31. "There are thousands...." *Lawrence Telegram,* August 22, 1929.
32. "Do you really...." *Evening Tribune,* August 22, 1929.
33. "It's one now...." *Boston Globe,* August 25, 1929.
34. "Thelma never...." Bill Todd, April 22, 1991.
35. "I left Hollywood...." *Los Angeles Examiner,* September 11, 1929.
36. "I thought I could...." Palmer, *History of Hollywood* (Hollywood: Palmer, 1938).
37. "I feel absurd...." *Movie Mirror,* March 1932.
38. "She drank...." Lina Basquette, interview, December 17, 1990.
39. "I can't do...." *Los Angeles Examiner,* August 14, 1930.

Chapter Three

1. "We all...." Joe Cobb, interview, December 16, 1979.
2. "She'd get...." Dorothy Granger, interview, May 31, 1991.

3. "Very intelligent...." Anita Garvin, interview, September 7, 1987.
4. "She sparkled...." Harry Mines, interview, July 9, 1986.
5. "Roland was an odd...." William Bakewell, interview, October 19, 1987.
6. "He was a very odd...." Thompson, *Between Action and Cut* (Metuchen, NJ: Scarecrow, 1985).
7. "It was a very...." Lina Basquette, interview, December 7, 1990.
8. Roland West. Publicity biography, Academy Library.
9. "Made their first dimes...." Loos, *The Talmadge Girls* (New York: Viking, 1978).
10. "A galaxy...." Ibid.
11. "I am fifteen...." *Los Angeles Evening Herald,* May 5, 1913.
12. "There has been...." *Los Angeles Times*, May 6, 1913.
13. "White lies." *Los Angeles Record*, May 5, 1913.
14. "Did he make any...." Ibid., July 18, 1913.
15. "Who is Jewel Carmen?" *Photoplay*, July 1917.
16. "Where is that...." *Motion Picture Magazine*, November 1918.
17. "Destroyed in a fire...." *New York Times*, April 28, 1925.
18. "There's not a star...." *Variety*, March 17, 1926.
19. "My dear cousin...." Roland West Collection, Academy Library.After Margaret Van Tassel left the stage, she never returned to acting, despite her son's success and connections. She traveled with E.E. Bellamy, her second husband. They moved permanently to Los Angeles in 1930. For a while, the couple lived at 777 S. Westmoreland Avenue. Margaret died in Los Angeles in 1936 in the Bellamy home at 1133 W. 77th St. at age 72 (obituary, *Los Angeles Times*, August 5, 1936). Cora Van Tassel's early life was quite successful. According to an article in the *New York Times* (October 4, 1896), Cora inherited $300,000 from A.T. Van Tassel, a wealthy uncle who was a businessman. However, she was only allotted an allowance of $50 per week until her 30th birthday. The money was entrusted to the care of Norman Kelly, described as a millionaire. They produced *Tennessee's Pardner* in New York City. At age 23, after she fell in love with William Sherman, her guardian forcibly returned her to Cleveland. Indignant, Cora vowed to initiate a lawsuit and obtain her inheritance. She later toured the country in various productions and wed Francis Fleming. Cora died at 325 W. Bowdoin Place in Seattle on November 29, 1925. The cause of death was listed as "illuminating gas poisoning — accidental." Cora's occupation was given on her death certificate as "medium," indicating she was a spiritualist in her later years. Her remains were cremated and she was buried in Seattle (Death Certificate, State of Washington, Center for Health Statistics).
20. "I do not care...." Ibid. The Wests' residence had a second entrance at 17520 Revello.
21. "He had some...." Thompson, *Between Action and Cut* (Metuchen, NJ: Scarecrow, 1985).
22. "If Roland West...." *Exhibitor's Herald World*, March 16, 1929.
23. "Jolt-packed...." *Variety*, April 10, 1929.
24. "Producers usually...." *Exhibitor's Herald World*, April 20, 1929.
25. "To remain permanently...." Roland West Collection, Academy Library.
26. "Dear cousin Roland...." Ibid.
27. "Dear friend Roland...." Ibid.
28. "There is no...." Ibid.
29. "Dear Roland...." Ibid.
30. "Dear Allie...." Ibid.
31. "Everything Theatrical...." Ibid.
32. "Dear mother...." Ibid.
33. "We received...." Ibid.
34. "I recently...." Ibid.
35. "Dear H.E." Ibid.
36. "I don't know...." Ibid.
37. "Una Merkel...." William Bakewell, interview, October 19, 1987.
38. "Dear Efe...." Roland West Collection, Academy Library.
39. "The changing of Thelma Todd's name...." *Every Week Magazine*, September 26, 1931.
40. "I have always...." Ibid.
41. "Hal Roach is pretty burned up...." *Los Angeles Examiner*, September 7, 1931.
42. "I don't want to...." *Every Week Magazine*, September 26, 1931.
43. "By a process...." Ibid.
44. "I think it is every...." undated, *Public Ledger*, 1931.
45. "I have noticed...." Roland West Collection, Academy Library.
46. "I'll take a trip...." *Los Angeles Examiner*, December 18, 1935.
47. "I only had...." Ibid., September 18, 1931.
48. "Have laid...." Roland West Collection, Academy Library.
49. "Thelma found, too...." *Photoplay Magazine*, February 1932.
50. "Not impressive...." *Variety*, November 24, 1931.
51. "A physical wreck." *Los Angeles Examiner*, December 17, 1935.
52. "Port of missing men," *Boston Globe*, December 17, 1935.

Chapter Four

1. "Numerology shows...." *Motion Picture Magazine*, September 1931.
2. "Austin Parker...." *Hollywood Reporter*, November 11, 1931.
3. "How are you...." *Motion Picture*, August 1931.
4. "Domineering roughneck...." Broccoli, *When the Snow Melts* (London: Boxtree, 1998).
5. "I used to play...." William Bakewell, interview, October 19, 1987.
6. "Her stripping...." *Variety*, April 19, 1932.
7. "She told my mother...." William Todd, interview, February 12, 1991. "She and my mother were very close ... They talked a lot. She told my mother, 'I made a big mistake marrying Pat De Cicco.' She realized that when she was married to him about only a month. Alice thought he was a handsome, dashing man."
8. "What the hell...." Greg Blackton, interview, September 8, 1991.
9. "The blonde menace...." *Los Angeles Examiner*, September 10, 1932.
10. "She suffered...." Ibid., January 24, 1933.
11. "We'd all fight...." Bert Wheeler, oral history, Columbia University.
12. "Ida, dear...." Ida Lupino, interview, October 23, 1983.
13. "Now that...." *Hollywood Reporter*, May 23, 1933.
14. "After Thelma...." Ibid., June 1, 1933.
15. "Thelma Todd and Dennis...." Ibid., June 15, 1933.
16. "Poor Pat...." *Los Angeles Examiner*, July 6, 1933.
17. "I'm still Thelma Todd...." unidentified clipping, Bill Todd scrapbook.
18. "Is that the best...." Ibid., July 10, 1933.
19. "Keep all worthwhile...." Roach Collection, Warner Archives.
20. "When did the...." *New Movie*, March 1933.
21. "I was supposed...." *Film Fan Monthly*, March 1971.
22. "Husbands...." *Hollywood Reporter*, September 18, 1933.
23. "Harsh and opprobrious...." Divorce Complaint, February 23, 1934.
24. Casidria Mae Whitehead (1903–1989). Public documents use both Mae and May for her first name; however, Mae is correct. Mae Whitehead was a devoted employee of Thelma Todd. Although she identified herself as a personal maid, she was much more. Today she would be termed a personal assistant. Mae accompanied Thelma to work at studios and even drove the expensive Lincoln Phaeton from the Wests' garage to the café, a skill likely acquired from her husband, Philip E. Whitehead, a chauffeur in the motion picture industry. A photograph shows her on the set at Roach Studios with Thelma, Patsy Kelly, and others. Mae was privy to Thelma's private life and witnessed her tempestuous marriage to Pat De Cicco. She loyally testified as a witness for Thelma in divorce court. Mae was so trusted by Thelma that she was allowed her own key to Thelma's apartment at the Sidewalk Café. A photograph of Mae at the grand jury hearing shows her stylishly dressed with *MW* monogrammed on her purse. Mae and her husband lived in a home at 1642 West 36th Place, as recorded in city directories. She later worked for Patsy Kelly.
25. "As a result...." *Los Angeles Examiner*, March 3, 1934.

Chapter Five

1. "He is a Socialist...." *Los Angeles Examiner*, October 10, 1934.
2. "We didn't meet...." Ibid., December 5, 1934.
3. "America's admiration...." Ibid., May 5, 1934.
4. "True they cannot...." Ibid., April 22, 1934.
5. "I deny ever...." *Los Angeles Times*, August 19, 1934. Like most screen performers, Thelma avoided public political affiliation, to ensure wide popularity.
6. "I need my own...." Ibid.
7. "In 1931, my father...." William Todd, interview, February 12, 1991.
8. "I realized...." *Film Pictorial*, August 17, 1935.
9. "Pay $10,000...." Thelma Todd FBI File.
10. "I want it distinctly...." *Pittsburgh-Post Gazette*, March 6, 1935. Joseph Dunn left the FBI and became a private investigator. In 1936, he was hired by attorney Moses Polakoff, defense lawyer for Lucky Luciano. Dunn met two prostitutes in Los Angeles on behalf of Polakoff. The women had testified against Luciano during his trial. Flo Brown and Mildred Balitzer had gone to California to start a new life but were soon back on narcotics and without funds. They recanted their testimony. Joe Dunn watched the women while Polakoff prepared Luciano's appeal. Justice McCook rejected the recanting affidavits as "a fraud on the court...poisonously false," as found in William Donati's *Lucky Luciano* (Jefferson, NC: McFarland, 2010).
11. "You have failed...." Thelma Todd FBI File.
12. "She told...." William Todd, interview, February 12, 1991.
13. "Dear Sir...." Thelma Todd FBI File.

14. "Well Lyman...." Ibid.
15. "This is the...." Ibid.
16. "That Commissioner...." Ibid.
17. "Pay $10,000...." Ibid.
18. "We are giving...." Ibid.
19. "So far...." *Los Angeles Times*, August 30, 1935.
20. "That man...." Thelma Todd FBI File.
21. "I have received...." *New York World-Telegram*, August 26, 1935.
22. "It is with deep...." Thelma Todd FBI File.
23. "Please put a piece...." Ibid.
24. "My dear Georges...." Hal Roach Collection.
25. "Lyle was...." Lina Basquette, interview, December 17, 1990. Basquette recalled the event as a few days before her death, but the date is unclear.
26. "I hear...." *Illustrated Daily News*, December 24, 1935.
27. Billy Wilkerson owned and wrote for *The Hollywood Reporter*. The trade publication made him a powerful player in the motion picture industry. Beside Café Trocadero, he owned the popular nightspots LaRue and Ciro's. Wilkerson was a gambler who sat down to play high stakes poker with Joe Schenck, Sam Goldwyn, and other studio executives. The Flamingo in Las Vegas was his idea. He remained the main shareholder until Ben "Bugsy" Siegel threatened to kill him. Siegel's "vision" to build the Flamingo is one of the great myths perpetrated by Las Vegas lore and hoax films. Wilkerson's fascinating life is recounted in *The Man Who Invented Las Vegas*, written by his son, W.R. Wilkerson III (Beverly Hills, CA: Ciro's Books, 2000).

Chapter Six

1. "2:05." *Los Angeles Times*, December 20, 1935.
2. "Four hours...." *Los Angeles Examiner*, December 18, 1935.
3. "Don't drink...." Ibid.
4. "I think you should...." *Los Angeles Examiner*, December 29, 1935.
5. "I didn't think you'd...." Ibid.
6. "We'll go...." Coroner's Inquest, December 18, 1935.
7. "Goodbye...." Ida Lupino, interview, October 23, 1983.
8. "Never mind...." Coroner's Inquest, December 18, 1935.
9. "She has been murdered...." *Venice Evening Standard*, December 21, 1935.
10. "It's that heart...." *Los Angeles Times*, December 17, 1935.
11. "She was if...." *Illustrated Daily News*, December 17, 1935.
12. "It's awful...." *Evening Herald and Express*, December 17, 1935.
13. "There is absolutely...." *Evening Outlook*, December 16, 1935.
14. "Unusual circumstances." *Evening Herald and Express*, December 17, 1935.
15. "I recall...." *Los Angeles Times*, December 18, 1935.
16. Dr. Edwin Larson. His office was at 6504 Crenshaw Boulevard. After Thelma's death, the estate was billed for $30, for five office visits for undisclosed treatment. There was no billed visit for December, so either Thelma paid the fee or Larson's comments refer to her last visit on November 4. On October 29, the bill states "office visit and refraction — $10.00," for a likely eye exam. Larson's remarks raise questions. Why would he test her for heart problems? Were there symptoms? Alice mentioned earlier fainting spells and a diagnosis of a heart murmur. Did the fainting return?
17. "She was...." *Evening Herald and Express*, December 17, 1935.
18. "On other...." *Illustrated Daily News*, December 17, 1935.
19. "Until last...." *Washington Herald*, December 20, 1935.
20. "Hollywood...." *Evening Herald and Express*, December 19, 1935.
21. "At thanksgiving...." *Hollywood Citizen News*, December 17, 1935.
22. "She gave me...." *San Francisco Chronicle*, December 21, 1935.
23. "She seemed...." *Los Angeles Examiner*, December 17, 1935.
24. "For the first...." *Venice Evening Vanguard*, December 17, 1935.
25. "Thought I'd be...." *Evening Tribune*, December 17, 1935.
26. "Lawrence and its...." Ibid., December 20, 1935.
27. "She was a favorite...." *Los Angeles Times*, December 17, 1935.
28. "I know you must have...." Roach Collection, Warner Archives.
29. "Thelma's just kidding...." *Los Angeles Times*, December 17, 1935.
30. "As it was...." *Evening Outlook*, December 19, 1935.
31. "But would...." *Los Angeles Examiner*, December 18, 1935.
32. "I know her...." *Evening Herald and Express*, December 17, 1935.
33. "Last Saturday...." *Los Angeles Times*, December 18, 1935.

34. "Nothing...." *Evening Herald and Express*, December 17, 1935.
35. "I am sure...." *Los Angeles Times*, December 30, 1935.
36. "Miss Todd...." *Washington Times*, January 4, 1936.
37. "About the size...." *Washington Post*, December 22, 1935.
38. "Holding hands...." *Washington Herald*, December 30, 1935.

Chapter Seven

1. "Please state...." Coroner's Inquest, December 18, 1935. Chief Medical Examiner-Coroner, County of Los Angeles. Pat De Cicco's surname is incorrect in the transcript. The subpoena sent to Thelma's personal maid was addressed to May Whitehead, but her first name is different in the transcript, where she is listed as Mae, the correct name.

Chapter Eight

1. "So far...." *Washington Herald*, December 19, 1935.
2. "The grand jury...." *Venice Evening Standard*, December 22, 1935.
3. "Your hasty...." *Evening Outlook*, December 20, 1935.
4. "I don't want any...." *Evening Herald and Express*, December 21, 1935.
5. "Dark complexioned...." *Washington Times*, December 19, 1935.
6. "The staunchest friend...." *Los Angeles Examiner*, December 19, 1935.
7. "I stepped...." Ibid.
8. "I have always...." *Evening Herald and Express*, December 19, 1935.
9. "The place is...." *Los Angeles Examiner*, December 20, 1935.
10. "I know because...." *Los Angeles Times*, December 20, 1935.
11. "Even as...." *Los Angeles Times*, December 20, 1935.
12. "She was one...." *Illustrated Daily News*, December 20, 1935.
13. "In the church...." *Evening Herald and Express*, December 20, 1935.
14. "Miss Carmen...." *Los Angeles Examiner*, December 23, 1935.
15. "I am not feeling...." Ibid., December 24, 1935.
16. "Sensational...." Ibid., December 24, 1935.
17. "During my party...." *Los Angeles Times*, December 24, 1935.
18. "It was said...." Ibid.
19. "This is Thelma...." *Los Angeles Examiner*, December 25, 1935.
20. "I never heard...." *Los Angeles Times*, December 25, 1935.
21. "There is going...." Ibid., December 25, 1935.
22. "What the hell...." *Hollywood Citizen News*, December 28, 1935.
23. "She had few...." *Evening Herald and Express*, December 28, 1935.
24. "Only kidding...." *Evening Outlook*, December 28, 1935.
25. "I never saw...." Ibid., December 25, 1935.
26. "A couple...." *Los Angeles Examiner*, December 28, 1935.
27. "The only thing...." *Evening Outlook*, December 25, 1935.
28. "Sometimes...." *Evening Herald and Express*, December 28, 1935.
29. "It is terrible...." Ibid.
30. "I never saw...." *Los Angeles Examiner*, December 31, 1935.
31. "Pulling out...." *Hollywood Citizen News*, January 2, 1936.
32. "She did not...." *Illustrated Daily News*, January 3, 1936.
33. "She said...." *Los Angeles Examiner*, January 3, 1936.
34. "If she had them...." Ibid.
35. "Threat after threat...." *Washington Times*, January 4, 1936.
36. "Thelma often told...." *Evening Outlook*, January 2, 1936.
37. "I would be the happiest...." *Washington Herald*, January 8, 1936.
38. "She turned...." *Illustrated Daily News*, January 3, 1936.
39. "I called Thelma...." *Los Angeles Examiner*, January 3, 1936.
40. "I definitely know...." Ibid., January 5, 1936. Catherine Hunter was one of Chaplin's close associates. When he wed Oona O'Neill in Carpenteria, California, in June 1943, there were two witnesses: Catherine Hunter and Harry Crocker.
41. "Very happy." Ibid., January 7, 1936.
42. "This grand jury...." *Hollywood Citizen News*, January 6, 1936.
43. "He treated...." Ibid., December 30, 1935.
44. "We were convinced...." Ibid., January 6, 1936.

45. "I will not...." *Evening Herald and Express*, January 8, 1936.

46. "The death has been...." Ibid.

47. "Beaten up...." Ibid., January 8, 1936.

48. The low price for the car indicates buyers purposely avoided it. Thelma had the luxury car regularly serviced at F.J. Sauer's garage at 15200 Beverly Blvd, Pacific Palisades (today W. Sunset). On November 27, 1935, Thelma bought four new white stripe tires and heavy duty Goodyear tubes for $169.95. The 1932 Lincoln Phaeton's engine number was KB1008.

Chapter Nine

1. "She tried...." Adam Todd, interview, March 8, 1991.

2. "Mental cruelty." *Illustrated Daily News*, October 27, 1939.

3. "At $30,000." *Evening Herald and Express*, November 28, 1940.

4. Werthheimer on Fox payroll, *New York Times*, March 14, 1941.

5. Harpo Marx wins $7,827, *Los Angeles Times*, March 11, 1941.

6. "Most of these...." *Los Angeles Examiner*, March 11, 1941.

7. "I won't have...." Ibid., March 20, 1941.

8. Tax deduction of $170,000, *Los Angeles Times*, March 18, 1941.

9. "A misfortune...." *Los Angeles Examiner*, March 20, 1941.

10. "I'm his friend." Ibid., April 1, 1941.

11. "It was a loan." Muir, *Headline Happy* (New York: Henry Holt, 1950).

12. "Chez Roland." *Los Angeles Examiner*, June 26, 1952.

13. "Several hundred...." *Los Angeles Times*, May 13, 1952.

14. "Roland told me...." *Los Angeles Examiner*, June 26, 1952.

15. "You're just...." *Variety*, October 25, 1978.

16. "Pat terrifies...." Vanderbilt, *Black Knight, White Knight* (New York: Knopf, 1987).

17. "I am home." De Cicco, Trial Testimony, Estate of Howard Hughes, Probate Court No. 2, January 12, 1978. The transcript was kindly provided by Pat Broeske, the biographer of Howard Hughes.

18. "Patsy never...." Rena Lundigan, interview, April 8, 1990.

19. "She had a...." Parish, *The Funsters,* (New York: Arlington House, 1979).

20. "He struck her...." *Los Angeles Magazine*, October 1976.

21. "He ran around...." *Los Angeles Magazine*, December 1987. I wrote to Hal Roach to confirm the accuracy of his comments, but he never responded. Roach died in 1992 at age 100.

22. "Thelma Todd back...." *Los Angeles Examiner*, January 4, 1935.

23. "Gambling interests." Ibid., December 20, 1935.

24. "Clean up Hollywood...." Ibid., July 29, 1932.

25. "At least 500...." Ibid., January 29, 1934.

26. "I would never...." William Studer, interview, June 5, 1991.

27. "She invited us...." *Variety, 49th Anniversary Issue*, October 1982.

28. "There are so many...." Bill Todd, interview, February 12, 1991.Bill Todd and his sister Edna Todd Bixby were pleased when I published *Ida Lupino*. The Todd family was incensed by *Hot Toddy*. The assertion that Thelma was involved in an affair with a notorious gangster was especially outrageous, since family members never heard Luciano's name before. *Ida Lupino* provided the factual account of what occurred the night of the Trocadero party. In 1998, I appeared in an episode about Thelma Todd for *Hollywood Mysteries and Scandals*. I asserted that if Alice Todd believed her daughter had been murdered, she would have moved heaven and earth to bring the killer to justice. Bill and Edna agreed. Thelma's cousins died in 2002, within a month of each other. Bill Todd's obituary noted that he had served with gallantry in the U.S. Navy during World War II. He served on a minesweeper and received numerous medals, including the American Theatre Medal, the European-African Middle Eastern Theatre Medal (2 stars) and the Asiatic-Pacific Theatre Medal. Both brother and sister were devoted to the memory of their famous cousin. While in Lawrence, I briefly spoke with Shirley Raymond, Thelma's cousin, now deceased. However, she said that she had "no recollections. I was so young then." Alice and Thelma had been fond of Shirley. In fact, Alice gave Shirley one of the rings Thelma had worn the night of the Trocadero party. After her death, Shirley's vast collection of Thelma Todd and Hollywood memorabilia was sold at auction.

29. "The police, however...." *New York Times*, October 28, 1935. Luciano left the Waldorf on October 29. He was soon reported to be in Atlantic City and by November 2 was in Miami. Detective Brennan was honored by Mayor La Guardia for his service in the Luciano prosecution. Detective Brennan was an honest cop. Aboard the train to New York Brennan became concerned when Luciano and Detective Stephen Di Rosa conversed in Italian. He told them to stop it. When they ignored him, Brennan took out his blackjack. "Lay off that stuff," he said to Di Rosa. Soon after, in a separate case, Di Rosa was caught passing confidential information and demoted. See Donati's *Lucky Luciano: The Rise and Fall of a Mob Boss* (Jefferson, NC: McFarland, 2010).

30. "Requiring...." *Chicago Daily Tribune*, November 2, 1935.

31. "On the afternoon...." Lucania File, police report, New York City Municipal Archives.

32. "When I left...." *Washington Star*, April 3, 1936.

33. The Siegel theory. There is no evidence that Ben Siegel and Thelma Todd ever met. Siegel was supposedly a powerful crime figure in Los Angeles; yet, according to press reports, when his associate Al Smiley opened Club Esquire at 9015 Sunset on May 27, 1937, the police closed the restaurant the next day because it did not have a liquor license; it never reopened. Once in charge of the Flamingo project, Siegel spent enormous sums but failed to satisfy the gangster investors whose money he spent. The investors, including Meyer Lansky, had Siegel murdered. Siegel and Lansky were called "executioners" by Ed Reid, the author of *The Green Felt Jungle* (New York: Trident Press, 1963). If Lansky believed his reputation had been sullied, he could have sued for defamation; however, he did nothing. He died in 1983.

34. Luden arrest. *Classic Images*, July 1987.

35. Jewel West death. Social Security Death Index.

36. "Well, it's been years...." Rudy Schafer to Benny Drinnon, correspondence, 1999. Benny Drinnon, the moderator of the Thelma Todd Fan Club, stayed in touch with Rudy who signed the club's petition asking Turner Classic Movies to show more Thelma Todd films in 2003. The club was successful and TCM started broadcasting Thelma Todd movies. Rudy left an interesting glimpse into the past. Schafer and his wife were prominent antique dealers. He died in 2007. Special thanks to Benny Drinnon for providing Rudy Schafer's memories.

37. A. Ronald Button. Obituary, *Los Angeles Times*, February 5, 1987. Button became Republican State Central Committee chairman in 1953 and was selected for the national party post, a position he held for three years. At the time of his death, at age 83, Button suffered from Alzheimer's disease.

38. "Certain people were...." Ida Lupino, interview, October 23, 1983. Lupino insisted Thelma suffered from serious heart disease and even provided the name of the physician who treated Thelma in London; nevertheless, she agreed that Thelma's death was an accident caused by carbon monoxide poisoning. Lupino had a lifelong interest in medicine and told her close friend Harry Mines she regretted her lack of formal education, a situation that prohibited her from becoming a doctor.

39. "She was very affectionate, loveable." William Todd, May 2, 1991.

Bibliography

Books

Balio, Tino. *The Company Built by the Stars.* Madison: University of Wisconsin Press, 1976.

Basquette, Lina. *Lina: DeMille's Godless Girl.* Fairfax, VA: Denlinger's Publishers, 1990.

Blesh, Rudi. *Keaton.* New York: MacMillan, 1966.

Broccoli, Cubby. *When the Snow Melts.* London: Boxtree, 1998.

Cole, Donald B. *Immigrant City.* Chapel Hill: University of North Carolina Press, 1963.

Donati, William. *Ida Lupino.* Lexington: University Press of Kentucky, 1996.

_____. *Lucky Luciano: The Rise and Fall of a Mob Boss.* Jefferson, NC: McFarland, 2010.

Dorgan, Maurice. *History of Lawrence, Massachusetts.* Lawrence: Dorgan, 1924.

Edmonds, Andy. *Hot Toddy.* New York: William Morrow, 1989.

Foster, R.F. *Modern Ireland.* New York: Penguin, 1988.

Fowler, Will. *Reporters.* Malibu, CA: Roundtable, 1991.

Heimann, Jim. *Out with the Stars.* New York: Abbeville Press, 1985.

Kaufman, J.B. "Fascinating Youth: The Story of the Paramount Pictures School." *Film History* 4.2 (1990): 131–151.

Lasky, Jesse. *I Blow My Own Horn.* New York: Doubleday, 1959.

Leavitt, Thomas. *Mill Owners and Missionaries.* Lawrence: White Fund, 1975.

Loos, Anita. *A Girl Like I.* New York: Viking, 1965.

_____. *The Talmadge Girls.* New York: Viking, 1978.

Maltin, Leonard. *Movie Comedy Teams.* New York: Signet, 1970.

Moldea, Dan. *Dark Victory.* New York: Viking, 1986.

Muir, Florabel. *Headline Happy.* New York: Henry Holt, 1950.

Munden, Kenneth W., ed. *The American Institute Catalog of Motion Pictures Produced in the United States.* New York and London: Bowker, 1971.

Palmer, Edwin. *History of Hollywood.* Hollywood: Palmer, 1938.

Paris, Barry. *Louise Brooks.* New York: Knopf, 1989.

Parish, James. *The Funsters. New York:* Arlington House, 1979.

Reid, Ed. *The Green Felt Jungle.* New York: Trident Press, 1963.

Skretvedt, Randy. *Laurel and Hardy.* Beverly Hills: Moonstone Press, 1987.

Sullivan, Ed. *Chaplin Vs. Chaplin.* Los Angeles: Marvin Miller Enterprises, 1965.

Talmadge, Margaret. *The Talmadge Sisters.* Philadelphia: Lippincott, 1924.

Thompson, Frank, ed. *Between Action and Cut.* Metuchen, NJ: Scarecrow, 1985.

Underwood, Agness. *Newspaperwoman.* New York: Harper and Brothers Publishers, 1949.

Vanderbilt, Gloria. *Black Knight, White Knight.* New York: Knopf, 1987.

Wilkerson III, W.R. *The Man Who Invented Las Vegas.* Beverly Hills, CA: Ciro's Books, 2000.

Wolfe, Donald H. *The Black Dahlia Files.* New York: ReganBooks, 2005.

Newspapers

Boston Globe, Boston Evening American, Commercial Appeal, Hollywood Citizen News, Hollywood Reporter, Lawrence Eagle Tribune, Lawrence Evening Tribune, Lawrence Telegram, Los Angeles Examiner, Los Angeles Evening Herald and Express, Los Angeles Illustrated News, Los Angeles Times, New York Daily News, New York Times, New York World-Telegram, Pittsburgh Post-Gazette, San Francisco Chronicle, Santa Monica Evening Outlook, Variety, Venice Evening Outlook, Washington Herald, Washington Times

Magazines

American Cinematographer, Classic Images, Every Week Magazine, Exhibitors World Herald, Film Fan Monthly, Film Pictorial, Motion Picture, Illustrated Daily News, Los Angeles Magazine, Motion Picture Classic, Movie Mirror, New Movie Magazine, Photoplay, Picture Play, Screen Book

Index

Page numbers in **_bold italics_** indicate illustrations.